BEFORE IDENTITY

BEFORE IDENTITY

The Question
of
Method
in
Japan Studies

RICHARD F. CALICHMAN

Published by State University of New York Press, Albany

© 2021 State University of New York

All rights reserved

Printed in the United States of America

No part of this book may be used or reproduced in any manner whatsoever without written permission. No part of this book may be stored in a retrieval system or transmitted in any form or by any means including electronic, electrostatic, magnetic tape, mechanical, photocopying, recording, or otherwise without the prior permission in writing of the publisher.

For information, contact State University of New York Press, Albany, NY
www.sunypress.edu

Library of Congress Cataloging-in-Publication Data

Name: Calichman, Richard, author.
Title: Before identity : the question of method in Japan studies / Richard F. Calichman.
Description: Albany, NY : State University of New York Press, Albany, 2021. | Includes bibliographical references and index.
Identifiers: LCCN 2020045640 (print) | LCCN 2020045641 (ebook) | ISBN 9781438482132 (hardcover : alk. paper) | ISBN 9781438482149 (pbk. : alk. paper) | ISBN 9781438482156 (ebook)
Subjects: LCSH: Japan—Study and teaching. | Education—Philosophy. | Identity (Philosophical concept) | Kafka, Franz, 1883–1924.
Classification: LCC DS806 .C275 2021 (print) | LCC DS806 (ebook) | DDC 952.0072—dc23
LC record available at https://lccn.loc.gov/2020045640
LC ebook record available at https://lccn.loc.gov/2020045641

10 9 8 7 6 5 4 3 2 1

Contents

Acknowledgments		vii
Introduction		1
Chapter 1	Remembering Kafka: Between Murakami Haruki and Komori Yōichi	9
Chapter 2	The Double Pull of History and Philosophy: Reading Harootunian	57
Chapter 3	The Question of Subjectivity in North American Japanese Literary Studies	107
Coda	Some Brief Remarks on Responsibility	181
Notes		189
Bibliography		209
Index		215

Acknowledgments

For some time, the process of writing a book has been like swimming underwater: the experience is at once pleasurable and frightening, and one yearns for the moment when one can finally resurface and recommence one's relationship with the far less demanding element of oxygen. Now that I have arrived at such a moment, I must attend to academic protocol and thank publicly those whose gifts and kindnesses I cherish primarily privately. Friends and colleagues whose insights have helped improve this manuscript include: Michael Bourdaghs, Pedro Erber, Mayumo Inoue, Ted Mack, Cliff Rosenberg, and Atsuko Ueda. I would also like to give particular thanks to Jon Solomon: the years have brought distance and differences, but many of the thoughts expressed in the following pages originated from our past discussions. Parts of the work were delivered as a conference paper at Cornell University in 2017 and as a public lecture at the University of Chicago in 2018, and I am grateful to Joshua Young and, again, Michael Bourdaghs for organizing these events.

At SUNY Press, I have been extremely fortunate to receive the help of Christopher Ahn and James Peltz. I am also indebted to the two anonymous readers whose perceptive comments encouraged me to rethink certain aspects of my argument.

The book is dedicated to Naoki Sakai: with respect and gratitude.

Introduction

In the following pages, I attempt to set forth what might be considered a divergent or dissenting approach to Japan studies, one primarily concerned with the question of method rather than the more traditional focus on objects. It must be immediately added, however, that there is nothing unique about either Japan or Japan studies that would prevent my remarks from conceivably being applied to other branches of area studies as well. The study of area is typically established on the basis of the unit of the individual nation-state—e.g., French studies, China studies, etc.—and this national unity is given substance by appeal to a unified people, culture, and language. This very division of knowledge, I contend, is intrinsically nationalistic. Regardless of whether the individual scholar comes to treat the problem of nationalism, his or her participation in the discourse of area studies already reinforces the overall sense of national oneness. In order to examine the root of this problem, attention must be directed to the general manner in which difference and identity are conceived and institutionally organized. With particular focus on the region of area studies known as "Japan," I aim to show that our thinking of such sites must be placed on a more rigorously critical footing.

How, then, might one contribute to the formation of a critical Japan studies? This is the question that motivates the writing of this book. As goes without saying, such a question did not arise out of thin air; on the contrary, it is ineluctably a response to the dynamics of the North American field of Japan studies that I have witnessed and participated in for nearly two decades now. Certainly there is much to commend about the current scholarship in this field, and there can be little doubt that the discipline as a whole has continued to evolve in such a way as to become more critically self-conscious and finely attuned to the politicality inherent in any project of knowledge. A glance at recent publications in the major subfields of

1

modern literature and history, for example, reveals a powerful and ongoing scrutiny of the various instances of Japanese nationalism and imperialism. The critical impulse that shapes this work also informs the converse of such scholarship, in which various manifestations of *resistance* to nationalism and imperialism receive sustained attention as a way to better engage with issues of ethics and politics. Distinguishing itself from the work produced in the early decades of the Japan studies field following the end of World War II, contemporary scholarship continues to build on the theoretical insights that gradually began to appear in the 1980s. Such schools of thought as poststructuralism, Marxism, feminism, postcolonial studies, psychoanalysis, and queer studies now form an unmistakable presence in the diverse investigations into modern Japanese phenomena, functioning as valuable tools with which to understand Japan more globally and with greater conceptual sensitivity. This trend can be said to signal the establishment of a properly critical Japan studies.

At the same time, however, questions linger as to the nature of this theoretical-critical progress. It is to assess the state of these advancements that I examine the general problem of method. Method, from the Greek *hodos*, or "way," names the path upon which the subject of knowledge enters the domain of its objects. However, if we are to avoid the trap of a subjective formalism in which a set of theories already formulated in advance can simply be applied to any and all Japanese objects, then it must be admitted that this methodological path originates in the object itself. In the particular context of Japan studies, does this mean that the method most befitting the object is to be found in Japan? Such a position would appear to bring us close to the notion of "Asia as method" (*hōhō to shite no Ajia*) as introduced by the social critic and China scholar Takeuchi Yoshimi.[1] Yet it is clear that in these questions of knowledge one cannot suddenly leap to an empirical Japan as the real, extradiscursive site upon which to anchor a methodology. Rather, focus must be directed to the very relation between Japan as an empirical entity and our subjective representations of it. At this more general level, prior to any attachment to this or that particular Japanese object, the central question of how the subject of Japan studies constitutes its various objects comes into view with greater clarity. From this vantage point, I believe, it will be possible to better evaluate a scholarship whose critical spirit appears in the compounded form of enhanced political awareness and more probing theoretical insight.

To confront the question of method, one must recognize the insufficiency of treating the subject-object relation in Japan studies in purely synchronic terms. This discipline possesses a distinct individual history, and the most effective means of understanding its methodological issues is to study the diverse ways in which these matters have been handed down to us from the past. Of course, the presence of methodological issues in the field can be traced to multiple points outside of Japan studies, but in order to comprehend the manner in which these issues have been reflected and internalized, as it were, one needs to analyze the course of their reception in diachronic fashion. A conceptual history, then, which aims at showing how past attempts at theoretical-critical engagement represent challenges to received frameworks and patterns of thought that continue to confront us in the present. In this sense, one of my principal claims in this book is that the past, in its demise or passing, persistently haunts our research in the present. Because of differences in terminology, references, and objects of inquiry, it is easy to overlook these recalcitrant vestiges of the past. It is precisely in order to shed light on the residual presence of past forms of Japan studies that I have decided to focus on the general question of method. In point of fact, I sought as part of my previous study of Abe Kōbō, *Beyond Nation: Time, Writing, and Community in the Work of Abe Kōbō*, to indicate a certain continuity in methodological approach to this writer between an earlier era of Japan studies and its contemporary form.[2] The present volume aims to extend the scope of this type of inquiry, following philosophical strands in the subfields of both literature and history, so as to ideally bring about an acknowledgment that the problematic conceptual frameworks of the past have not been entirely vanquished but indeed continue to inform much present-day scholarship.[3]

A careful examination of past methodological issues will serve to render more explicit the difficulties that attend our present attempt to place Japan studies on even firmer critical ground. For the concern is that the various appeals to theoretical schools or factions, together with the widespread adoption of a more theoretical vocabulary, might not fully achieve the desired goal of advancing the discipline along the lines of greater ethicopolitical awareness and increased conceptual acuity. Despite the best of intentions, the ghost of an earlier Japan studies, as characterized by Orientalist projections and theoretical naiveté, might still haunt present-day scholarship. My point is that an understanding of the current status of Japan studies might be gained by directing attention to past forms of this discipline with an eye to unearthing, beyond the surface level of theoretical references, certain larger conceptual structures that continue to undergird research. I am aware that a metacritical shift from the study of Japanese objects to an examination of the attempts at theoretical objectification on the part of Japan scholars will not be greeted, to say the least, with universal approbation. The field of Japan studies is a small one, and it seems reasonable to expect that my theoretical analyses of the theoretical analyses undertaken by several scholars of literature and history will be seen as mere personal attacks, a sign of individual animus rather than scholarly integrity. This risk will be assumed primarily for two reasons. First, it seems unduly restrictive to conceive of the objects of inquiry in Japan studies as necessarily "Japanese." Precisely by widening the scope of possible objects in this field to include entities that may not be immediately identifiable in such fixed national (cultural, racial, ethnic, etc.) terms, I would like to draw attention to an irreducible level of arbitrariness in the meaning of what is called "Japan." Secondly, my suspicion is that the theoretical turn in Japan studies that began in the 1980s has not sufficiently called into question many of the presuppositions that continue to structure the field. Without a conceptual engagement at this more fundamental level, the incorporation of theoretical research exposes itself to the possibility of mere ornamentation. In many instances of scholarship, the strategic use of a term or proper name can be seen to function as a facile substitute for actual intellectual engagement. It is in order to avoid this trap and investigate those concepts that forcefully govern scholarly inquiry that I have chosen to discuss theoretical readings of the recent past.

From the standpoint of the present, it is impossible to view the past as a simple exteriority. To say that the present is partially a product of the past is to in effect acknowledge that one is oneself internally inhabited or occupied by past forces. In the context of Japan studies, this raises the important question of inheritance. Regardless of whether one desires to or not, or indeed whether one is consciously aware of it or not, contemporary scholars of Japan have already inherited certain conceptual frameworks and modes of thought from the institutional past, and these serve to create a line of diachronic continuity that ensures that Japan studies remains at all times essentially close to itself. At issue here is the elusive notion of reception: does one receive this inheritance from the past passively or actively?[4] If we receive such transmission in a strictly passive sense, then it seems we are condemned to repeat this legacy in more or less the same terms. In this way, individual scholars of Japan studies can be seen to function as conduits in the larger project of institutional replication. The line that began in the past works itself through one's participation in the present to create in turn an even more formidable inheritance for future scholars. In the very *act* of reception, however, the opportunity arises to inflect the inheritance differently. Yet such intervention requires that one be able to evaluate the content of this heritage, and such capacity is not necessarily guaranteed in a field that is committed less to conceptual reflection than to the organization and explication of its empirical objects. For the fact remains that the inheritance, despite its apparent grounding in factual knowledge, is indeed conceptual through and through. The field codifies its rules and practices through this medium, and it is only by subjecting these to a rigorous theoretical examination, I believe, that the value of the inheritance can be properly assessed.

In chapter 1, "Remembering Kafka: Between Murakami Haruki and Komori Yōichi," I attempt to clear a kind of path between the famous novelist and the renowned literary critic so that an exchange of ideas might freely take place. Here I am simply repeating Komori's own gesture of creating a dialogue with Murakami as set forth in his polemical 2006 book, *Murakami Haruki ron: 'Umibe no Kafuka' wo seidoku suru* [On Murakami Haruki: A close reading of *Kafka on the Shore*]. As the title makes clear, this work constitutes a response to Murakami's 2002 bestselling novel, *Kafka on the Shore*. It is well known that Murakami is the object of considerable opprobrium from leftist intellectuals in Japan, and Komori's unforgiving treatment of his fiction can be said to mark the zenith (or perhaps nadir) of that trend. While my own view of Murakami is that he is an occasionally entertaining if steadfastly mediocre novelist, I am suspicious of moralistic attempts to regard his work as something akin to evil, as Komori insistently does in his study. Such unflinching confidence in matters of ethics and politics strikes me as antithetical to the very nature of ethicopolitical decisions, for these decisions must take place within time, and the radical difference that "is" time prohibits any stable recourse to rules or precedents upon which to model behavior. From my standpoint, the subject who claims knowledge of what is ethical and what is not represents a very classical form of subjectivism, and philosophy throughout its history has sought to determine man as subject precisely as an attempt to shield him from the incessant contingency and singularity of the world. After tracing this subjectivism back to Komori's early works, I provide my own reading of Murakami's novel in order to demonstrate that the subject is inescapably inscribed within a milieu of spatiotemporal difference that it is unable to fully master.

Chapter 2, "The Double Pull of History and Philosophy: Reading Harootunian," shifts the disciplinary terrain from literature to history by focusing on the wide range of writings by the eminent intellectual historian of modern Japan, Harry Harootunian. One of the great virtues of

Harootunian's work lies in its persistent engagement with philosophical questions. In a field that views historical inquiry primarily in terms of an objectification of past events, Harootunian recognizes that the elusive force of the past is such that it precedes such objectification, thereby indelibly marking the historian in ways that exceed the epistemology of the traditional subject-object relation. It is because of this insight that Harootunian is drawn to issues of methodology and time. After showing how Harootunian's project is unfortunately misrecognized in the attacks on his work by the scholars David Williams and Andrew Gordon, I provide a close analysis of Harootunian's thinking of the relation between time and space, locating a certain inconsistency. For Harootunian, the time-space binary is provocatively determined along ethicopolitical lines, and I attempt to unravel some of the difficulties that arise as a result of this decision. I then undertake a reading of Harootunian's unreservedly affirmative interpretation of Imamura Shōhei's 1970 film, *Nippon sengoshi: Madamu Onboro no seikatsu* [History of postwar Japan as told by a barmaid], so as to better grasp the nature of his position on ethics and politics. As in my reading of Komori, the general element of time reappears in this context and provides a clue to a certain temptation of prelapsarianism that I detect in Harootunian's work. I conclude the chapter by following the logic of Harootunian's repeated critiques of the philosopher Martin Heidegger. While Harootunian insightfully discovers a rejection of what might be called the messiness of sociality in Heidegger's thought, I argue that his underestimation of the philosopher's notion of ecstatic temporality has powerfully negative consequences for his own attempt to rehabilitate the concept of presence.

While chapter 1 focuses on the work of one of the most influential literary theoreticians in Japan and chapter 2 on the writings of undoubtedly the most theoretically ambitious and astute scholar of Japanese history in North America, for chapter 3 I could find no single figure of similar stature and orientation in the field of Japanese literature in North America. As a result, I decided to consider the research of three major scholars teaching at the most prestigious universities with the aim of identifying their principal theoretical contributions to the discipline. Rather than form three separate chapters, however, I gradually came to recognize a profound level of commonality that joins their otherwise disparate scholarship: the question of subjectivity. Despite considerable differences in their respective research objects, it is the underlying problematic of method that acts as the agglutinative force that allows their work to be regarded as conceptually similar. A methodology centered on the subject will be forced to reduce the complexity and multiplicity of the world to the status of object, and in this way a certain essential unruliness of literature will come to be domesticated. The literary text might still be expertly handled according to the dominant conventions of the discipline, but it is undeniable that something of precious conceptual value will be lost.

In the first section of this chapter, "Subjectivity and Retroactivity," I examine Tomi Suzuki's 1996 study of the I-novel, *Narrating the Self: Fictions of Japanese Modernity*. At the methodological level, Suzuki announces that her work represents a radical break from previous I-novel scholarship because she focuses not on textual presence but rather on the untimely act of retroactive reading. While I fully agree with the importance of this move, the notion of retroactivity nevertheless sets loose something like a general disturbance in her text, and Suzuki is forced to arbitrarily—if revealingly— restrict this notion's scope of effectivity to narrow literary phenomena, thus preserving the integrity and substantial presence of Japanese cultural identity. In the next section, "Subjectivity and Binding," I pursue a reading of Alan Tansman's two major works: the 1993 *Writings of Kōda Aya, A Japanese Literary Daughter* and the 2009 *Aesthetics of Japanese Fascism*. For Tansman, the essential core of fascism is determined as binding, or *musubi*, from the original Roman term *fasces*. Binding is fascistic because it threatens what is held to be the primordial unity and identity that defines each individual qua individual. Tansman marshals a wide array of theoretical sources to support his fundamentally subjectivist claim of the sanctity of the individual, and he does not hesitate to criticize such philosophers as Heidegger and the Kyoto School's Nishida Kitarō for what he regards as their quasifascist attacks on individual identity. In a manner similar to my response to Suzuki and her treatment of retroactivity, I show in my discussion of Tansman that this notion of binding must be logically generalized: far from being excluded as the binary contrast of individualism, it functions as the necessary condition upon which a thinking of individuality first becomes possible. The concluding section of the chapter, "Subjectivity and Alterity," develops an analysis of Dennis Washburn's 1995 *The Dilemma of the Modern in Japanese Fiction* together with his 2007 *Translating Mount Fuji: Modern Japanese Fiction and the Ethics of Identity*. I locate in Washburn an underlying paradox whereby his avowed goal of formulating a critique of nationalism is offset by his commitment to a traditional view of spatiality as structured by the duality of inside and outside. As a result, the notion of identity that appears in the title of his later monograph is conceived in such a way that what is seen to be "indigenous" to Japan, as he refers to it, can only be opposed to that which is posited as "foreign." This methodological decision, which affirms an inheritance that belongs as much to metaphysics as it does to common sense, is never questioned as such. What is thus foreclosed is the chance to interrogate nationalism at a more fundamental level so as to discover its conceptual complicity with the very establishment of the field of Japan studies.[5]

By way of conclusion, let me express my hope that this book will contribute to a rethinking of some of the most basic premises in Japan studies. The very ubiquity of these premises lends them the value of a common sense so deeply rooted that it often governs our thinking invisibly, without us being explicitly aware of their nature and considerable force. These premises do not originate in us as autonomous subjects but rather precede us; they form part of the tradition of Japan studies that substantially shapes the way research is conducted, inscribing us as part of a longer historical chain and at times bringing us uncomfortably close to those earlier and less exalted instances in the field that we might otherwise insist are now dead and buried. By viewing conceptual thought beyond the level of contingent attachment to an empirical scholarship that is itself held to be unshakably grounded, one uncovers the possibility of more fully opening Japan studies to its outside.

Chapter 1

Remembering Kafka

Between Murakami Haruki and Komori Yōichi

My job is to arrange things in the right order. I make sure that results come after their causes. I make sure that meanings don't get conflated with each other. I make sure that the past comes before the present. I make sure that the future comes after the present. Well, I suppose it's alright if things get a little out of order.

—Murakami Haruki[1]

Introduction

The astonishing domestic and international success of Murakami Haruki's 2002 novel, *Umibe no Kafuka* [Kafka on the shore], would be critically appraised several years later by literary critic Komori Yōichi in his 2006 book-length study, *Murakami Haruki ron: 'Umibe no Kafuka' wo seidoku suru* [On Murakami Haruki: A close reading of 'Kafka on the shore']. Komori, who first rose to prominence in the field of modern Japanese literature in 1988 with the publication of two widely influential works, *Buntai to shite no monogatari* [Narrative as literary style] and *Kōzō to shite no katari* [Narration as structure], declares that Murakami's novel must be understood contextually on the basis of the historical aftermath of 9/11. Noting that the novel was published exactly one day prior to the first anniversary of the series of terrorist attacks that occurred in the United States on September 11, 2001, Komori writes, "The very act of the book's publication played a performance that momentarily recalled to readers the memory of 9/11, which took place in the real world, only to then draw their consciousness into the fictional world of [Murakami's] own novel, making them forget that memory."²

Echoing the criticism of Murakami's oeuvre by a number of other left-wing critics, Komori specifically faults *Umibe no Kafuka* for its effacement of historical memory. Certain writers, as for example Natsume Sōseki, help us apprehend the past with greater depth and urgency by virtue of the sophistication of their fictional techniques as well as their general awareness of the politicality inherent in the act of literature. Murakami, by contrast, diverts the reader's attention away from the demands of the past by creating what Komori regards as a politically vacuous fictional world. While the external fact of the novel's publication date may have been strategically intended to evoke some type of historical linkage with the events of 9/11, the internal dynamics of the work appear, from Komori's perspective, to erase that link by preying upon the reader's consciousness, displacing his or her focus on historical memory, and encouraging a lack of vigilance in the form of historical forgetting.

In his denunciation of Murakami, Komori finds support in the words of the novelist Kakuta Mitsuyo. Writing in the literary journal *Gunzō* in 2002, Kakuta describes reading *Umibe no Kafuka* while watching television coverage of the previous year's 9/11 terrorist attacks. As she reports, the anxiety produced by these two activities was of such intensity that she considered canceling a trip abroad for fear that her plane might be targeted; similarly, she recalls a friend's inability to open the seal of a parcel of books sent from the United States out of concern that the box may contain traces of anthrax bacteria. Kakuta concludes that her sense of fear stems from what she refers to, in a striking phrase, as Murakami's "intention of unintentional violence" (*bōryokuteki na ishinaki ishi*).³ Komori emphasizes this fear by contrasting it with the overwhelmingly positive reception of the book in Japan, where readers have consistently described it as providing a sense of "solace" (*iyashi*) and "relief" (*sukui*). How is it possible that Murakami's novel can yield such contradictory readings? For Komori, Kakuta's response to *Umibe no Kafuka* represents a minority voice that must not be drowned out by the vast number of readers who, in the wake of 9/11, turn to the novel for a sense of reassurance and emotional comfort in the face of an otherwise frightening historical reality. The widespread acclaim for the novel instills in Komori a "strong apprehension" and "powerful sense of crisis," as he writes, for he views this response as symptomatic of an increasing political apathy found throughout present-day Japan.

Komori notes that the publication of *Umibe no Kafuka* was accompanied by an extensive marketing campaign that deployed various resources from the internet. Moreover, the commercial pressures brought to bear on readers received tacit support from the Japanese government. Here, Komori refers to remarks made shortly after the book's appearance by the psychologist Kawai Hayao, who as director of the Agency for Cultural Affairs (*Bunkachō*) played a leading role in Japanese national education. Praising *Umibe no Kafuka* as "great narrative fiction," Kawai goes on to quote a passage that appears at the end of the novel about "looking at the painting and listening to the wind" as image-based activities that are somehow capable of endowing life with a greater sense of purpose and meaning.[4] Komori critically summarizes Kawai's words as follows: "Emphasize images rather than language, and particularly such corporeal or pre-reflective (*shintaika sareta*) images as 'listening to the wind.'" In his response to Kawai, Komori once again appeals to the notion of consciousness: "If language is consciousness, then images encompass the realm of the unconscious, and corporeal or pre-reflective images are linked even more deeply to this unconscious realm."[5]

In his reflections on historical memory as well as in his engagement with the views of Kakuta Mitsuyo and Kawai Hayao, Komori is keen to stress the importance of critical vigilance in our approach to *Umibe no Kafuka*. With the support of a variety of commercial and state forces, Murakami's novel has achieved unprecedented recognition at a historical juncture in which the events of 9/11 and the subsequent "War on Terror" have produced a sense of increasing global instability. A rigorous understanding of *Umibe no Kafuka* must begin by situating the work against the background of this larger violence: "In those countries where *Umibe no Kafuka* has become popular, a common social and spiritual pathology has been spreading since '9/11' in 2001, and the novel has been consumed as a commodity that brings about 'relief,' 'succor,' and 'solace' for that pathology. It is the standpoint of the present book that we must not accept this situation as 'something positive.'"[6] This large-scale "pathology," Komori argues, reveals certain problems endemic to contemporary society, problems that require rational analysis so that we may better grasp its causes and possible forms of treatment. The false promise of emotional consolation held out by Murakami's novel must be resisted, for it encourages a form of complacency and even infantilization that leaves intact our existing sociopolitical structures. In this regard, Kawai's focus on sensory images is dismissed as a mere withdrawal from conscious political engagement in favor of an unconscious acceptance of institutional reality. Komori regards the unconscious as a site of prereflective corporeality in which consciousness remains stunted, prevented from developing beyond the limits of the body such as to expand its critical faculties and achieve greater awareness of the surrounding world. Consciousness is associated with historical memory, and this is contrasted with the forgetting of the past and dulling of critical vigilance that appear initially in *Umibe no Kafuka*, but is then repeated in Kawai's celebration of the novel as well as, more generally, the work's global commercial success. Komori's project in *Murakami Haruki ron: 'Umibe no Kafuka' wo seidoku suru* consists in awakening the reader from the slumber of this unconscious forgetting so that we may confront literature and the historical reality that encompasses it with a greater responsibility to the past.

Reflections on Method

In order to better grasp the stakes of Komori's approach to Murakami's novel, we must first consider the broader issue of Komori's methodological commitments in his understanding of literature. Some of the clearest examples of the theoretical foundations that undergird his interpretative practice are found in two early works, *Kōzō to shite no katari* and *Dekigoto to shite no yomu koto* [Reading as event]. In the former text, Komori undertakes an analysis of literature on the basis of the interrelated notions of writing and reading. He examines these notions in the course of explicating the literary formalism of the modernist writer Yokomitsu Riichi, as can be seen in the following extended passage:

> It is no exaggeration to claim that the logical cornerstone of Yokomitsu's 'formalism' is to be found in the single word 'writing' (*moji*). For example, such contemporary French thinkers as Roland Barthes, Jacques Lacan, Julia Kristeva, and Jacques Derrida have made a radically conceptual expansion of the word *écriture*, with its everyday meanings of written language, written letters, writings, the act of writing, and handwriting. Just as they have sought to enact a structural shift in the world's knowledge of this term, so too did Yokomitsu try to construct a theoretical strategy for his notion of 'formalism' by expanding the concept of 'writing.' . . . He poses the question of readership in the process of receiving 'writing' in the form of linguistic 'traces' or residual 'material forms' that are severed

from the 'author' as parent in the sense of the source of expression. . . . As Yokomitsu states, 'We look at a newspaper. Yet *even without looking at it*, the newspaper contains *merely forms in the sense of engraved writing*, which appear simply *like meaningless stones*. Now *when we look at that newspaper, we for the first time perceive the content determined by this writing*, which *originating in the forms of engraved writing* as arranged in the newspaper is *completely different from stones*'. . . . In this sense, the 'writing' that is 'simply like meaningless stones' appears as spatialized 'material forms' that are completely different from 'language' that appears in the process of expression whereby the expresser tries at each instant to grasp the temporal succession of consciousness. . . . In order to once again recover this 'object's' function as language, that is, in order to restore to life dead language or the linguistic corpse, 'we' readers must 'look' at that 'writing.' Only when the reader 'looks' at 'writing,' perceives it in its status as 'writing,' sets in motion its interpretive codes and contexts as linguistic signs, incorporating it into his own continuous flow of consciousness in the Bergsonian sense of *durée*, can we 'for the first time' 'perceive the content determined by this writing, which is completely different from stones' that exist, and which emerges from 'the forms of writing.' This is Yokomitsu's claim.[7]

At first glance, these lines may appear to have little in common with Komori's critical reading of Murakami. While the contexts are indeed quite different, there can nevertheless be discerned an underlying attention to what might be called *ideological concealment* that is pivotal to Komori's project. Just as the widespread reception of *Umibe no Kafuka* in terms of "solace" and "relief" masks a dynamics of violence, as Komori indicates in referring to Kakuta Mitsuyo's response to the novel, so too does the traditional understanding of writing and reading depend upon a concept of expressionism. This is a concept centered on the ideal of communicative transparency that dismisses the possibility of misreading and misunderstanding as mere empirical accidents that do not impinge upon the essential transmission of meaning in intersubjectivity. As Komori recalls, such expressionism posits "the 'author' as parent in the sense of the source of expression." Whatever temporal or spatial gap may come to intervene in the relation between the parent-author and child-text must be regarded as strictly provisional, for the latter in its status as emissary or representative of the former can in principle only give itself through the larger identity shared between these two. Because the text contains within it the core of meaning as intended by the author, it presents itself as intelligible to the reader. As a vehicle of expression that is initially animated by the author, writing awaits the reanimation of the reader, whose understanding of the author's original meaning is enabled by the fact that the act of reanimation in reading is ultimately nothing more than a repetition or doubling of—that is to say, a return to—the source. For Komori, the animation of meaning that unites the otherwise distinct acts of writing and reading conceals the complex manner in which writing *presents itself* to be read.

According to Komori, this classical notion of expression comes to be disturbed by Yokomitsu Riichi's strategic expansion of the concept of writing—an expansion that Komori compares to the theoretical development of the otherwise everyday term *écriture* in contemporary French thought. The rethinking of writing takes as its point of departure the interstitial space that exists between the writer as source of meaning and the reader as its intended recipient or destination. In this account, what is given to the reader are merely the "traces" (*konseki*) or "material forms" (*busshitsuteki keishiki*) that remain after being "severed" from the author. What has come to be naturalized as a simple transmission of meaning from writer to reader is now discovered to contain an element of materiality that risks being overlooked in this model of intersubjective communication. In his example of the newspaper, Yokomitsu stresses that the page of print "contains merely forms in the sense of engraved writing (*chōkokuteki na moji*), which appear simply like meaningless stones." Komori conceives of this material remainder of writing in the specific terms of death and spatiality: the traces left by the original writer are nothing more than "dead language," a "linguistic corpse" that in and of itself signifies nothing. From the time they appear in the world, detached from the animating temporality of the writer, such lifeless marks give themselves strictly as instances of bare spatiality: "The 'writing' that is 'simply like meaningless stones' appears as spatialized 'material forms' that are completely different from 'language' that appears in the process of expression whereby the expresser tries at each instant to grasp the temporal succession of consciousness." Just as writing signals a passage from temporal life to spatial death through the expressive act in which language leaves the writer and falls into the material world, so too can writing once again rise to the level of meaningful language (as opposed to "meaningless stones") through the animating act of reading. As Komori concludes, "Only through the reader's *durée* . . . that is, the setting into motion of consciousness in the form of time, can 'writing' in the sense of the non-linguistic spatial object for the first time be restored to life in the form of language."[8]

Komori's elucidation of Yokomitsu's formalism through focus on the concept of writing represents a vital theoretical intervention that raises the level of discourse on Japanese literature considerably beyond the limits of traditional empirical scholarship. Nevertheless, we would be remiss not to point out that certain problems do appear in his reading of Yokomitsu, problems that are not merely restricted to this or that particular object of inquiry but indeed form part of Komori's general method of literary interpretation. Despite his attempt to liberate the question of writing from a narrow expressionist conception in which the parent-author is posed against the child-text over which he retains full control, Komori replicates this same binary framework in both his sympathetic or productive approach to Yokomitsu and his far more critical commentary on Murakami. Komori is by no means unaware of the trap of binarity, as can be confirmed, for example, in his early study *Buntai to shite no monogatari*, where he criticizes Freud for "attempting to describe the binary opposition between man and woman as the binary between the penis and vagina, presence (*genzen*) and absence."[9] As we witnessed in his attack on Murakami, however, Komori follows a broadly Manichean approach in his reading of *Umibe no Kafuka*. The novel is grasped *either* as a source of comfort and emotional relief, as can be seen in the work's general reception as well as in the remarks of the psychologist and government bureaucrat Kawai Hayao regarding the book's putatively therapeutic value, *or* as a site of violence that provokes fear, as attested to by the novelist Kakuta Mitsuyo and confirmed by Komori's own impressions. No doubt Murakami's work has given rise to a wide array of responses, but Komori seems intent on narrowing the range of possible readings to the unilaterally adulatory or the no less unilaterally negative or disparaging. Given that a literary text is at issue here, however, the oppositional structure of Komori's reading (either/or, for or against, good or bad) immediately raises the question of whether *Umibe no Kafuka* or indeed *any* work of fiction can justly be seen through such a reductive lens.

This presentation of Murakami's novel in such starkly contrastive terms lays the groundwork for more specific instances of binarity. From Komori's perspective, *Umibe no Kafuka* is to be denounced for its violent erasure of historical memory. This work, as he remarks in lines previously quoted, "momentarily recalled to readers the memory of 9/11, which took place in the real world, only to then draw their consciousness into the fictional world of [Murakami's] own novel, making them forget that memory." Here memory is conceived in an exclusively dualistic sense, such that it can only be "recalled" (*sōki saseta*) or forgotten ("making them forget": *wasuresasete iku*). Memory is not regarded as taking place along a spectrum in which the act of recall always remains vulnerable to forgetting, just as forgetting might at any time suddenly yield to recall. The possibility of relationality between memory and forgetting, whereby each remains essentially exposed to the other in a kind of mutual contaminatability, appears to be foreclosed in advance. Indeed, Komori's unduly rigid conception of memory eventually leads him at one point in his reading of Murakami to propose a literary typology between "Novels that Recall Memory and Novels that Omit Memory,"[10] as he entitles a chapter section in his book. In this view, the interrelated questions of time and subjectivity in their indispensable role in memory come to be dismissed in favor of a purely objectivist account according to which certain things in the world in and of themselves give rise to memory while other things are innately or naturally disposed to erase it.

In the foregoing passage, the opposition between memory and forgetting is reinforced by the division between the exteriority of what Komori calls the "real world" and the interiority of Murakami's "fictional world." Consciousness, which Komori insists should be authentically directed to the former, falls into inauthenticity when seduced or "drawn into" (*ishiki wo hikikomi*) the latter. Yet consciousness itself becomes subject to this same operation of binarity, as Komori seeks to rigorously distinguish it from the unconscious. "If language is consciousness," as he argues, "then images encompass the realm of the unconscious." Claims such as this readily point to the problems inherent in dualistic thinking, since the complex phenomenon of language can in no way be reduced to consciousness, just as images are never restricted to the level of the unconscious. As with all binary relations, these sets of opposed terms do not exist in any abstract, neutral space outside of subjective intervention. On the contrary, Komori at a certain moment in time—that is to say, in all contingency—makes a *decision* in his critical reading of Murakami that the text of the latter is to be associated with the unconscious, corporeal or prereflective imagery, interiority, the fictional or imaginary (*kyokō*), emotional solace, and forgetting. These terms are given a straightforwardly negative valuation. Opposed to them stand the values that Komori puts forth as positive, in the sense of that which is ethically and politically just: consciousness, language, exteriority, the real world (*genjitsu no sekai*), critical vigilance, and memory. Now these two conceptual chains, it must be pointed out, cannot be understood as separated in any absolute sense. Rather, a schema of development secretly links them together, such that consciousness and the various traits allied to it will be posited as the ideal telos or endpoint toward which the unconscious and its associated traits must strive, failing which they are summarily condemned to a position outside of or beneath this normative site of ethics and politics.

Despite the different issues under discussion as well as the diverse stances adopted vis-à-vis the object of inquiry, Komori's reading of Yokomitsu Riichi broadly follows this same mode of approach. On the one hand, this reading sheds important light on the elusiveness of meaning in the context of intersubjectivity. In a powerful gesture, Komori reminds us that the relation between writer (author) and reader hinges upon the medium of expression that exists between these two figures. If communication is enabled by this medium, then the material vehicle that is writing also, paradoxically, threatens that communication by calling attention to the dual acts in which language spills forth from the expressive writer only to then be reabsorbed by the attending reader. As Yokomitsu declares, the reader is not confronted with any pregiven linguistic meaning but merely with "meaningless stones" that need to be actively reanimated so that they may return to their original intelligibility. On the other hand, however, Komori's elaboration of Yokomitsu's notion of writing remains grounded on the same binary that informs his analysis of Murakami. The series of oppositions that are mobilized in the treatment of *Umibe no Kafuka* now comes to be replaced by those of time versus space and life versus death. Significantly, the privileged role assigned to consciousness remains unchanged. The attack against the ideology of expressionism proceeds by demonstrating that the tremendous power over meaning wielded by the parent-author must in fact be supplemented, at a different time and place, by the reader's restorative act of reanimation.

Before examining the binary operation that supports this rethinking of writing, let us quickly note that Komori's sensitivity to the strange powerlessness of the writer constitutes an abiding feature of his work. Already in 1988 in the opening pages of *Kōzō to shite no katari*, for example, we find the following passage: "Even in the process of choosing his context and codes, or even when he tries to read a certain unified message, the flesh and blood author can never 'present' himself before the reader as a linguistic subject who controls his discourse."[11] This same emphasis on the writer's lack of potency reappears nearly two decades later in *Murakami Haruki ron: 'Umibe no Kafuka' wo seidoku suru*, although here the remarks are limited to the particular genre of the novel: "The special quality of the novel as genre lies in the fact that even the author cannot force a specific manner of reading upon the reader."[12]

The central problem of Komori's interpretation of Yokomitsu is that the notions of time and life are linked with a conception of subjective interiority that is posed against the material world of objects understood primarily in terms of spatiality and death. Here Komori doesn't appear to realize that the conceptual expansion of *écriture* in contemporary French thought was motivated by the need to account for the essential limitations of subjectivity, to rethink more fundamentally the relation between man and the world such that the latter remain irreducible to the otherwise penetrative theoretical vision of the former. The recognition of writing in its silent materiality helps us better grasp the meaning-producing acts of both the expressive writer and the supplementary reader. In particular, Komori seeks in his reading of Yokomitsu to underscore a crucial displacement in the production of meaning from the writer to the reader. Following the standard view of expressionism, it is the writer who must be regarded as the source or "parent" of meaningful language. Because the writer embeds this core of meaning in the vehicle of writing, the reader's task is merely to passively receive it, and upon this reception the act of intersubjective communication can be said to reach achievement. In Komori's expansion of Yokomitsu's initial expansion of the notion of *moji*, however, it is now the reader who takes center stage. Since the writing being read is here seen to be radically stripped of meaning, consisting merely of a carcass of marks that remains after the departure of the writer, the reader is no longer capable of passively internalizing these marks in the form of language. Directly to the contrary, the reader must now actively transform these mute "spatialized 'material forms,'" raising these "meaningless stones" to the proper level of language.

Hence, the privilege accorded to the reading subject lies in his ability to overcome the initial resistance of materiality and achieve meaning. Komori's aim is to shift the site of production of meaning from the writer to the reader, thereby calling attention to the long history of neglect suffered by the reader, whose active role in the reading of writing was illegitimately dismissed as nothing more than passive reception. It is not difficult to see here a kind of dialectical reversal in which, following Hegel's account of the bondsman (slave) eventually triumphing over the lord (master) through his labor on the thing, the reader finally liberates himself from the false tyranny of the writer through the negativity of his labor on the text.[13] As with all such reversals, however, the point is to see beyond the mere play of surface effects and grasp the substance of the change being wrought. Just as Hegel's dialectic finds its resolution in a more developed form of mastery, the transition from writer to reader leaves in place, albeit in an implicitly more advanced form, the core activity of subjective animation in the production of meaning. In other words, the subject is determined on the basis of his ability to transcend worldly materiality and raise it to the level of spirit. The inferior status of writing in the form of "meaningless stones" derives from its inability to signify, that is, to reflect its identity in and of itself. In this sense, the materiality of writing is no different from that of any other physical thing in the world. Only through the gaze of the reader can writing assume its true status not as a mere physical object but rather as a privileged spiritual product: "In order to once again recover this 'object's' function as language, that is, in order to restore to life dead language or the linguistic corpse, 'we' readers must 'look' at that 'writing.' Only when the reader 'looks' at 'writing,' perceives it in its status as 'writing' . . . can we 'for the first time' 'perceive the content determined by this writing, which is completely different from stones' that exist."

This "look" of the reader is nothing other than the theoretical vision required to penetrate brute matter so as to identify the spiritual core of meaning that resides latently within it. In Komori's account, the reader's encounter with these initially unintelligible marks is one in which time confronts space. Following Yokomitsu, Komori finds that worldly or material writing is devoid of time and that it only comes to be temporalized and thus swept up into the spiritual process of signification through the theoretical act of the reader. What was hitherto dead is now restored to life (*saisei suru*) by the reader's consciousness. Prior to its encounter with the reader, writing was only writing that did not yet know itself as writing; it was thus unable to reveal its essential "content" (i.e., meaning), which remained locked within it, hidden from the view of others. This death, in the sense of a merely corporeal, prereflective materiality, can only be sublated and returned to life by the sovereign consciousness of the reader, whose look "sets in motion [writing's] interpretive codes and contexts as linguistic signs, incorporating it into his own continuous flow of consciousness." This very classical form of subjectivism, centered on the life-giving powers of consciousness, never seems to be questioned. Here we must recall Komori's privileging of consciousness in his condemnation of Murakami, for the latter's work is associated with the sphere of the unconscious in such a way that it loses sight of external reality and falls prey to historical forgetting. Above all, however, the subjectivism that informs Komori's reading of Yokomitsu appears most sharply in his reduction of time to the domain of subjective interiority. As he claims, "Only through the reader's *durée* . . . that is, the setting into motion of consciousness in the form of time, can 'writing' in the sense of the non-linguistic spatial object for the first time be restored to life in the form of language." From this perspective, the unsettling movement of time, which is capable in its effects of overturning all logical or rational order, comes to find stable accommodation within consciousness. Time is required in the conscious operation by which the materiality of writing is spiritualized, purified of its dross, and rendered into meaningful language. No doubt this is true, in a certain sense, but it is also to severely underestimate the ability of time to distort any and all conscious acts performed by the subject. If time, in its radical alterity, only appears at each moment as other to itself, then Komori seems to place excessive faith in subjectivity and the power of consciousness to master worldly exteriority.

Having examined certain methodological features in *Kōzō to shite no katari*, let us now turn to the 1996 text *Dekigoto to shite no yomu koto*. In this work, Komori presents a meticulous and highly inventive reading of Sōseki's 1908 novel *Kōfu* [The miner], a text that in fact features prominently in Murakami's *Umibe no Kafuka*.[14] The opening pages of *Dekigoto to shite no yomu koto* consist of a general or formal account of reading, one that lays the groundwork for the particular approach Komori adopts in his interpretation of Sōseki. As Komori writes:

> The act of *reading* is nothing other than following writing (*moji*) with one's eyes and recognizing it as signs that express words. However, this apparently simple act is an extremely complex process. Our vision distinguishes the different shapes of each black ink stain printed on the white paper, cognizing these as writing in the sense of something more than stains. We send this visual cognition to consciousness, where writing in the form of icons is transformed into voice as auditory images that represent the units of language (*kotoba no tan'i*). As the memory of these auditory images continues in duration, we shift our vision to the next form of writing, again allowing voice to emerge from the icon. We gradually come to form words and phrases or sentences by connecting and disconnecting these icons as fixed units.
>
> When we compose words, of course, we must connect vocalized images into a unit that evokes some type of meaning while distinguishing them from other parts, thus making the movement of consciousness all the more complex. In the act of *reading*, we transform writing to voice, proceed from the previous form of writing to the next form of writing, from the previous

sound to the next sound, from the previous word to the next word, while durationally continuing the memory of this prior information as new information is being introduced, and finally disconnecting and connecting and connecting and disconnecting these at various levels. This activity appears as a flickering process of the bewilderingly multiple and different levels of the movement of consciousness.

This movement is one that proceeds on the basis of the flow of time from the past through the present and continually onward into the future. At the same time, it also involves the ceaseless recall of past memories into the present, thus continually engaging multiple layers of memory with present consciousness . . .

In reading, what is first of all thrown before one is nothing other than a site composed of a textual series of writings. From the instant my consciousness as reader begins to interact with this site, time begins to flow and the textual space begins to appear. This is also when both the expresser and the reader simultaneously manifest themselves. The language previously written by the expresser enters within the site of consciousness of the reader, and through this there occurs the generation of meaning (*imi seisei*). This also entails that the language existing within the consciousness of the reader is projected to the textual site constituted by the expresser. Thus an instantaneous distortion and protrusion in the site of the spatiotemporal continuum. What takes place there is the *event*.[15]

This passage further develops the account of writing and reading offered in the analysis of Yokomitsu that appears in *Kōzō to shite no katari*. Komori's fundamental understanding of the relation between writing and reading as an active site of contestation between writer and reader remains unchanged. Whereas the earlier analysis focused specifically on Yokomitsu's conception of writing, here the stress is unequivocally on reading, with the suggestion that this notion will play a crucial role in the engagement with Sōseki. Paralleling his demonstration that the act of intersubjective communication must pass through the materiality of writing, Komori now shows precisely how the dynamics of reading involve a potentially disorienting bilateral movement of time. The flow of time that he identifies runs sequentially from past to future—we "proceed from the previous form of writing to the next form of writing, from the previous sound to the next sound, from the previous word to the next word"—such that we find ourselves at each instant virtually overwhelmed by new stimuli; it is in order to render such stimuli intelligible that the reverse movement takes place, as we are forced to constantly reach back into the past and establish connections between the externally new and that older new that has now been safely internalized in memory. In Komori's description, consciousness appears continually under siege in the act of reading, for this bilateral movement of time requires an intricate coordination between the sense of sight, which is directed to the textual marks found in the outside world, and the faculty of memory, which by contrast is directed internally to the contents of consciousness itself.

Despite his acute understanding of the act of reading, Komori nevertheless insists on conceptualizing this process within the restricted framework of subjectivity. All too quickly the question of reading is reduced to the figure of the *reader*, and this reader receives the external stimuli of written marks that have their source of transmission in the *author*, or *expresser* (*hyōgensha*), to use Komori's term. As should be evident, this figuration of the general or fundamental activities of writing and reading effectively limits these latter to the human. In truth, however, there is nothing intrinsically human about these acts. As we saw earlier in Komori's examination of Yokomitsu, a "conceptual expansion" of the notion of writing is enacted following the example of certain contemporary French thinkers. The decision Komori makes to expand upon Yokomitsu's initial expansion of the concept of *moji* nevertheless falls short of considering the interrelated questions of writing and reading beyond the traditional category of the human. Indeed, this treatment of writing and reading not in terms of ontology (i.e., the incessant movement of being determined in its generality as acts of inscription that call forth a re-acting or response in the form of reading) but in the far more confined sphere of the subject yields a diminished thinking of time that fails to account for the many ways in which writing and reading, precisely, exceed subjectivity. I have already touched upon the limited nature of Komori's conception of time, but in the above passage on reading we encounter the following lines: "In reading, what is first of all thrown before one is nothing other than a site composed of a textual series of writings. From the instant my consciousness as reader begins to interact with this site, time begins to flow and the textual space begins to appear."

Exactly as with *Kōzō to shite no katari*, the attention to time appears strictly as an attempt to explain the inner workings of consciousness. The cognition of material inscriptions as language, that is, as something more than black ink stains on white paper, requires time. For Komori, significantly, time is not seen as a general element that essentially disturbs the intelligibility and meaning production necessary for reading; on the contrary, time is that which makes reading possible. The reason for this conviction in the subject's ability to appropriate time in making sense of the world can be found in Komori's conception of origins. As we quoted, "From the instant my consciousness as reader begins to interact with this site, time begins to flow and the textual space begins to appear" (*soko ni dokusha de aru watashi no ishiki ga kakawarihajimeta shunkan kara, jikan ga nagarehajime, tekusuto no kūkan ga genshō shihajimemasu*). In other words, time begins its flow not in the world, since external objects are regarded as lifeless forms of brute spatiality, but in the subject, and particularly in consciousness, for consciousness is seen as that part of the subject which is most essential to his subjectivity. According to this view of reading, the opening of consciousness coincides with the opening of time itself. However, what if we were to conceive of time as *excessive* to the subject, that its beginning somehow takes place prior to the commencement of consciousness and that it continues its flow long after consciousness has completed its assigned task?

In *Dekigoto to shite no yomu koto*, Komori's interest in the question of succession appears specifically in the act of reading whereby subjective focus is forced to constantly shift from one form of writing (or sound and word) to the next. This movement of consciousness echoes that already found in the act of writing or expression, where, as Komori reminds us in *Kōzō to shite no katari*, "the expresser tries at each instant to grasp the temporal succession of consciousness (*ishiki no jikanteki na keiki*)." Komori's attention to the notion of succession as it structures the interrelated acts of writing and reading is certainly admirable—such analysis is otherwise virtually absent in studies of Japanese literature—but he unfortunately fails to examine this question in a general sense beyond the narrow borders of the subject. It must be pointed out that this omission is somewhat unusual in a book that aims to thematize the complex notion of the event (*dekigoto*), for events occur only in their spatiotemporal inscription, and such space and time can in no way be limited to the domain of subjective interiority. In order for one event to follow another in temporal succession, there must be present an element of negativity that enables the death or passing of a singular moment to be reborn as a different moment that comes after it. No temporal movement is possible without this negativity, which, to use Komori's language, radically "disconnects" or severs (*setsudan*) one moment from the next while nevertheless "connecting" (*ketsugō*) them in the form of an extended line or chain. What is foremost at issue in succession is the interrelationship between time and space, for the power of time to negate each moment as it newly arises requires a minimal trace of spatiality that receives this negation and remains, or is carried over, in its wake. Yet this survival of the spatial trace over temporal negation is exceedingly fragile: not only has this exposure to the difference of time stripped the trace of any persisting identity, but the very condition of survival for the spatial trace is that it be continually exposed to temporal difference.[16]

Given this condition of survival for the trace in the context of temporal succession, it is clear that there can be no necessity for the trace to survive into the future. In order for the spatial trace to remain from the past into the future, it must pass through the negative or differential force of time, but this passage also threatens to erase the trace at every moment. There is no guarantee that the trace will *necessarily* be carried over into the future, for all that we are establishing here in this account of succession is the *possibility* for the trace to remain. This distinction between possibility and necessity bears important implications for Komori's understanding of memory. Let us recall that, in the foregoing passage from *Dekigoto to shite no yomu koto*, memory is asked to play a crucial role in the act of reading: there must be a "ceaseless recall of past memories into the present" in order for consciousness to render intelligible the constant stream of new information that otherwise threatens to overwhelm it. Memory, in its broadest sense, signifies the retention of the past into the future. Here the question arises as to why, given the tenuous nature of this retention, Komori insists on conceiving of memory solely in its successful functioning within the overall machinery of reading. Rigorously speaking, it is always possible for there to occur a momentary lapse of memory, of which the subject might indeed remain unconscious but that would nonetheless negatively impact the outcome of reading. If the retention of the past is constantly exposed to the possibility of its erasure, why does Komori place so much faith in the reader's capacity to overcome both the materiality of writing and the possibility of forgetting in the successful achievement of meaning? The answer, undoubtedly, is this: given that the opposition between life and death corresponds to the distinction between man (consciousness) and the world of material objects, *it is because subjective consciousness is endowed with the power of life that the negativity intrinsic to temporal succession can be neutralized*. Any malfunctioning of memory, and thus of reading, can thus be dismissed as a mere accident that may occasionally befall consciousness but is not essentially related to the operation of consciousness itself. From

Komori's perspective, man's mastery of reading is simultaneously a mastery over time, for the life of consciousness is such as to effectively make use of the negativity of temporal difference in the service of meaning.

Succession requires that the past be retained strictly on the condition that it not pass into the future identically as itself. Traditionally, identity refers to the capacity of an entity to persist as itself over time. Given that each moment of time emerges in its singularity as radically different from all other moments, however, identity must be seen as a kind of surface effect that conceals underlying elements of difference. Just as the essential erasability of the trace sheds light on certain problems with Komori's conception of memory, so too does the negativity intrinsic to succession come to unsettle his presentation of the self-identical unit in the context of reading. As he describes in *Dekigoto to shite no yomu koto*, "We send this visual cognition to consciousness, where writing in the form of icons is transformed into voice as auditory images that represent the *units* of language. . . . We gradually come to form words and phrases or sentences by connecting and disconnecting these icons as *fixed units*. When we compose words, of course, we must connect vocalized images into a *unit* that evokes some type of meaning." These lines reveal the considerable weight borne by the notion of the unit in the reading subject's cognition of language. Regardless of whether the content of these units is made up of icons or vocalized images, the formation of the unit as such testifies to the activity of consciousness in its raising of external, material inscription to the level of internalized, meaningful language. Through its repeated acts of "connecting" and "disconnecting," consciousness organizes the data of reading into discrete units that, identical in and of themselves, can be distinguished from other units. This ordered division of identity and difference ensures that the operation of linguistic cognition remains a smooth one. Once again, attention is directed exclusively to the possibility of reading. If the notion of the unit were to be exposed to time, then the movement of succession would quickly reveal that the unit, in its positivity, is violently pulled apart by forces exerted at once from the past and the future. In this sense, time can be regarded as that which exceeds all acts of organization, that is to say, all subjective forming or *uniting* of identity in its opposition to difference. Consciousness is certainly capable of creating a host of positive linguistic units composed of icons and vocalized images, but these units necessarily depend for their survival on the general movement of temporal succession, which may at any moment come to negate them in the form of disfigurement or erasure.

Umibe no Kafuka: Writing, Secret, Event

Having examined certain issues that emerge in the context of Komori's larger methodological commitments, let us now turn our attention specifically to his reading of Murakami Haruki's novel *Umibe no Kafuka*. Our analysis of the difficulties that subtend both *Kōzō to shite no katari* and *Dekigoto to shite no yomu koto* will help us better evaluate various aspects of Komori's approach to Murakami. Such evaluation, however, requires that we first develop a fundamental understanding of some of the conceptual issues at work in Murakami's novel. This is especially true, for instance, with regard to the concept of writing. As any reader of Murakami's work will attest, *Umibe no Kafuka* takes as one of its most pervasive themes the issue of writing. Understood in the quotidian sense of this word, writing appears as a central element that simultaneously links and separates the book's two protagonists, Tamura Kafka and Nakata Satoru. As a result of a childhood accident, Nakata has lost the ability to read and write, a deficiency that is repeatedly emphasized throughout the novel. In contrast, the youth Kafka is presented as a bibliophile whose zeal for the written word leads him, upon running away from home, to a small, privately owned library in Shikoku where he spends his days reading. The vast archival of writing presented by the library—"collections of Japanese literature, world literature, and individual writers, classics, philosophy, drama, art history, sociology, history, biography, geography," as Kafka marvels[17]—provides a means of historical access to other writers across differences in time and space. More immediately, it is through the library that Kafka is introduced to Saeki, a woman who acts as the director of the library and who devotes her time to recording her own personal history in the extensive journal she keeps.

Already we can glimpse in this introductory sketch of the novel that writing is depicted as maintaining an intimate relation with history. This relation encompasses both the large-scale history of geopolitical events, which are typically affiliated with the public sphere, and the considerably more minute, less recognizable events that make up individual history, which is correspondingly associated with the private domain. Indeed, one of Murakami's aims in *Umibe no Kafuka* appears to be showing how these two types of history are in fact complexly interwoven, such as to render difficult any determination of where the precise boundary between the public and the private might be drawn. If the act of writing is linked to history, however, this is not simply because writing may be used to develop factual accounts of the past or perhaps thematize the question of historical reflection. Conceived in this restricted manner, it would be possible to distinguish certain forms of writing as historical and other forms as existing outside of the scope of history. In a more general sense, however, writing is historical because it marks the differential movement of time. To claim, following the typical standpoint adopted in historiography, that all writing is necessarily historical insofar as it takes place within time unfortunately makes of time a kind of universal container that is merely filled in by events, which are thus reduced to the level of content. In its abstraction, this image fails to account for the dynamic movement of succession that at every moment articulates time as radically other to itself. The only way to mark this difference or alterity is by *writing*, understood now beyond its everyday sense to signify a spatial remainder of the past that has come to survive into the present. It thus follows that writing, even prior to revealing this or that particular meaning, signifies in the first instance the passage of time.

Why is this insight into the essential temporality of writing so important for a reading of *Umibe no Kafuka*? Murakami's work appears in the realm of literature, it might be argued, and this affiliation makes all conceptual or philosophical reflection on the novel unsuitable or, at worst, irrelevant. In defense of our approach, it can be seen that *Umibe no Kafuka* itself makes appeal to philosophical discourse in its reference to the notion of memory in Bergson and the twin concepts of subjectivity and self-consciousness in the work of Hegel. Komori effectively repeats Murakami's gesture in his *Murakami Haruki ron: 'Umibe no Kafuka' wo seidoku suru*, as his reading of the novel proceeds through support from such diverse thinkers as Freud, Derrida, Foucault, and Lacan. More crucially, however—and this is a point where Murakami and Komori would undoubtedly find themselves in agreement—the distinct genres or disciplines of literature and philosophy cannot be regarded as essentially unrelated. As soon as a literary text employs the word *is*, for example, it reveals its involvement in the general question of ontology. To be sure, the nature of this involvement may vary widely depending upon the explicit or implicit treatment of this issue, which itself relates to a range of other problems traditionally posed in philosophical discourse. In the specific dialogue conducted by Murakami and Komori, the question of ontology appears in the divergent views offered regarding the status of discrete beings or entities as either identically present to themselves or in some sense already divided from within such that present identity can only be determined as a derivative or belated effect. As should be apparent, this question of being is intimately linked to the problematic of time, and we have already reviewed the particular way in which Komori conceives of time in his account of consciousness. Komori's methodological decision to privilege consciousness as the core feature of subjectivity in man's relations with the world immediately establishes his commitment to a certain philosophical tradition, and the question this implicitly raises is whether Murakami also belongs to this tradition or if his work must instead be considered otherwise. From our perspective, the unmitigated negativity that characterizes Komori's response to Murakami serves to reveal in a particularly illuminating way the depth of his subjectivist convictions. By following Komori's close reading of Murakami, we aim to better grasp the specific limitations of his theoretical approach as well as the blind spots of subjectivism more generally.

If we were to repeat the conceptual expansion of writing that Komori finds in Yokomitsu and that he further develops, we could tentatively determine writing as that which links time and memory. In *Umibe no Kafuka*, this more general sense of writing appears most significantly in the instance of trauma: some type of disturbance has taken place in the past and has created painful effects that continue to survive into the present. In parallel chapters, Murakami describes such trauma suffered by his protagonists as a result of two incidents of violence that are separated by a span of over a half-century. In the case of Nakata, this event is retrospectively identified as the "Rice Bowl Hill Incident," which occurred at approximately 10:00 a.m. on November 7, 1944. At that time, Nakata and his classmates were participating in an outdoor excursion, where they had climbed a hill and were foraging for mushrooms, when suddenly the group of students fell unconscious. All the pupils regained consciousness shortly thereafter except for Nakata, who upon awakening several weeks later was discovered to have suffered severe memory loss as well as lasting cognitive impairment. In his depiction of this accident, Murakami establishes an important connection between memory and writing, since Nakata has experienced these two losses simultaneously.[18] What is of particular interest, however, is that Murakami will go on to narrate a series of attempts by which others seek to retroactively make sense of this event. These attempts, as he describes in great detail, are carried out through the medium of writing. In this sense, the association between memory and writing comes to be deepened by going beyond the level of individual trauma suffered by Nakata to include a larger reflection on how past events can be understood once they have already vanished.

Writing emerges as the sole means of gaining access to this past, which has otherwise completely disappeared. The multiple forms of writing required to apprehend the past are repeatedly stressed by Murakami. Evidence of this can be found, for example, in the interview with the psychiatrist Tsukayama Shigenori. This interview is taped, and the transcription appears in a US Army Intelligence Report that is titled, numbered, and dated May 12, 1946. In the broader context of the novel, the questioning of Tsukayama appears in chapter 8 as the third and final interview conducted and partially reproduced, following those of Okamochi Setsuko, Nakata's teacher (chapter 2), and Nakazawa Jūichi, a local physician (chapter 4). As the novel carefully notes, the transcribed interviews appear as the result of a series of prior acts: questioning is conducted by a Lieutenant O'Connor and interpreted by a Sergeant Katayama before the documents are finally prepared by a Private Cohen. Murakami's point here seems to be that the transmission of information must pass through a range of often unseen mediations before reaching its intended target or destination and that such waypoints can at any moment produce a kind of swerving or veering effect at the level of meaning. While the source of this information is of course the testimony itself, these words, which derive from the actual witnessing of the event as it unfolded over time and as it marked itself on the witnesses' consciousness, find themselves constantly remarked. The presentation of evidence takes time, Murakami emphasizes, and this passage of time relentlessly exposes what is presented to the threat of loss or difference. In the transcription of the taped interview with Tsukayama, for example, the reader is informed that "documents 271 and 278 are missing (*kesson*)."[19] In point of fact, however, such disappearance has already been announced in the form of the various redactions explicitly marked in all the interviews.

Upon being questioned as to the possible causes of the Rice Bowl Hill Incident, Tsukayama replies,

> Also we knew that no poison gas, whether man-made or naturally occurring, would act like this, leaving no traces whatsoever in the body. Especially when you're dealing with children, who are more sensitive and have a more delicate immune system than adults, there would have to be some afteraffects that remain in the eyes or mucous membranes . . . So what we were left with were psychological problems, or problems dealing with brain function. If this incident had been caused by such internal factors, then it would naturally be extremely difficult to search for these traces through internal medicine or surgery. The traces would be invisible and unquantifiable.[20]

Tsukayama reveals in these lines that the notion of writing as it relates to time must be grasped beyond the traditional, narrow sense of this term. Just as his testimony required for its presentation a passage through a series of intermediate acts, all of which to some degree *marked* his words, actively producing an element of difference within them as they underwent changes in time and space, so too does he now engage with the problem of the trace (*konseki*) as it inscribes itself on the varied surfaces of the human mind and body. Once again, writing is identified as the privileged mode of return to the past. In concrete terms, an as-yet-unexplained event has taken place, but in its very passing or demise it has nevertheless traced out a path that remains legible in the present. If Nakata and his classmates were in fact victims of a poison gas attack, then it is assumed that residual elements of poison would still be detectable in their bodies despite the subsequent evaporation of the gas. In this way, a path would be created from the past to the present, and understanding of that past event would in principle be achieved by following that road back from the present to the point of its original emergence. As Tsukayama emphasizes, a determination of the cause of the Rice Bowl Hill Incident is facilitated in the case of physical traces as opposed to psychological traces, as the former can be rendered more visible and quantifiable through the existing tools of medical technology. As a psychiatrist, Tsukayama would doubtless agree that psychological trauma also creates effects that manifest themselves over time, and that in certain instances we may determine the nature of the past events that caused such trauma by examining the various symptoms that reveal themselves in the present. Even prior to this opposition drawn by Tsukayama between the physical (external) and psychological (internal), however, writing appears as that which allows a link to be established between the present and past.

The quandary that Tsukayama gestures to in his remarks is that, on the one hand, we must return to the past, we must follow the path that the past has already traced out for us in order to understand both it and the present that is its extension; and yet, on the other hand, the irreducible fact of the past's disappearance renders this return journey impossible, for there can be no guarantee that these traces of the past will ever yield the past itself. In *Umibe no Kafuka*, the past discloses itself strictly as a secret. Indeed, we can see this already in the series of interviews involving Tsukayama, Okamochi, and Nakazawa. The documents that contain these interviews are classified as "Top Secret" (*gokuhi shiryō*),[21] as the novel specifies, and one of the often-overlooked paradoxes of Murakami's work is how this secret nonetheless comes to be exposed. If time only appears in the very moment of its disappearance, then each instant of the past may be understood as a secret in that it no longer remains to present itself to us as it identically was. Government documents may or may not be classified as secret—this is strictly a matter of empirical contingency—but the past event of the Rice Bowl Hill Incident that they recount must necessarily be determined as a secret insofar as it belongs to the past. In order to expose this secret, Murakami appears to suggest, the event must be repeated. Hence the use of the tape recorder during these interviews, a device that is also referred to in the opening pages of the Kafka narrative, where the text specifically indicates that the Sony Walkman the youth decides to take with him when running away from home is equipped with an audio recording function. By doubling this image at the very beginning of the novel—the phrase *rokuon no dekiru* ("can record sound") clearly echoes that of *rokuon tēpu shiyō* ("the use of a tape that records sound")[22]—Murakami invites us to consider the question of how time allows itself to be captured so that we may in some sense recover it once it has gone. Despite its inherent evanescence, sound may prolong its life in a variety of ways: through human memory, the use of artificial recording devices, and the presence of an echo chamber, among others. A past sound necessarily retains its status as secret because no subsequent repetition of it can ever purely repeat the past time in which it appeared, which indeed forms an essential part of that sound itself. And yet the *same* sound can be reproduced at a later time, upon which its original secrecy will be at least partly violated. In *Umibe no Kafuka*, the very possibility for the past secret to be repeated implies that a certain level of violence or violation is paradoxically necessary for us to better understand, and thus protect, its secrecy.

If the past remains a secret, then certainly no retrospective examination of the Rice Bowl Hill Incident will ever fully explain its mystery. However, Murakami's point in the early part of the novel is not simply that this event ultimately resists all attempts to unlock and decipher it. The very repetition of this event in the form of recorded and archived interviews creates new events that may at any time assume a life of their own. What is at issue here is the complex question of how an event may unfold or develop over time and space. If the various repetitions of the Rice Bowl Hill Incident are determined as essentially part of this incident itself, then it becomes extremely difficult to identify the event's precise boundaries or parameters. Already Murakami tacitly poses this question to the reader when he depicts this incident, which originally took place in 1944, as only first recognized within the framework of the novel two years later in 1946. Each recurrence of the event enhances it and inflects it differently. Indeed, the event's unfolding puts constant pressure on the subject's ability to comprehend it within the most typical spatiotemporal coordinates. The incident in question originally took place in the space identified as Rice Bowl Hill at approximately 10:00 a.m. on November 7, 1944. As this event unfolded, however, it assumed a kind of viral quality that allowed it to spread immediately and unpredictably to other times and spaces. Readers are informed that investigations into the incident were conducted "from March to April 1946 . . . in [name deleted] County, Yamanashi Prefecture" as well as, in the distinct case of Tsukayama, "over a three-hour span at the GHQ of the Supreme Commander for the Allied Powers in Tokyo."[23] The final report issued by the US Army Intelligence Section is dated May 12, 1946. The incident subsequently comes to be revived twenty-six years later in the form of a remarkable letter dated October 19, 1972, sent from Miss Okamochi, Nakata's teacher, to Dr. Tsukayama. Finally, the document containing the interviews, which had previously been classified as "Top Secret," and which, as we are told, "is now kept in the National Archives in Washington, D.C.," is released to the general public (*ippan kōkai*) in the year 1986.[24]

In its singular mode of appearing, the Rice Bowl Hill Incident reveals its ability to survive its own death as a temporal event by extending itself across different times and spaces. As we discussed, such acts as questioning, interpretation, and document preparation were instrumental in the retrospective identification of the event as itself. At each step in which the event came into its own self-presentation, the possibility appeared for it to be rendered otherwise, for it to receive some type of external imprint or stimulus that would come to be absorbed within the very interiority of the event and form part of its identity. In this regard, the various levels of mediation required for the event to initially gather within itself the interviews and organization of documents merely reappear at a later, more advanced stage when the event is effectively reshaped by Okamochi's letter, transplanted to the United States, and made available to a general readership—where, particularly in light of its generality, it may continue its afterlife in ways that cannot be anticipated. This logic of the event to which Murakami points, however tacitly or obliquely, is so challenging for thought because it involves at its core a recognition that the event, in its taking place, never takes place punctually. Here it is essential to avoid the trap of thinking repetition according to its most standard formulation as occurring strictly *after* another event that precedes it. In the marking of spatiotemporal difference that is its taking place, the event never fully occurs or exhausts itself at an identifiable time and place. That is to say, the event discloses the fact that it can never be entirely adequate to itself. It is indeed precisely because of its essential insufficiency or inadequacy that repetition can become possible at all—*not* in the sense of something that can be seen as simply separated from that which it repeats but rather, much more disturbingly, as a spatiotemporal extension of that original occurrence itself. Because the event is never definitively present to itself, it is forced to undergo repetition, which has the inevitable effect of transforming or disfiguring it, such that the event may always arrive at a point at which it is no longer recognizable even as itself. In the Washington, DC, of 1986, having survived the crossings of time, an ocean, and a national language, the Rice Bowl Hill Incident discovers that it can now only give itself in its identity as radically other to itself.

One fails to understand the strange logic of the event if one insists on conceiving of its repetition along the lines of common sense as merely a *two* that befalls or quantitatively adds to an earlier *one*. As a general principle, prior to any of its spatiotemporal instantiations, the event is incomplete, not entirely present to itself. It is in order to achieve that presence that the event must depart from itself and its concrete emergence at a particular time and space and repeat itself elsewhere. The threat that this essential itinerary of the event poses to conventional forms of historical and literary scholarship should be apparent, for the event in its multiple recurrences functions to constantly displace the normal spatiotemporal frameworks used to identify it. In a reading of *Umibe no Kafuka*, for example, is it possible to determine the proper site of the Rice Bowl Hill Incident strictly as Yamanashi Prefecture, when one considers that the unconscious Nakata was subsequently taken to a military hospital in Tokyo, where the intelligence report describing the event was also presumably composed before this same document was then sent to be archived in Washington, DC? Similarly, must we identify the proper year of this occurrence as 1944 when the Rice Bowl Hill Incident only truly came into its name in 1946, before then undergoing a decisive change in 1972 because of new information that came to light in Okamochi's letter, only to finally gain release to the general public in 1986, when it receives the chance to continue its itinerary in the unanticipatable future?

In Murakami's novel, the second incident of violence, which repeats in significant ways the Rice Bowl Hill Incident that preceded it by over half a century, involves the youth Kafka. Just as the Rice Bowl Hill Incident is first presented to the reader in its aftermath, after the initial event has emerged only to then vanish, so too does Kafka suddenly appear at the beginning of chapter 9 bearing the effects of an as-yet-unexplained episode of violence.

> I notice something dark on the front of my white T-shirt, shaped like a huge butterfly with wings extended. I try brushing it away, but it won't come off. I touch it and my hands come away strangely sticky. In order to calm down, I consciously take my time and remove my dungaree shirt before lifting my T-shirt over my head. Under the flickering fluorescent light I realize what it is—darkish blood that has seeped into the fabric. The blood is still fresh and wet, and there's a lot of it. I bring it close to smell, but there is no smell. Some blood has been spattered on the dungaree shirt that I wear over my T-shirt, but only a little, and the traces are not so obvious on the dark blue fabric. But the blood on the white T-shirt is extremely fresh and vivid. I wash the T-shirt in the sink. The blood mixes with the water, staining the white porcelain sink red. No matter how hard I scrub, though, the traces of blood won't come out. I'm about to toss the shirt into the garbage can, then decide against it. If I throw it away, then some other place would be better . . . I take some soap out of my toilet kit and wash my hands. They're still trembling a little, but I take my time, carefully washing between my fingers. The blood has even gotten under my fingernails. With a damp towel, I wipe away the traces of blood that have seeped onto my bare chest.[25]

This event, which plays a central role in our understanding of developments in the Kafka narrative (which appears throughout the novel in the odd-numbered chapters), parallels the Rice Bowl Hill Incident in its creation of lasting effects that shape the course of the Nakata narrative (which appears, correspondingly, in the even-numbered chapters). Both episodes are marked by violence, but whereas the Rice Bowl Hill Incident has claimed the child Nakata as its most obvious victim, the above incident involving Kafka is described more ambiguously in that the text never states with any finality whose blood has been shed. The question of the trace emerges in the earlier incident through Tsukayama's use of the word *konseki*, but here it appears with the term *ato*, which in its *on-yomi* pronunciation forms the *seki* of *konseki*. This term is mentioned three times in the foregoing passage, and the fact that Murakami writes it not with Chinese characters but rather in the *hiragana* syllabary functions to reinforce its link to the homophone *ato*, which contains both the spatial sense of "behind" and the temporal sense of "after" or "later." As we saw in the case of *konseki*, the trace structures temporal difference by binding the past, which is no longer, with the coming of the future, which is not yet.

In the interview with Tsukayama, the psychiatrist reminds his questioners that past trauma, whether physical or psychological, manifests itself not in its original or proper identity but solely in its effects, which appear necessarily after the traumatic event has gone. In similar fashion, the above depiction of a highly agitated, bloodstained Kafka focuses on the traces of blood, since they are the most palpable remnants of the violent episode that has otherwise vanished. This blood *marks* him—it stains both his shirts, his chest, and his fingernails—but what this means most immediately is that the past has somehow survived its passing and written itself upon him. As Kafka discovers, this writing is not easily effaced: "No matter how hard I scrub, though, the traces of blood won't come out." Even if those traces were to completely disappear, however, the very traumatic quality of this event has now marked itself upon Kafka in the form of memory. The tracing of the past assumes multiple forms, and indeed Tsukayama tells us this several pages (and over a half-century) earlier in the scientific distinction he makes between physical traces and psychological traces. If the external traces that mark Kafka can eventually be washed off, the more invisible, internal traces may continue to linger. Here it is not simply that Kafka, in an act of consciousness, has successfully internalized or spiritualized these material traces, thereby demonstrating in classical fashion the superiority of the subject over the world of objects. On the contrary, what the question of the trace in *Umibe no Kafuka* asks us to think is the manner in which time, in its differential movement, incessantly writes itself upon man even as he continues to subjectively internalize the outside world.

It is this general structure of the trace that demands to be thought. The past event, whose identity is yet to be established, writes itself upon material things (Kafka's two shirts) as well as upon the human, both in a physical sense (the youth's chest and fingernails) and in a spiritual or psychological sense (his memory). The point is not merely that the world of objects, in its materiality, has the capacity to resist the subject's act of internalization in the form of memory. Man's rewriting of the objective world (the physical shirts) as or in terms of the subjective world (the mnemonic image and concept of the shirts) certainly takes place, but it takes place, significantly, in an infinitely broader context of writing that can at any time *overwrite* the subject's own acts of inscription. Here again the link between time and writing presents itself in all its force. In the above passage from *Umibe no Kafuka*, it is noteworthy that the notion of time is referred to twice: "In order to calm down, I consciously take my time and remove my dungaree shirt before lifting my T-shirt over my head" and "I take some soap out of my toilet kit and wash my hands. They're still trembling a little, but I take my time, carefully washing between my fingers." Conceived in its broadest sense, Kafka's "taking of time" in his encounter with these traces is possible strictly because time has originally been given to him to take.

Yet time constantly eludes the subject's attempts to master it and domesticate its effects—to, as we showed in the case of Komori, effectively put it to use in the service of meaning as created by consciousness. For Komori, the subject has the power to consciously set time in motion through the active transformation of writing into language. In the model of writing and reading that he constructs, the dual points of origin and destination are determined in advance as situated within the subjective interiority of the writer and reader. By contrast, our presentation of *Umibe no Kafuka* in terms of the relation between time and writing as marked in the event reveals that these activities of writing and reading take place primarily in the world, beyond or *in excess of* the restricted domain of subjectivity. It bears emphasis that this distinction between the world and the subject cannot be understood according to any binary oppositionality that would pose a simple, material exteriority against a more mediated, or enfolded, interiority, for this very division between world and man is itself a product of the subject. Indeed, we have already encountered such conception in Komori's interpretation of Yokomitsu's notion of writing. It thus becomes necessary to think about writing more fundamentally as that which encompasses in its movement both man and the material objects of the world.

The event whose effects have so unsettled and bewildered Kafka does not end when the youth finally collects himself and leaves the shrine, where he has (exactly as with Nakata over a half-century earlier) regained consciousness. Given that what is at issue here are traces, the question of precisely when and where an event begins and ends remains essentially elusive. The traces that Murakami describes are of blood, certainly, but they are also of the event "itself" as it presents itself differentially across time and space. Significantly, the first repetition of these traces takes place, after Kafka has exited the shrine and taken a cab to a convenience store where he will meet Sakura, when he doubles himself by looking at his own reflection in the window glass: "I look at myself reflected in the glass. My hair is still a bit of a mess, but the traces of blood on my dungaree shirt are barely noticeable. Even if someone were to notice them, they would appear as nothing more than a stain."[26] These traces next surface slightly later at Sakura's apartment, first physically in reference to Sakura—"She looks at the T-shirt that I take out of my backpack. She carefully inspects the residual traces of blood that couldn't be washed out"—and then psychologically, as Sakura has in the meantime now disposed of the bloodied shirt, and Kafka finds himself haunted by the mental image that remains of it and has indeed replaced it: "After she turns out the light and gets in bed, I climb into my sleeping bag, shut my eyes, and try to go to sleep. But sleep is impossible. Stuck to the back of my eyes are the traces of blood on my white T-shirt."[27]

Once the physical T-shirt is destroyed, then its only mode of return to Kafka is through the internalized medium of memory. What can be seen here is the same viral quality that earlier launched the Rice Bowl Hill Incident to different times and places in its unpredictable itinerary. The bloodied shirt, and with it the earlier causal event that still remains a secret and must await its future determinations, thereafter appears at the site of Ōshima's mountain cabin when Kafka is reading what appears to be Hannah Arendt's *Eichmann in Jerusalem*: "I shut the book, lay it on my lap, and think about my own responsibility. I can't help it. My white T-shirt was soaked in fresh blood. I washed the blood away with these hands, so much blood the sink turned red. I imagine I'll be held responsible for all that blood."[28] In assuming his guilt in a crime of which he has no memory, Kafka is not so much consciously recalling the bloodied T-shirt to memory as he is unconsciously suffering its visitation. Regardless of whether or not he wishes to remember this object, the object, in a sense, clearly wishes to remember him. The object, and the traumatic event that is its cause, have not yet had their fill of Kafka and so must continue to haunt him until the point at which this energy reaches exhaustion. Finally, toward the end of the novel, Kafka finds himself back at Ōshima's cabin where he comes across a butterfly while walking along a forest path: "A huge black butterfly about the size of my palm flutters into my line of sight. Its shape resembles the traces of blood on my white T-shirt. The butterfly appears from the shade of the trees, slowly moves through space, and then once again disappears in the shade of the trees."[29]

Crucial in this final passage is the description of the butterfly's alternating movement of appearing (*araware*) and disappearing (*kiete iku*) as it "moves through space" (*kūkan wo idō shite*), as Murakami writes. As we have seen, this spatial movement is necessarily also a temporal movement.

The physical butterfly that Kafka glimpses along the forest path involuntarily triggers within his memory a mental image of the earlier bloodstain. Implicitly the line of flight traced out by the butterfly is linked to the line formed by the series of differential spatiotemporal instantiations that constitute the self-presentation of the otherwise concealed and secretive event of past violence. Exactly as with the Rice Bowl Hill Incident, this event discloses to us that it is essentially divided from within. Its original taking place was never fully present, and this strange insufficiency necessitated that the event be repeated along an itinerary that comes to include a convenience store, the young woman Sakura, the transgender librarian Ōshima and his mountain cabin, and finally Adolf Eichmann and the question of historical responsibility. Here it is imperative to grasp that these differential markings or traces that allow the event to at one time "appear" and then "disappear" do not exist in any way external or accidental to the event itself. Because the event itself can never fully be itself, it exists only in the line that it traces out over the course of its various instantiations, a line that continues to trace itself out in the coming of the future (and which, therefore, the subject can never entirely get ahead of). Yet this line, whose successive points can never be determined in advance, is also never one. In its development, this line constantly forms new lines, the content of which cannot simply be reduced to the "original" line. Thus the event of bloodshed, whose identity remains unknown, comes to touch upon *as essentially part of itself* such otherwise distant and apparently unrelated matters as, for instance, sexuality (Sakura masturbates Kafka on the night of his visit), Plato (Ōshima relates to Kafka the theory of three sexes as found in the *Symposium*), and various ethicopolitical issues revolving around Nazism and the Holocaust.

Reading a Close Reading: The Question of Ethics

Despite writing extensively on the notion of the event in his *Dekigoto to shite no yomu koto*, Komori fails to realize that serious reflection on this notion requires first of all a radical departure from classical ontology. In other words, the event never simply *is*. Without taking the step outside of ontology, one runs the risk of falling back into a precritical empiricism in which events are conceived in what appears to be their individual identity and self-presence as fundamentally separate from other events. Appealing to the traditional distinction between identity and difference, moreover, the unique power that is capable of identifying this elemental unity of the event is determined as consciousness, seen here as the most intrinsic feature of subjectivity. Indeed, the attachment to ontology and the privileging of consciousness must be understood as complementary: the integrity and self-presence that allow something to exist as itself, as opposed to something other, correspond at the deepest level to the subject's own conscious recognition of itself as a being that persists identically over time without any essential infraction of difference. Because the subject knows itself in its identity, in other words, it is able to distinguish itself from other things as well as individual things from one another. In the pages of *Murakami Haruki ron: 'Umibe no Kafuka' wo seidoku suru*, the loss of this ability to consciously differentiate one thing from another will come to be severely criticized by Komori. Quoting Kafka's internal monologue that "my ability to think had really diminished. I can't think coherently. . . . Things in my head are all intertwined and entangled. I can't tell the difference between *something* and something else,"[30] Komori writes:

> What has been completely stripped from the youth Kafka here is the human ability to think rationally, such as to inquire linguistically into causal relations as expressed by the question, 'Why?' In other words, this forms a set with the deregulation of the 'authoritarian personality' while erasing the 'democratic personality.' The psychological state in which one says, 'I can't tell the difference between *something* and something else,' is nothing other than a situation of regress in which one can no longer distinguish between the 'permissible' and 'impermissible.' The memory of this taboo as previously given by the surrounding adults has been erased or perhaps executed.[31]

The scene in which Kafka expresses these thoughts is openly framed by violence: while walking along the forest path, the youth encounters two deserters from the Japanese Imperial Army who, miraculously unaged and still dressed in military uniforms, explain to him the correct technique used to kill one's enemy with a bayonet. As part of his now well-known claim that *Umibe no Kafuka* represents an unethical "novel of execution" (*shokei shōsetsu*), Komori attempts to make a critical intervention in what he believes to be the work's active endorsement of violence. This intervention requires that one possess the ability to distinguish between moral and immoral codes of conduct. The soldiers' graphic discussion of disembowelment is seen by Komori as indicative of a dangerous breach of ethics, a breach that he locates throughout the novel, as for example in the famous cat-killing scene with Johnnie Walker or in the allusions to violence in such classic literary works as *The Arabian Nights* and Franz Kafka's "In the Penal Colony." Physically exhausted by his walk through the forest, Kafka finds himself unable to follow the words of the two soldiers with any sense of cogency. From Komori's perspective, this lapse of mental acuity signals a threat to rationality and logical ways of thinking, a threat that he associates with a loss of subjective autonomy and thus a greater propensity to submit to various forms of authority. Drawing on Adorno's distinction between the "authoritarian personality" and "democratic personality," Komori posits a firm link between reason and ethics. The value of the question "Why?" lies in its ability to lead individuals back to the realm of logical causality as well as to foster a heightened sense of critical vigilance. Failure to pose this question is regarded negatively as a sign of "regress" (*taikōteki jōkyō*), such that one becomes incapable of distinguishing both right from wrong (or what is socially "permissible" and "impermissible") and "something from something else." The unethical man, in other words, is he who lacks reason; conversely, the ethical man is determined to be identical to the reasonable man. More precisely, a man is ethical because he is able to reasonably distinguish right from wrong. In Komori's view, such a figure must be seen as the ideal telos toward which all others who are in an arrested state of "regress" are to strive. In this developmental model that posits a certain type of reason and ethics as normative, the youth Kafka is judged to be inadequate.

Previously we called attention to Komori's conception of the unit in his description of the conscious act of reading. The unit is the minimal element of identity; it is that which maintains its unity despite all temporal flux. This conviction in the persisting unity of the unit is of course central to Komori's commitment to classical ontology, according to which individual entities are held to exist as essentially distinct from one another. This view can be fruitfully contrasted to Kafka's anguished description of his thinking as one in which things "are all intertwined and entangled. I can't tell the difference between *something* and something else." The words Murakami uses here to describe this disorderly mesh or intermingling are *karamiai* (絡み合い) and *motsureteiru* (縺れている). As we can see in the *ito-hen* or "thread" radical that ties these two verbs together, Kafka's thoughts are confused because of the existence of a web of diverse strands that cannot be easily untied. Unlike the unit, these strands or threads have no punctuality; that is, they cannot be determined as a point that presents itself identically within time and space. Whereas the identifiable point that is the unit constitutes the simple or indivisible origin from which all things extend and to which they can thus be reduced, the "intertwined and entangled" nature of strands signifies that the minimal element of things, whether material or mental, is irreducibly complex and divided from within. This is the reason why the act of differentiation is so difficult. In reading Kafka's admission that "I can't tell the difference between *something* and something else," Komori all too quickly interprets this difficulty as a sign of deficiency within the subject. In his view, this deficiency represents a suspicious departure from normativity. The difficulty experienced by the subject in clearly distinguishing one thing from another creates a kind of domino effect that unfortunately pushes such diverse notions as humanity, reason, language, causality, politics, ethics, and memory into the realm of the abnormal.

What if, however, the difficulty of *decision*—that is, following this word's Latin root of *caedere*, of "cutting" or "severance"—was not originally located within subjective interiority but rather conceived far more generally as stemming from the complex, threaded way in which all things present themselves? If individual things only reveal themselves in the mode of intertwinement and entanglement with other things, how can I be sure that the results of my decisions or distinctions are as I intend them to be? If things in their interthreadedness give themselves not fully as themselves but partially otherwise, then it is always possible that my identification of that which needs to be decided might be entirely mistaken. That is, I might subjectively believe that I am deciding one thing when in fact I am deciding something else. Here we begin to see the limitations of Komori's account of consciousness and particularly of his ethicopolitical desire to conceive of consciousness as something like a ground or foundation of decision. If things in the world are grasped as identically present to themselves, then the act of decision or distinction (i.e., cutting) comes to be shorn of its complexity. Because I know, as a conscious subject, the identity of the things to be distinguished—rationally, what is the cause and what is the effect; politically, what is authoritarian and what is democratic; ethically, what is permissible and what is impermissible—the moment at which I actively sever one thing from another is surreptitiously preceded by an earlier moment of knowledge in which the difference between these things already becomes clear to me. In which case, the act of distinction reveals itself to be in truth an act of application, for my rational, political, and ethical decisions are made on the basis of knowledge that I have already acquired regarding the identity of that which is to be distinguished. A formula or blueprint has been composed by consciousness in advance, and this allows me to ascertain what is rational and what is not, what is politically progressive and what is not, and what is ethically just and what is not.

By tying together reason and ethics, Komori in effect strips the moment of decision or distinction of its inherent temporality and contingency. As soon as the act in which the subject cuts into the world is conceived as governed by consciousness and knowledge, then it becomes relatively easy to determine the actions of myself and others as either properly or improperly rational, political, and ethical. Here let me clarify that I am not offering a defense of what appears to be the youth Kafka's inability to coherently distinguish different things from one another. On the contrary, my point is that the cutting that is at issue in the act of distinction takes place necessarily always, but that one loses sight of this general force by restricting this act to the level of consciousness. When, for example, Kafka thinks to himself, "Things in my head are all intertwined and entangled. I can't tell the difference between *something* and something else," is he not in fact distinguishing certain things from others? In order to say the phrase "things in my head," must I not first decide if this head belongs to me or not, thereby implicitly distinguishing myself from other beings? Similarly, is not a distinction being made between that which is "intertwined and entangled" and that which appears in its simplicity and unity strictly as itself? When I say that "I can't tell the difference between *something* and something else," am I not determining this inability in contrast to, or in distinction from, the ability to register such difference? Indeed, even to admit my inability to distinguish one thing from another requires that I first recognize this distinction so as to comprehend my inability to make it.

My general point is that being itself is a movement of cutting understood in the sense of articulation. And here we return to the crucial questions of time and succession—questions that Komori, as we witnessed earlier, attempts to think within the limited framework of subjective interiority. If time in its negativity only presents itself as irrevocably other to itself, then this self-presentation is in truth a constant cutting or division of itself from itself. Man, understood here beyond the traditional subject-object distinction that Komori inherits, has no choice but to participate in this differential cutting. In the strongest sense of these terms, this is what is meant by decision and distinction. These acts of cutting produce difference in the world: once a decision or distinction is made, the world, to however minimal a degree, finds itself irretrievably transformed as a result. In contrast to the thinking of distinction put forward by Komori, the subject can never be fully conscious of the decisions and distinctions he makes. As a general principle, every moment of man's existence can be seen to be punctuated by the cutting indicated in these acts. Despite Komori's intent to portray *Umibe no Kafuka* as a "novel of execution" that actively condones violence, the fact is that the restriction of distinction to consciousness has the inevitable effect of excluding—through an act of violence or execution, to borrow his hyperbole[32]—everything in the decision that exceeds consciousness and of which consciousness remains, precisely, unconscious. Just as, in the account of reading developed in *Dekigoto to shite no yomu koto*, Komori seeks to reduce time to the time of consciousness, so too does he now, in *Murakami Haruki ron: 'Umibe no Kafuka' wo seidoku suru*, attempt to reduce the movement of cutting or differential articulation to the act of conscious distinction. In both cases, an infinitely greater force can be seen to precede consciousness, one that continues to produce effects within the otherwise inviolate domain of consciousness itself.

What is particularly noteworthy in Komori's linking of reason and ethics is his formulation of a developmental model in which normativity comes to be measured by the individual's distance from what he calls in the above passage "regress." In order for a society to function normally, there must be established laws and customs through which individual members may learn to distinguish between what is "permissible" and what is "impermissible." Kafka's inability to make such distinction is condemned as a moral failure, one that Komori associates with a forgetting of social norms. As he states, "The memory of this taboo as previously given by the surrounding adults has been erased or perhaps executed." In accordance with the binarity that, as we have shown, constitutes an abiding feature of Komori's thought, the reference here to "regress" and "adults" points to a conception of family and society in which reasonable and ethical adults are accorded the privilege of governing, and those who require governing are children, whose as yet uncultivated mental and ethical faculties place them in a position of underdevelopment. In *Murakami Haruki ron: 'Umibe no Kafuka' wo seidoku suru*, Komori devotes many pages to this issue of child development, since he believes that the youth Kafka has suffered a childhood trauma that has rendered him susceptible to fantasies of violence—particularly sexual violence. The root of this trauma is Kafka's abandonment by his mother at an early age, a period that Komori finds to be critical to the success of a child's acquisition of language. As he claims, "Abandoned by his mother at the age of four, the youth Kafka was robbed of the opportunity to receive stories in the form of a causal series through the mediation of the voice as uttered by flesh and blood humans. Beginning with his mother, familiar adults would have regaled him with tales of old and read picture books to him."[33]

In Komori's account of child development, the child begins life in an initial "state of undifferentiation between self and other (*jita mibunka na jōtai*) vis-à-vis the mother,"[34] who provides for all the physical and emotional needs of her offspring. This primal state of identity is abruptly terminated with the appearance of language, which Komori determines to take place in the child at approximately three or four years of age. The process of language acquisition is crucial to the child's overall cognitive development. As Komori notes above, stories told or read to the child are instrumental in fostering a basic sense of causality, such that one learns to identify causes in their distinction from effects, and vice versa. Even more significant, however, is the child's formation of a unified sense of self, and this is achieved primarily through the linguistic ability to refuse or reject: "It is precisely the voiced 'No!' that represents the first step to becoming a human being with an independent personality."[35] Again what is at stake here is the human capacity to clearly distinguish one thing from another. By saying "No!" to adults, the child reinforces his identity as an autonomous individual who is not to be confused with any other individual. If the bedtime stories that a child hears are essential to the development of rudimentary logic and reason, as Komori maintains, the child's insistent "No!" functions doubly as an incipient claiming of subjective identity and the emergence of a protoethical sense that is centered on the value of protest. Through the act in which the child linguistically differentiates himself from others, he in fact commences a form of relationality with the other who is expected to understand and respect that declaration of autonomy. As Komori concludes, "For human beings in the sense of creatures with a command of language (*kotoba wo ayatsuru*) . . . thinking that connects cause and effect, i.e., causal or rational thought, first becomes possible when the child, who previously had merely been confined to language in the form of magic words for which there could be no argument, now separates self and other and seeks responsibility (*ōtō sekinin*) from the other."[36]

It should be evident that this view of childhood development makes a variety of questionable assumptions that are never rigorously scrutinized. Limiting the scope of inquiry exclusively to the question of ethics, however, let me identify two conceptual difficulties with Komori's account. First, the assertion that the child's life is characterized originally by the presence of undifferentiated identity, which is only subsequently lost in the separation characteristic of language acquisition, is a claim that merits closer attention. There exists a long tradition in both metaphysics and theology in which what is posited as the good (happiness, unity, immediate communality) is held to precede evil (suffering, separation, abstract society). Inheriting this tradition, certain communalist accounts derive their ethical force in overcoming what is widely agreed to be the fallen state of contemporary society so as to return to an earlier time in which the violent *cut* of difference had not yet emerged. In Komori's analysis of Kafka, the youth's deviation from normalcy is seen to result from a loss that effectively disrupted a prior state of wholeness. "Abandoned by his mother at the age of four, the youth Kafka was robbed of the opportunity to receive stories in the form of a causal series through the mediation of the voice as uttered by flesh and blood humans. Beginning with his mother, familiar adults would have regaled him with tales of old and read picture books to him," as Komori writes. In these lines, the original health and propriety of presence is figured not only in the mother, whose disappearance Kafka mourns, but also in the notions of the voice and physical proximity as appear in the words "flesh and blood" (*namami*) and "familiar" (*shinkin*). For Komori, the legitimate form of child development consists in a group of adults surrounding the child and comforting him through the reassuring sound of their voices and the touch, sight, and smell of their bodies. While such a family scene can never hope to repeat the initial bliss of the womb, it nevertheless attempts to approximate it through the consolidation of family unity. In Kafka's case, however, it is precisely this reassuring closeness of which he is "robbed" (*ubawareta*) through the traumatic event of his mother's abandonment. The violence of the loss of mother, and with it the accompanying traits of voice and physical proximity, has created a corresponding propensity for violence in Kafka when we encounter him in the novel more than a decade later.

Komori thus attempts to trace back what he regards as the perversion and aberrance of Kafka's character to an earlier trauma that decisively impaired his process of language acquisition, consequently rendering him unable to distinguish things in a rationally sound and ethically just manner. In Komori's account, Kafka's life appears to be divided between a period of normalcy and a period of violent deviation. Significantly, however, these two stages are not presented as symmetrical, for the evil that is deviation is seen as supervening upon an earlier instance of good. The question this raises pertains directly to Komori's relation to Murakami. Murakami clearly seems to view Kafka more generously than Komori is prepared to allow,[37] and at first glance this might appear to be due to their different conceptions of loss. The collapse of an otherwise normal, sound childhood following the abandonment of the mother is actively linked by Komori to deficiencies at the interrelated levels of reason and ethics, and this negative depiction of Kafka represents a departure from Murakami's openly sympathetic portrayal of his character.

In point of fact, however, *Umibe no Kafuka* can be found to adhere to precisely this same prelapsarian logic. In the beginning was the good, this logic assures us, and only through a subsequent fall was the good spoiled and innocence lost. Murakami distributes this view among a variety of characters and scenes in the novel. Early in the text, for example, Ōshima relates to Kafka the classical Greek theory of three sexes:

> In ancient times people weren't just male or female, but one of three types: male/male, male/female, or female/female. In other words, each person was made out of the components of two people. Everyone was happy with this arrangement and never really gave it much thought. But then the gods took a knife and cut everybody in half, right down the middle. So after that the world was divided into just male and female, the upshot being that people spend their time running around trying to locate their missing other half.[38]

This notion of an originally pristine whole that later suffers damage reappears in the description of Nakata's shadow, which was violently halved as a result of the Rice Bowl Hill Incident. This incompleteness of self-identity is observed by the cat Ōtsuka, who suggests that Nakata try to regain that earlier part of himself: " 'What I think is this: You should give up looking for lost cats and start searching for the other half of your shadow.' "[39] In accordance with these two examples, Nakata's friend, the truck driver Hoshino, at one point finds himself reflecting on the painful turn his life has taken:

> Hoshino was drawn back to his childhood. He used to go to the river every day to catch fish. Nothing to worry about back then, he reminisced. Just live each day as it came. As long as I was alive, I was *something*. That was just how it was. But somewhere along the line it all changed. Living turned me into *nothing* . . . But the longer I've lived, the more I've lost what's inside me—and ended up empty.[40]

Finally, and perhaps most obviously to readers of Murakami's novel, Miss Saeki, the library director who becomes Kafka's lover, speaks about the tragedy of her past youthful romance in a late scene that takes place immediately before her death:

> I was born nearby and fell deeply in love with a boy who lived in this house. I couldn't have loved him more, and he was deeply in love with me. We lived in a perfect circle, where everything inside was complete. Of course that couldn't go on forever. We grew up, and times changed. Parts of the circle fell apart, the outside world came rushing into our private paradise, and things inside tried to get out.[41]

Despite the varied circumstances of these remarks, the logic presented is entirely consistent. Throughout *Murakami Haruki ron: 'Umibe no Kafuka' wo seidoku suru*, Komori repeatedly attempts to mark the difference between his own ethical conception of literature and the unethical and depoliticized work that is Murakami's *Umibe no Kafuka*. As our reading reveals, however, both Komori and Murakami subscribe to a prelapsarian logic in their thinking about ethics. In these two texts, the present time is depicted as grievously inadequate, and the only remedy or salvation for this lack of presence is seen to be a return to an earlier time of plenitude. In the case of Komori's Kafka, the youth's various aberrancies are traced back to a childhood event of loss that shattered the original good associated with the immediacy (the voice, the physical body) of the mother. In exactly the same way, Murakami's portrayal of Ōshima, Nakata, Hoshino, and above all Saeki illustrates that good in the sense of happiness and wholeness must be understood as originary. The loss of an initial unity of two beings within one body (Ōshima), the loss of the natural fullness of one's shadow (Nakata), the loss of childhood pleasure such that one's sense of self comes to decline from "something" to "nothing" (Hoshino), and finally the loss of a past love through physical death (Saeki): all of these concrete examples draw upon the same conception of evil, in the sense of suffering and separation, as that which tragically befalls an earlier good. Yet this logic does not in and of itself derive from ethics. To be sure, ethical viewpoints of various stripes have long found conceptual support in this logic.[42] But the idea that present negativity originates from a positive or determinate event (e.g., the abandonment of the mother, the punishment of the gods, the Rice Bowl

Hill Incident, the disappearance of one's childhood, the death of a lover) belongs most fundamentally to a traditional understanding of time, according to which the negativity required for the passage from one *now* to the next emerges only upon the demise of that *now*. In other words, the negativity intrinsic to time is located strictly outside the positive, unitary presence of the *now*. Despite Komori's repeated references to time throughout the entirety of his work, he fails to realize that negativity cannot simply be exiled from the unit, understood here in the sense of the minimal element of presence. And indeed, the most crucial consequence of this essential unexilability on the part of negativity is that the unit never really *is* a unit.[43]

The second difficulty of Komori's account of ethics relates to the developmental model he employs as a means of charting the transition from an uncultivated, unethical position to a position of full ethical presence. For Komori, as we have seen, the successful formation of an individual as an ethical being is necessarily also an achievement of reason. The ethical, rational individual, moreover, is one who has realized his full potential as a "human being in the sense of a creature with a command of language." Here let us recall the link that Komori earlier established between language and consciousness, which he determined positively as an advancement over mere imagery and the unconscious. In this normative conception of subjectivity, an individual's command of language forms an essential part of his command over himself. The overcoming of any unconscious elements that might threaten to lead him astray along dangerously unethical or irrational paths indicates above all the triumph of self-mastery. In this conception, the attainment of a proper form of subjectivity leads inexorably to a higher form of intersubjectivity:

> Upon becoming a human being in the sense of an independent creature with a command of language, what is now most important is that one can use language to transmit as well as to make the other—i.e., the other from whom one has been differentiated (*bunka shite shimatta tasha*)—understand and be convinced by one's own desires and thoughts. If these are rejected by the other, then one can consider the reasons for this rejection and be convinced by them while clarifying their cause and effect. If one is unable to be convinced by them, then one can use language to again ask the other. This is the method by which people interact without the intervention of violence upon the other.[44]

In other words, the subject arrives at full subjectivity by achieving autonomy or "independence" (*jiritsu shita*) from others[45] with whom he can use language rationally, calculating the various causal elements of their communication, and through this process help create a normal form of intersubjectivity characterized by the absence of violence. Particularly revealing in this intersubjective framework is Komori's claim that it precludes "the intervention of violence upon the other." This ethical absence of violence is directly contrasted to the unethical presence of violence he finds throughout the pages of Murakami's *Umibe no Kafuka*, and that takes the form of not only physical violence but also violence against reason (and, as we saw earlier, the related violence against memory). Hence the repeated criticisms of the novel for its "false causal relations," its "unclear causal relations," the fact that it contains "no acceptably rational causal relations whatsoever," and also displays an "utter lack of rational grounding," etc.[46] These accusations of irrationality, it must be stressed, target various scenes that appear in what is, after all, a work of fiction: it is worthwhile to consider whether literature should be upbraided for its failure to uphold the standard of reason. More importantly, however, Komori doesn't appear to consider the possibility that reason and violence are not essentially antagonistic, and that on the contrary reason itself might be seen to harbor certain elements of violence whose lack of visibility makes them no less virulent.

If violence is regarded by Komori as antithetical to reason, language, and consciousness, then one might respond by asking whether this conception of violence is not in fact violent toward the irrational, prelinguistic, imagistic, and unconscious. In what we now recognize as a recurring gesture in his work, the ethical and peaceful come to be posed in all purity as the opposite of the unethical and violent. Yet is not such a pure notion of duality itself violent? This suspicion seems especially justified when ethical issues are treated on the basis of a developmental model in which progress is measured, precisely, by the effectiveness of the violence exercised against those elements determined as "regress." Only by destroying things deemed inferior—and thus excluded from the scope of reason and ethics—can progress be achieved. In this regard, it should come as no surprise to see Komori introduce the notion of spirit in his condemnation of Murakami's novel:

> First of all, the song "Kafka on the Shore" is based on a poem composed by Miss Saeki, but the text doesn't engage the "spirit" signified by the words of the poem; rather, everything is distilled into an image of the "oil painting," which is a form of pictorial

representation in its status as a visual image. In this way, the song is forced to regress to a state of non-linguistic cognition. That is, it is forced to regress to a world that is strictly one of sensory perceptual (*chikaku kankakuteki*) experience, which appears prior to language acquisition; it is a regression to the world of the newborn infant, to a relation of undifferentiation between self and other vis-à-vis the most familiar, care giving adult as represented by the mother. . . . The "love" between the youth Kafka and Miss Saeki that the author Murakami Haruki depicts through the mediation of the "oil painting" is nothing more than an act whereby each projects onto the other their own sensory perceptual fantasies while discovering them within one another. What is thoroughly concealed in this process is all spiritual existence, namely, the spiritual essence or nature (*honsei*) that they possess as human beings in the sense of creatures with a command of language. Here there exists no encounter with alterity, in any sense of the word. Rather, the "love" found in *Kafka on the Shore* is based on the rejection and negation of the other in its being as other.[47]

In these lines, spirit (*seishin*) appears as representative of the uniquely human achievement of language in the form of signification. Komori originally appropriates this term from the novelist Mizumura Minae's reading of Sōseki's 1907 work *Gubijinsō* [The poppy],[48] but he interprets it in such a way that it becomes virtually synonymous with language itself. From Komori's perspective, the words in Miss Saeki's poem "Kafka on the Shore" should rightly draw attention to her ability, as a "human being in the sense of a creature with a command of language," to actively create this spiritual product. Yet he finds that Murakami utilizes what is essentially a bait-and-switch tactic in diverting attention from the poem to the oil painting that hangs in Kafka's room, a painting that is also called *Kafka on the Shore*. This diversion is condemned by Komori because it represents an untenable decline from the heights of spirit to the lowliness of physical being. The painting, as he describes it, is merely "a form of pictorial representation in its status as a visual image." Rather than indicating the spiritual progress of language, the painting points only to an unfortunate "regress to a state of non-linguistic cognition (*higengoteki na ninchi*)." This state of nonlinguistic cognition is then equated to sensory perception, which, as Komori specifies, precedes (*izen no*) the process of language acquisition. This shift to the issue of language acquisition allows Komori to conjoin the otherwise quite disparate realms of epistemology and child development. Given its primitive status as a nonlinguistic artifact that relies strictly on sensory perception, the painting now signifies "a regression to the world of the newborn infant, to a relation of undifferentiation between self and other vis-à-vis the . . . mother." Precisely the same demotion of status occurs in the case of love. The relation between Kafka and Saeki cannot be accurately characterized as love because it lacks the "spiritual essence or nature" that is a necessary condition for authentic love to develop. Instead, the baseness of their physical desire for one another condemns these lovers to a state of inauthentic love, which, because it is insufficiently spiritual, comes to be linked to the merely immediate or unformed level of sensory perception. Quoting the novel's depiction of their lovemaking as an act in which "everything takes place in silence," Komori concludes: "It is clear that there is in the relationship between Miss Saeki and the youth Kafka a thorough rejection of engagement through language—that is, through spirit."[49]

The attack on sensory perception is motivated by the desire to think the human subject as uniquely capable of mediating the world through language. In this regard, the immediacy of sensory perception must be criticized, since human beings of course share the ability to receive sensory data from objects with all other animals. Yet Komori has no choice but to be moderate in his criticism, for sensory perception is necessarily *also* recognized as the first stage in the formation of language. Spirit, that is to say, requires the raw material of the world in order to begin operating, and this operation consists of the gradual filtering or screening out of those impurities that are considered excessively worldly such that, at the end of this process, spirit encounters only itself. Here we must point out Komori's remarkable consistency in conceiving of language in this manner. To recall, *Kōzō to shite no katari* offers a description of writing in the form of *moji* as "meaningless stones" whose materiality must be simultaneously overcome and uplifted in order to attain its properly spiritual status as language. In *Dekigoto to shite no yomu koto*, similarly, the act of reading commences with the recognition of ink stains as inchoately linguistic, and "[w]e send this visual cognition to consciousness, where writing in the form of icons is transformed into voice as auditory images that represent the units of language." For Komori, this passage that departs from the unformed materiality of "meaningless stones" and reaches its endpoint in the fully formed "units of language" is nothing other than the movement of spirit.

It is puzzling how Komori wishes to think about ethics on the basis of a developmental model without pausing to consider the violence inherent in the concept of development itself. In its classical formulation, spirit is not simply opposed to matter; it actively *requires* matter in order to violently consume it and thereby sustain its own spiritual life. This violence is twofold, for it appears both in the interiorization of matter and in the distance thus created between spiritual progress and material "regress." In this sense, Komori's attempt in the foregoing passage to link spirit with the notion of alterity is especially striking. Denouncing Kafka's relationship with Saeki as insufficiently spiritual, Komori states, "Here there exists no encounter with alterity, in any sense of the word. Rather, the 'love' found in *Kafka on the Shore* is based on the rejection and negation of the other in its being as other." The final phrase here is *tasha ga tasha de aru koto*, and this appeal to identity, to the being (*de aru*) of identity, is necessary for Komori because his conception of love requires above all that the lovers understand and accept each other as who they truly are, as opposed to merely projecting that desired identity upon one another ("nothing more than an act whereby each projects onto the other their own sensory perceptual fantasies while discovering them within one another," as he writes). At stake here for Komori is something like the ethical ground of love, and this ground is itself grounded upon the notion of identity. In this view, no love is possible without first identifying the other as who he or she is in their difference from myself. The recognition of alterity consists in accepting this difference from myself, and this entails that the other presents him or herself to me in the particular identity that is their otherness—an otherness that may in turn be distinguished from my own otherness vis-à-vis them.

Once again, however, Komori unfortunately neglects to fully reckon with the unsettling effects of time. If spirit is linked with ethics, then alterity, rigorously understood, is that which escapes the ethical. This is so because alterity by definition only gives itself as *other* to itself. In other words, as soon as the other presents himself or herself to me as who they truly are, they are no longer *other*. According to its most traditional determination, identity is that which allows something to persist strictly as itself through time. In his desire to set forth a code of ethics based on mutual respect and acceptance between human beings (i.e., a humanist ethics), however, Komori all too quickly conflates the notion of alterity with that of identity. Far from allowing itself to be joined to identity, however, alterity names the movement of difference, but this difference goes beyond the dimension of particular identity as it exists between individuals to include even self-identity. Because nothing can ever persist identically as itself through time, alterity asserts itself as a force. Despite the best ethical intentions, Komori's claim that "there exists no encounter with alterity" in the relation between Kafka and Saeki must be false since there can never be an absence of alterity. One *must* encounter it, whether one likes it or not, whether one is conscious of it or not. If there is time—again, time understood in its generality beyond the time of consciousness delimited by Komori—then there is necessarily alterity, for time can only appear in its difference or division from itself. Prior to referring to another human individual, then, the notion of alterity points in its most fundamental sense to the differential movement of time.

Conclusion

It might be tempting to read our intervention in the dialogue between Murakami Haruki and Komori Yōichi as a theoretical defense of the former, an attempt to unearth those conceptual riches that are otherwise overlooked or perhaps even willfully ignored in Komori's unforgiving critique. We have already suggested, however, that Murakami at certain moments appeals to the same prelapsarian logic as Komori does, and that what appears to be divergence or disagreement may in fact conceal underlying commonalities. To say that *Umibe no Kafuka* is a complex text is ultimately not saying very much: if one thinks the notion of text on the basis of its Latin root, *textus*, or "tissue," which in turn derives from *texere* in the sense of "to weave," then one is faced with a web consisting of multiple strands tied together in such a way as to resist any pure reduction to simplicity or unicity. Indeed, we sought to demonstrate this very point in our analysis of the youth Kafka's description of his confused thoughts as "all intertwined and entangled." Komori reads these lines as evidence of a dangerous lack of reason and ethics on the part of the subject. However, we attempted to draw the discussion back to the more fundamental level of time and ontology in order to call attention to an essential heterogeneity that disturbs all identity, including (but not limited to) subjective identity. In precisely the same way, Murakami's novel presents itself as strangely incommensurate with itself. As can unfortunately be seen throughout Murakami's corpus, *Umibe no Kafuka* contains elements of a rather indulgent form of popular psychology and popular philosophy, to say nothing of its considerable debt to the various clichés of young adult fiction. Komori shows himself to be keenly aware of Murakami's faults as a writer, and this is hardly surprising given his extraordinary sensitivity to the literary text. Nonetheless, if a text is to be recognized in the fullness of its textuality, then one must acknowledge the presence of inconsistencies in *Umibe no Kafuka*, inconsistencies that at times challenge our understanding of concepts that inform the discourses of both literature and philosophy.

One of the central challenges posed by Murakami's work concerns the notion of identity. Beyond the scope of cultural studies, which insists on viewing this term from the empirical standpoints of psychology and sociology (thereby reinforcing the hold of subjectivism), identity must instead be grasped in its link to time and the ability of an entity to remain strictly itself despite the constant incursion of difference. According to the law of noncontradiction, an entity must be identical to itself if it is to *be* at all. Hence entity X cannot be both X and not X at the same time. In *Umibe no Kafuka*, however, one finds repeated transgressions of this apparently self-evident principle. As Kafka tells Saeki, for example: "I am there, but it's not me." In her letter to Dr. Tsukayama, Okamochi confesses that she physically beat the child Nakata, "but it wasn't me who was there." Somewhat later in the novel, the adult Nakata attempts to confirm the identity of Johnnie Walker: "So you're a foreigner and also not a foreigner." Responding to Nakata's confusion, Johnnie Walker remarks, "You are no longer yourself. . . . That's a very important point, Mr. Nakata. A person is no longer himself." This disturbance of unified identity, however, is in no way limited to the human. As Ōshima explains to Kafka when they are driving back from the mountain cabin: "But nature is in a certain sense unnatural. Serenity is in a certain sense threatening. One must have a kind of preparation and experience in order to really accept such antimonies."[50]

The "antinomies" (*haihansei*) in which the *de aru* (is) is seen to share or coexist with the *de nai* (is not) reveal that entities can never be fully present or adequate to themselves. Given that all entities must exist in time, they remain essentially vulnerable to the negativity inherent in succession whereby one moment appears in the very same gesture by which it disappears and thus gives way to another. Contrary to Komori's conception of alterity, this *other* moment can never be absolutely separated or "distinguished" from the moment that immediately precedes it. Despite his considerable gifts as a literary critic, Komori's attachment to the canonical account of time and being prevents him from reading *Umibe no Kafuka* as anything but an aberration of subjectivity. From his standpoint, the subject must above all distinguish, he must cut clearly and distinctly, and the objects of his distinctions include subject versus object, man versus world, good versus evil, and "something" versus "something else." The singular tool that enables the subject to identify what is to be distinguished is consciousness, which allows man to develop reason and ethics—thereby creating a further distinction between spiritual progress and material "regress." If *Umibe no Kafuka* doesn't adhere to this logic, it is not because Murakami wishes to resist development and remain at the level of immediacy, a charge that Komori frequently levels against him.[51] On the contrary, the novel shows that the cutting or articulation that lies at the heart of distinction is necessarily already underway. It is this general movement of cutting that is so threatening to a thinking that grounds itself on the centrality of the subject. In the subjective cutting of the world that is distinction, incision appears to be regulated by consciousness. In this way, things can be unambiguously distinguished from one another because they exist as originally present to themselves in the integrity of their identity. Once cutting is shown to exceed the limited scope of subjective consciousness, however, this very identity that differentiates one thing from another begins to crack and suffer distortion. Whatever other faults can be found in Murakami's novel, this insight into the primal deformation of identity must be recognized and remembered.

Chapter 2

The Double Pull of History and Philosophy

Reading Harootunian

> Because it is not solely the present, past, and future of empty time that constantly mingle with one another but also the true, lived time of the present, the time present to consciousness forms a complex weave of warp and woof.
>
> —Harry Harootunian[1]

Introduction

Among the various lines or lineages that can be identified in the field of Japan studies, those traced out by the work of Harry Harootunian must be regarded as particularly vital. From his groundbreaking research on early modern Japan, *Toward Restoration: The Growth of Political Consciousness in Tokugawa Japan* and *Things Seen and Unseen: Discourse and Ideology in Tokugawa Nativism*, to his most recent study on global Marxism, *Marx After Marx: History and Time in the Expansion of Capitalism*, Harootunian has worked indefatigably to promote greater theoretical reflection in the discipline of Japanese history and beyond.[2] For several decades now, Harootunian has been one of the most powerful voices to call attention to the need in Asian studies to go beyond a narrow, positivistic scholarship and engage with a variety of concepts and methodological frameworks that help us better understand "Asia" and its associated phenomena in more general and rigorous terms. In this regard, whether one explicitly recognizes this fact or not, all contemporary critical-theoretical research in the field remains indebted to Harootunian's work; it *repeats* that work in ways that might extend or even complicate it but that nevertheless always remains in dialogue with it.

As Harootunian demonstrates throughout his writing, the relationship between positivistic research and theoretical reflection cannot be grasped as one of simple exteriority. If positivism claims that all cognitive meaning of subjective statements depends upon their objective, empirical verifiability, then Harootunian will call into question the subject's ability to transcend its own individual biases and register such external data in a purely transparent and rational manner. The positivist fallacy lies in the subject's conviction that the acquisition of objective knowledge is a neutral or value-free operation. For Harootunian, this conviction is not only untenable; it is, at bottom, a disavowal of the subject's own limitations with regard to truth claims. These limitations, however, cannot be explained merely at the level of individual psychology. On the contrary, the inability of the subject to directly access the external world of things must ultimately be attributed to the fact that the subject is a historical being, and that its knowledge is at every instant mediated by the vagaries and contingencies of history. As a result, the field of Asian studies, insofar as it remains governed by this methodology of positivism and its core assumption of objective, empirical verifiability, will be condemned by Harootunian as insufficiently historical.

In the particular context of Japan studies, for example, the objects of knowledge that are presented for inquiry already appear marked as Japanese. Do these markings inhere originally in nature or are they rather the derivative result of cultural or historical processes that, for ideological reasons, attempt to naturalize themselves and so conceal their own intervention? Traditionally, research in Japan studies will implicitly posit the various properties of the Japanese artifact (e.g., literary work, historical movement, etc.) as historical and thus arbitrary—the artifact may be determined as X but also possibly as Y, depending on differences in context and perspective. From Harootunian's standpoint, however, such historicization in fact covertly removes the Japanese object or artifact from historical consideration. In this division between a thing and its properties, it is insufficient to historicize the latter if the former, given its predetermination as *Japanese*, remains exempt from history. As Harootunian frequently reminds us, however, this difference is not exclusively a matter of epistemology. On the contrary, the operation by which the particular property or attribute "Japanese" comes to be regarded not as an extrinsic property of the thing but rather as an intrinsic or essential part of the thing itself represents the workings of ideology at their most subtle. The slippage of "Japanese" from property to thing is less an epistemological error than a symptom of modernity and the formation of the nation-state. It is because Japan studies fails to interrogate its objects at this fundamental historical level, Harootunian believes, that it remains complicit with the nation-state ideology of modernity.

Harootunian's work has been of inestimable value in allowing us to take a more critical view of the position of Japan studies in the broader context of modernity. But this work itself has rarely been subject to the same level of critical inquiry it so richly deserves. In what follows, I would like to begin to assess the theoretical positions staked out in Harootunian's research with particular regard to the question of the relation between history and philosophy. The challenge confronted by this present chapter lies in recognizing and taking account of the various merits of Harootunian's approach while nevertheless indicating what I believe are its methodological limitations. While many of Harootunian's insights are instrumental in enabling us to better grasp the diverse ways in which Japan studies has sought to foreclose larger, more fundamental questions of conceptuality, there can still be detected in his work certain moments in which that closure remains inadequately interrogated, thereby preventing us from exploring other paths of inquiry in which an opening beyond traditional forms of scholarship and thinking may be pursued. I will begin by examining two contestations of Harootunian's work, those by David Williams and Andrew Gordon, with the aim of assessing the legitimacy of these challenges on the basis of arguments presented in Harootunian's own writing. I will then turn to the more general issue of history and historiography in their relation to the discourse of philosophy so as to evaluate the particular nature of Harootunian's methodological contributions. This evaluation will traverse questions of ethics and politics before proceeding to a consideration of Harootunian's critical engagement with the thought of Martin Heidegger.

Challenges from Japan Studies

In his article, "Modernity, Harootunian and the Demands of Scholarship," David Williams offers a review of Harootunian's monograph *Overcome by Modernity: History, Culture and Community in Interwar Japan* (2000) while finding fault with such things as the author's archival research, prose style, factual knowledge, and conceptualization of fascism. Above all, however, it is Harootunian's theorization of Japanese modernity to which Williams sets himself in firm opposition. As Williams writes:

> Kyoto School thinkers such as Kōyama Iwao insisted that history had a plural character *because Japan's modernizing success had demonstrated the plural character of history* . . . This is the central intellectual insight of the Kyoto School on this subject. Here is where Japanese philosophy comes within shouting distance of the Western discourse on the Japanese miracle . . . Harootunian assumes that modernity is an irresistible force that roars down a single path to which all societies must, willy-nilly, conform. In making this assumption, he is an uncompromising Marxist, that is an unreconstructed Eurocentrist. He thinks that Westerners invented the modern world and that is the end of the matter. It was inevitable, therefore, that Japan would be overwhelmed by Western modernity. Harootunian has closed his mind to any other possibility. Hardly any of the Japanese thinkers examined in this book agree with this assumption. Some believe that modernity can be deflected or outwitted or perhaps even stopped. Others hold that alternative modernities are possible. The wartime Kyoto School, for example, was convinced that a Japanese form of modernity—one consistent with many Japanese values and most of its ambitions—was achievable. Guided by this conviction, the Kyoto School metaphysically anticipated the post-war triumph of the Japanese economic miracle. Between 1952 and 1992, a specifically Japanese form of modernity was achieved in defiance of Anglo-American economic logic and business practice. Japan did modernize but it was not overcome by Western modernity. In this sense, the aspirations that inspired the wartime deliberations of the symposia on "Overcoming Modernity" and "The Standpoint of World History and Japan" were fulfilled after 1945 in ways that Harootunian cannot explain.[3]

For Williams, history cannot be regarded in universal terms, particularly when it is the West that has shaped this discourse in such a way as to unilaterally arrogate to itself the position of both historical center or protagonist and the telos of historical progress. If the West represents the telos toward which history advances, then that advancement can be measured by the degree to which history departs from the East, gradually eliminating its receding traces in the course of the civilizing process. Historically, the West's self-determination as the privileged agent of progress and civilization has taken place through a concomitant determination of the East as the site of backwardness or barbarity. In this regard, as Williams recognizes, modernization has come to be seen as synonymous with Westernization itself: it is the historical process through which the West raises the East beyond itself so that it may decisively overcome its tendencies of stagnation and insularity and become part of a global movement of development. Williams attacks Harootunian because he views the latter's conception of modernity as unwittingly complicit with this Eurocentric tradition and its unfounded claims of superiority vis-à-vis those cultures located outside the West. Williams marshals the support of the Kyoto School to show that, contra Harootunian, history possesses a multiple rather than unified character, and that indeed the Kyoto philosophers' vision of a specifically non-Western form of modernity was subsequently achieved by Japan's record of economic success during the decades following World War II.

Unfortunately, however, Williams appears to misrecognize the central thrust of Harootunian's notion of modernity. For Harootunian, it is modernity that led to the formation of the nation-state system. To the degree that one can speak of Japan and the Japanese people on the basis of a discrete national identity, modernization is necessarily already underway. As, for example, Harootunian writes of the wartime "Overcoming Modernity" symposium referred to by Williams: "In many ways, the symposium was a continuation, by other means, of the struggle against an everyday life introduced by capitalist modernization that had been fiercely contested since the 1920s by all kinds of social and cultural theorists, writers, and thinkers, who saw in its growing hegemony both a dilution and diminution of an essential cultural endowment."[4] Here, Harootunian points to a contradiction that underlies much of the discourse on Japanese modernity: the "essential cultural endowment" so valued by Japanese intellectuals as to be anxiously regarded as jeopardized by the homogenizing force of modernization was *itself* a product of this same modernization. The modernization that saw the creation of an international system promoted the development of distinct national cultures: each of these cultures was recognized as different from other national cultures, but strictly on the condition that they were determined to be unified in and of themselves. Hence, the desire on the part of conservative intellectuals to safeguard Japanese culture could only arise from their own disavowal that such culturalism was entirely grounded on the movement of unification brought about by modernity.

When Williams criticizes Harootunian for his putative claim that "modernity is an irresistible force that roars down a single path to which all societies must, willy-nilly, conform," he fails to consider that, from Harootunian's perspective, the very formation of a specific "Japanese form of modernity" merely serves to confirm, rather than resist, the unifying or totalizing force of modernization. Williams doesn't appear to understand that the universalizing path of modernization takes place strictly through mediation. In this respect, there is no contradiction whatsoever between the modernizing movement of unification or homogenization and the differential formation of individual national cultures, since the latter functions precisely as the mediation through which the former comes to be effectuated. Williams sharply recognizes the historical violence of modernization as perpetrated by the West, but his attempt to resist that violence through appeal to a cultural particularism of the non-West—as for example "one consistent with many Japanese values," as he writes—remains caught within the universalizing logic of modernity. The point is *not* simply to support the East in its defense against the universal claims of the modern West, for, as the history of Japanese imperialism amply reveals, the very formation of a unified eastern identity takes place through a replication of the violence between a universalizing center and its colonial periphery.[5] Rather than subjectively identifying with one term or the other of this now antiquated geopolitical binary, it seems far more productive to critically examine the universalizing logic of modernity in the development of its particularist manifestations. Williams's project consists ultimately in reversing the terms of modernization so as to call attention to the historical injustices of Eurocentrism. Yet Harootunian, who has long been one of the most vociferous critics of modernization theory, astutely realizes the trap of such reversal and, identifying neither with the "East" nor "West," provides an analysis of modernity that accounts for the complex mediations through which its logic is unfolded.

Andrew Gordon provides a rather more balanced account of Harootunian's work in his review essay "Rethinking Area Studies, Once More." This article, which presents a critical discussion of the collected volume *Learning Places: The Afterlives of Area Studies*, coedited by Harootunian and Masao Miyoshi, focuses specifically on Harootunian's scholarship: not only are attacks directed at the book's introduction ("The 'Afterlife' of Area Studies," cowritten with Miyoshi) and Harootunian's contributing essay, "Postcoloniality's Unconscious/Area Studies' Desire," but the article concludes with a negative assessment of the "weakness" of his book *Overcome by Modernity*.

In order to provide a general sense of this debate, I quote the following passage from Gordon:

> A second vexing feature of the book is the tendency to set up straw men for attack. This is most striking in the blast leveled at a reputed obsession of traditional area studies with language mastery, reportedly seen in naive fashion as the magic key to knowledge of the Asian other: 'There is the presumption of the transparency of language as an unmediated conveyor of native truths and knowledge' (p. 11); and 'these two conditions [field work and language study] were inevitably seen as more than adequate substitutes or replacement for theory and methodology *as they still are*' (p. 162). I italicize the last four words for they are 'straw man' criticism at its worst. Tell us who these present-day scholars might be. I am sure some practitioners have been guilty as charged; and some may still believe it is possible to learn a language or two and thus apprehend the truth of Asia, pure and simple. But surely the vast majority of scholars in and around the area studies realm understand linguistic fluency to be a necessary tool, but by no means a sufficient one for important scholarship. Who would deny that language mastery is a crucial first step toward understanding?[6]

Referring in these lines to Harootunian's introduction and volume essay, respectively, Gordon warns against underestimating the importance of linguistic competency in the study of Asia. This point is presented together with a larger claim: Asian studies scholarship may have disproportionately stressed the value of language training in the past, but its contemporary form represents a more developed and sophisticated synthesis of elements drawn from theory and methodology. From Gordon's standpoint, Harootunian fails to acknowledge the significant qualitative improvements achieved by Asian studies during the past decades. Harootunian is thus guilty of "reductively collapsing decades of scholarship into a single polemic sweep and ignoring how much area studies scholarship has changed," as Gordon charges.[7] This insensitivity to the various advancements made in the field results in what Gordon describes above as a "straw man" type of argumentation in which the object of critique bears little resemblance to the actual state of scholarship. If indeed the current state of the field is the intended target of Harootunian's attack, then Gordon demands a greater level of specificity and concreteness from Harootunian in order to assess the validity of the latter's claims. This is the meaning behind Gordon's rebuttal, "Tell us who these present-day scholars might be." Individual scholars may yet exist for whom linguistic facility trumps the value of theoretical reflection, but surely the "vast majority" of researchers have moved beyond the disciplinary shortcomings of the past and now practice a more progressive form of scholarship.

It is not difficult to imagine that Harootunian would agree with Gordon that firsthand knowledge of Asian languages is instrumental in the context of Asian studies research. Harootunian's point, I believe, is less that such linguistic competency is negligible than that it has been, and unfortunately continues to be, excessively and even fetishistically valued relative to more general considerations at the level of theory and methodology. It is this move to generality that lies at the heart of Gordon's complaint, but I believe that this move is in fact central to Harootunian's argument concerning Asian studies. As for example Harootunian writes in *Learning Places*:

> Yet despite the confidence attending the establishment of area studies programs and its promise to grasp the totality of a region, its inaugural moment was marred by the absence of a definable object. Asia was simply an age-old cartographer's fantasy, reinforced by the necessities of World War II, referring only to itself in the expectancy that something out there will eventually correspond to it or be made to align with it. Vast professional organizations, college curricula, graduate training programs, and research institutes were organized around this substanceless something, as if it were an object, pledged to disseminating a knowledge even as the object vanished once it seemed we had a grip on it. (Post-coloniality has sought to avoid this embarrassment by disavowing totalities altogether but it has not solved the problem of the vanishing object.) With area studies Asia, for instance, was simply a process of naming but the names were as lifeless as the social science—geography—that once declared its reality and named its presence.[8]

It is important to recognize here that Harootunian's argument proceeds on both historical and philosophical grounds. In his account, the dream of Asian studies is to "grasp the totality of a region," and yet this totality remains elusive. It remains elusive not because research on Asia is thus far incomplete, thereby implying the existence of an ideal future moment in which this area, together with all the diverse phenomena it contains, might be known absolutely. On the contrary, this elusiveness appears for *essential* rather than *empirical* reasons. Harootunian refers to the belief held by Asian studies scholars that Asia can be posited as an empirical totality, and his response, crucially, is to raise the stakes of this debate beyond the level of empirical history to that of philosophical generality. In this sense, he can be said to enact a kind of hyperbolization in which the notion of empirical totality is in fact exceeded by a general claim that is not grounded in experience. Asia, Harootunian contends, cannot be understood as a "substance," "reality," or "presence." Of course the very notion of Asia derives from empirical discourse, but the assertion that the Asian object is, as he writes, "substanceless"[9] or "vanishing" is rather of the order of what Kant would call an a priori judgment, that is, it refers to knowledge that is universal and necessary, independent of and yet applicable to all experience. With this move to generality, Harootunian ensures that the positive empirical totality that is Asia must yield to the infinitely greater totality that is a priori judgment: regardless of the specific manner in which Asia appears in the world, it is at *all* times and *all* places without substance.

Once this generality is established, Harootunian's theoretical or methodological differences with Gordon can only multiply. For Harootunian, the core problem underlying the field of Asian studies is that in its theoretical naiveté it dogmatically assumes the real or empirical existence of a region called "Asia." The entire history of this discipline has been devoted to amassing greater quantities of information about Asia without ever rigorously questioning this inaugural assumption. Although Harootunian, in his role as historian, will analyze the material practices in which Japan has been discursively instantiated, closely following the concrete sociopolitical effects brought about by such activity, he nevertheless takes as his point of departure the otherwise abstract philosophical insight that Japan and Asia themselves are nonempirical, "substanceless" entities. Clearly Asian studies has experienced various intellectual and institutional changes throughout its history, but from his perspective these changes must not blind us to the field's founding assumption—one that continues to be reinforced in the present—that Asia is determinable as a substantial object. Gordon's accusation that Harootunian is insufficiently attentive to the field's changes, together with his demand that Harootunian specify exactly which present-day scholars might fall subject to his critique, unfortunately misses this general point. In this instance, the call for specificity too easily runs the risk of neglecting to consider those larger structures and paradigms that formatively shape the field. As Harootunian suggests, the very structure of Asian studies owes its existence to a disavowal of an originary philosophical insight, one whose generality far exceeds the scope of any given empirical totality. In this way, Harootunian can be said to remind Gordon that Asian studies must endeavor to remain close to the truth of this a priori judgment. This move to generality in no way comes at the cost of historical specificity, however. As Harootunian's work amply demonstrates, recognition of the originally nonempirical status of Asia rather opens the way for a more critical and far less insular form of Asian studies that is able to reflect on the contingency of its own foundations.

Haunting, Time, Space

Gordon's disagreements with Harootunian illustrate their very different methodological concerns. While Gordon upbraids Harootunian in a way that is revealing of his commitments at the level of empirical history, Harootunian makes an initial decision to conceive of Asia and its related phenomena in a radically preempirical manner, and this choice inevitably shapes the way in which he engages with historical materials. If Harootunian's recourse to a priori judgment will come to trouble Gordon's assessment, however, then this move may also be seen to complicate certain aspects of Harootunian's own project. Here, let us recall that Harootunian's thinking is above all devoted to what might be called the "concreteness of present experience," an expression that can equally be reversed to signify the "concrete experience of presence." In raising the issue of Harootunian's conception of the relation between history and philosophy, a preliminary question appears regarding the status of experience, which Harootunian reminds us is that which fundamentally determines our being as historical. The question is this: if what is called "Asia" can be shown to lack the "substance," "reality," and "presence" that empirical historiography erroneously ascribes to it, then what sort of consequences might be drawn regarding our understanding of other things in the world that similarly appear to give themselves in their immediacy? That is to say, in light of the importance of Harootunian's insight into the "substanceless" nature of Asia, what is the precise scope or generalizability of this claim? It seems clear that, in the context of Asian studies, Harootunian's argument is motivated by the desire to move beyond the fetishization of Asia in order to return to a more concrete level of experience. However, the claim that Asia is without substance is rather of the order of an a priori judgment, which means that its universality and necessity are not derivable from, or dependent upon, experience itself. If Harootunian's project, as we will see, consists of returning beyond the abstractions of ideology to the concreteness of lived experience, then how is it possible to issue a priori judgments?

In order to avoid misunderstanding, let me emphasize that these questions are in no way intended to doubt the value of a body of work that for several decades has been one of the leading examples of critical thinking and theoretical reflection in the field of Japan studies. Harootunian's attempt to more rigorously examine certain assumptions in historiography—using a form of argumentation more typically associated with the discourse of philosophy—allows us to better grasp the underlying complexity of the historian's relationship with the past. In this regard, it is important to realize that Harootunian's aims go well beyond the task of reconceptualizing Japanese modernity or exposing the empiricist prejudice that lies at the heart of Asian studies. While broadening the range of inquiry outside the traditional bounds of scholarship on Japan and Asia, Harootunian's work also seeks to investigate those ways in which the historian, whether he recognizes it or not, is already philosophically engaged with his various objects of knowledge. For Harootunian, the historical gaze into the past can only take place from one's position in the present, and this attention to the present brings to the fore the interrelated questions of time and experience. In what follows, I would like to pursue Harootunian's thinking at this level of conceptual generality in order to evaluate the success of his rapprochement between history and philosophy.

As a way of framing Harootunian's argument, I wish to first discuss this relation between history and philosophy through reference to a recent work, Ethan Kleinberg's *Haunting History: For a Deconstructive Approach to the Past*. In this study, Kleinberg draws extensively on the thought of Jacques Derrida in order to argue for a more philosophically grounded mode of historiography. Historians have avoided a rigorous confrontation with deconstruction, Kleinberg contends, because of their commitment to what he calls "ontological realism."[10] Inheriting the classical division between subject and object, now reformulated as the difference between epistemology and ontology, the historian views the past strictly as a past present in which the sense of reality yielded by the present through means of empirical data is then transferred back to the past. Epistemological uncertainty inevitably arises because of the distance between past events and our own position in the present, but this uncertainty is offset by our ontological certitude that these events actually happened at a specific time and place. In other words, while it is granted that historians may never fully understand *what* the past was in its identity, it is nevertheless determined *that* events in the past took place, and their mode of being can be grasped in terms of the present. It is this belief in the ontological reality of the past, that the otherwise absent *was* of the past remains accessible to the empirically grounded and verifiable *is* of the present, that Kleinberg wishes to call into question.

In order for the past event to be determinable as such, there must be an implicit understanding of events as originally present to themselves; while the passage of time invariably effaces that initial presence, the historian is convinced that this past present may nevertheless be recovered through the act of objectification. In this way, historiography can be said to triumph over the negative force of time. At stake here is the question of whether time merely distances the past event from our present perspective or, much more radically, negates the reality or being of the event in such a way as to essentially disturb the historian's operation of transforming this otherwise absent past into a viable object of knowledge. It is at this point where Kleinberg introduces the figure of the ghost: "[T]he place where conventional or scientific history breaks down is the place of the ghost—of haunting and of hauntology."[11] The ghost announces that the return of the past cannot be understood in terms of the binary relation between absence and presence. In contrast to the historian's belief that the reanimation of the past event takes place through an overcoming of distance or absence in order to reclaim the past in its original presence, Kleinberg argues that the past event was in truth never originally present. If the past event suffers temporal negation in its demise or passing, then that negation must already be inscribed within the interiority of the event itself. It is because of this disturbing "place of the ghost" within the heart of the past event that the event must be said to escape the order of presence and classical ontology and now be rethought, following Derrida's French pun, on the basis of *hantologie*.

Kleinberg's demand that historiography heed the philosophical imperative to inquire into its own conditions of possibility (which, as Derrida will always note, are inseparable from its conditions of impossibility) is instructive for our reading of Harootunian, for Harootunian is likewise deeply impatient with the historian's reluctance to pose questions that are fundamental to the acquisition of historical knowledge. Excessively attached to this or that particular historical object, the historian risks losing sight of the fact that his or her examination of the past involves above all the general question of time. As Harootunian comments at length in *Marx After Marx*:

An often acknowledged paradox of historical practice, whose knowledge has been organized according to categories denoting time and its passage from a "before" to an "after," is how little interest it has shown in actually addressing the question of time and temporality itself and its status in constructing the 'historical field.' . . . [S]ensitivity expressed by historians toward the temporal dimensions of history rarely exceeds the abstract measuring of time and its quantification in chronology, the marking of calendar time and the passage from one day to the next, contrasting dramatically with the commitment of philosophy, which, since Henri Bergson's and Martin Heidegger's project promising a "reckoning with time," had already embarked on a search for the forms of qualitative time. While this philosophical intervention has rarely assessed the relationship between time and capitalism (and thus history), more recent signs of interest have sought to make philosophy answerable to history and vice versa. This has entailed confronting the central role occupied by capitalism as the temporal dominant of modern society and thereby the need to address the effects of its structuring of time on history and politics. Such efforts invariably have converged on the incontrovertible observation that capitalism itself is, among other things, an immense conceptual organization of time. . . . In fact, this view matches precisely the contemporary experience of capitalism as an all-encompassing temporal rhythmology dedicated to ordering the different tempos of time with an unrelenting and inescapable circularity, which, accordingly, has truncated history itself, if not bracketing it altogether. . . . Capital's logic thus points to 'annihilating' history because it is posited on the eternality of the present . . .

The historian's indifference toward the problem of time, especially its agental aptitude, validates Jacques Rancière's observation that judgments like charges of anachronism reflect a misrecognition because the question of historical time is a philosophic one and cannot be resolved as if it were reducible to the methodology or epistemology of history. Moreover, the charge of anachronism constitutes a political dismissal of any expression of time that does not correspond to the order of a linear chronology since it belongs to another time to represent time out of joint. The identification of anachronism itself may well signal the fear of coexisting temporalities in a present pledged to obeying the rhythms of social normative time. For Rancière, the knotted question posed between the present of historical enunciation and the past it seeks to rescue concerns not a Rankean fidelity to the idea of reality that conformed to the 'way things were' but rather the status of the present's priority as the locus of history's representation. . . . Yet even before, Georg Simmel had already perceived how the present under capitalism had virtually been 'ontologized,' while Marx saw in it the housing of a vast, heterogeneous inventory and "conjuncture" of temporalities no longer stigmatized for having been cast out of time but rather as expressions of contretemps, simultaneous nonsimultaneities . . . contemporaneous noncontemporaneities or uneven times, and . . . time's turmoil, times out of joint, multiple temporalities, in other words, instances of *multiversum* testifying to untimeliness itself fully immanent to what constitutes normative social time. The supposed unity of time projected by capital and nation-state is a masquerade that invariably fails to conceal the ceaseless confrontation of different times. For Marx, these were instances of how time, or temporality, temporalized itself in the present, beginning with the process of production and reproduction where the colliding patterns of unevenness generated untimeliness and political struggle. . . . [I]t became evident that the past could not lay claim to the identity of being historical in itself but rather acquires this status through the mediation of the present.[12]

Harootunian diverges from Kleinberg in a number of significant ways, but what is common to both is the belief that historical practice does not take place outside of the discourse of philosophy. The disciplinary separation of historiography and philosophy has unfortunately produced in the former a severe narrowing of the field of inquiry such that historical objects are presented in their givenness in a manner that removes or abstracts these objects from a prior examination of their own constitution. To be sure, the selection of the historical object is to some degree subjective and contingent. Regardless of which particular object is chosen, however, the fact remains that *all* historical objects must, for reasons of necessity, emerge at a certain time in the past, survive their own temporal passing, and then appear to the historian in the now different or displaced time of the present. Failure to consider this mode of appearance in the object's itinerary from past to present leaves the historian open to charges of subjectivism, for the very enabling of historical objectification takes place in a fashion that ultimately calls into question any claims to subjective mastery vis-à-vis the past. In the context of historiography, it is the historian in his role as knower of the past who is seen as actively returning to the past to objectify the historical event. Even prior to this subject's operation of knowledge, however, it seems clear that the past has already shaped the present in which this act of historical objectification takes place. In this regard, the historian must be regarded as less the active subject of historical knowledge than as the passive recipient of the past's effects.

Harootunian is primarily interested in the deceptively complex relations that the past maintains with the present. "[I]t became evident that the past could not lay claim to the identity of being historical in itself but rather acquires this status through the mediation of the present," as he concludes with regard to Marx. Harootunian uncovers here a strange insufficiency of the past: in and of itself the past cannot be determined as historical, for it depends upon a present time located outside of or beyond itself in order to then belatedly, retroactively, become what it is. Hence the "lay[ing] claim to identity" must not be understood as coterminous with the actual occurrence of the past event. Historians might believe they are confronting the past as it was, Harootunian suggests, but such belief attests to nothing more than the objectivist bias that informs the field of historiography. From this disciplinary perspective, the past is determined to be the privileged site of the object. While the finite historian's knowledge of this object is necessarily partial, the object itself is seen to reside in the past, where it awaits the historian's approach. The task of the historian thus consists in returning to the past with the aim of liberating the object from the now obscure hold of its original occurrence, bringing it forth into the light of the present. It is in response to this objectivist model that Harootunian attempts to reconceive the present as something more than the departure point of historical inquiry. In turning his attention from the past to the present, he courts the risk of subjectivism. But Harootunian's point is that the objectivist model of historiography is already unknowingly centered on the subject. If the past requires for its historical identity the "mediation of the present," then the object is also forced to appeal to the subject in order to arrive at its proper objectivity. However, the goal of this critique of historiography is not merely to effectuate a reversal from past to present and object to subject. Rather, it consists in calling attention to the present as the unique site of identification, which Harootunian recognizes as the essential element of all historical inquiry.

Pivotal to Harootunian's confrontation with historiography is the issue of "[t]he historian's indifference toward the problem of time," as he argues. Whereas modern philosophy, as seen in the examples of Bergson and Heidegger, has sought to draw time back to its originally qualitative dimension, historiography has largely neglected any engagement with the subject of time despite the fact that its primary commitment remains the past. Because of its failure to explicitly pose the question of time, historiography condemns itself to relying upon the traditional interpretations of this concept. As a result, time is seen in the excessively narrow terms of quantification. This distinction between the temporally qualitative and quantitative to which Harootunian refers is grounded on the problem of measurement: unlike philosophy, historiography departs from the assumption that time is quantifiable and consequently employs such conventional units of measurement as the *day* while also making use of chronology and calendrical time. Just as the historian begins his investigation with the given historical object, failing to consider the conditions of possibility essential to its constitution qua object, so too does he now engage with this object on the basis of fixed units of measurement without first posing the question of time's measurability. The isolation of philosophical reflection from historical practice effectively allows the historian to examine the particular object without being concerned with such preliminary questions, which indeed appear from the standpoint of historiography as impractical and needlessly abstract. For Harootunian, however, it is this very desire on the part of historians to hastily turn to the concrete matter or content of history that appears as the height of abstraction. Historiography has illegitimately stripped the aspect of temporality from its temporal objects of inquiry, and this irony prompts Harootunian to bring about what might be called an enhanced philosophization of the historical field.

Yet this philosophization of history must take place, Harootunian insists, alongside a concomitant historicization of philosophy. It is in this double demand, I believe, that we can begin to grasp the considerable ambition of Harootunian's project. It is not just historians who should be taken to task for the disinterest they show in the enabling conditions of all historical inquiry; philosophers, too, must be chastised for their tendency to conduct their investigations as if in a historical vacuum. Hence the call to "make philosophy answerable to history," as Harootunian announces. In order to remind philosophy that its practice is not ahistorical, Harootunian turns to the subject of capitalism in its relation to time. Capitalism must be understood as the "temporal dominant of modern society" since it has, given both its global reach and molecular effects, entirely restructured our contemporary experience of the world. For Harootunian, the historical emergence of capitalism has brought about an immense violence with regard to how time is actually lived: "[T]he contemporary experience of capitalism as an all-encompassing temporal rhythmology dedicated to ordering the different tempos of time with an unrelenting and inescapable circularity, which, accordingly, has truncated history itself, if not bracketing it altogether." Two distinct forms of time are here introduced: historical time, which precedes the rise of capitalism and is as yet noncircular, and capitalist time, which in the force of its circularity has succeeded in reducing or suppressing the otherwise noncircular time of history. The triumph of the latter time over the former, moreover, has produced a politically dangerous notion of the "eternality of the present," in which existing modes of social reality are ideologically represented as permanent.

Harootunian's aim is to call attention to the unseen ways in which modern man's experience of time has become regulated and thus impoverished by the various technologies of capitalism. In this way, he seeks to liberate time so that its disturbing, disorienting potential can be unleashed and experienced anew. Following Marx, Harootunian describes this time as one that contains "contretemps, simultaneous nonsimultaneities . . . contemporaneous noncontemporaneities or uneven times, and . . . time's turmoil, times out of joint, multiple temporalities, in other words, instances of *multiversum* testifying to untimeliness itself fully immanent to what constitutes normative social time." This final point is especially important. The relation between the historical time of multiplicity and untimeliness and a capitalist time characterized by "circularity" and "unity" is not to be understood as one of absolute exteriority. Although during the course of modernity the latter appears to have vanquished the former, its victory is by no means decisive. One cannot speak of the *death* of historical time in this fateful encounter; on the contrary, historical time has managed to survive its defeat and remains immanent to capitalist time, which in its naturalization has now come to claim the status of "normative social time." Within or beneath capitalist time lurks (or, as Kleinberg would say, "haunts") historical time. No doubt the most significant consequence of this formulation is that what otherwise appears to present itself as the seamless "unity" of time in modernity is now shown to harbor a radical disunity and diffuseness.

It is here I would like to draw attention to a significant tension in Harootunian's argument. On the one hand, the crux of his thinking of time reveals itself to be a notion of fundamental untimeliness, in which time appears as essentially "out of joint." On the other hand, however, he insists on conceiving of this untimeliness on the basis of the present. Of the three modes or tenses of time—past, present, and future—Harootunian elects to give priority to the present. This present, of course, is utterly different from the "eternality" posited by capitalism, for it is constantly in dialogue with a past that remains irreducible to it. In mediating that past, the present comes to be informed by it, and this is the reason why the present, far from giving itself as unified, can be seen to contain within itself other times. Harootunian is keen here to stress the complex, multiple nature of the present. Historiography certainly recognizes that the present is a product of the past. However, it seems evident that Harootunian wishes to apply pressure to this insight in order to foreground the existence of various levels of unevenness, thereby emphasizing the political stakes involved in temporality in a manner quite unlike that of most historians. Nevertheless, it would not be unfair, following Harootunian's own logic, to ask exactly why the present receives such privilege. If, for example, the present can be shown to act as the site of mediation through which alone the past may become itself, then surely the same can be said of the past in its relation to the present. In Harootunian's discussion of this dyadic relation in the above passage, the formal or general rule that offers itself to extrapolation is that *all* forms of self-identity are constituted not through themselves but strictly through another. Hence we may equally conclude that it is the *past* that allows the present to come into itself. As goes without saying, the point here is not, contra Harootunian, that the present must ultimately yield to the greater force of the past but rather that both present and past necessarily participate in a more general logic that effectively robs each of any claim to original identity.

Harootunian is eager to give priority to the present, and yet in the same breath he allows us to understand why such privileging is in fact impossible. If all identity formation depends upon a prior movement of alterity or exteriority, then even such fundamental notions as present and past must be seen to adhere to this principle. Before the present appears as itself, then, a more general force of alterity is necessarily already underway. Here I want to underscore that this originary concept of alterity is not to be understood primarily along the lines of formal logic. Directly to the contrary, my claim is that originary alterity must be regarded as *the very movement of temporalization itself.* All temporal entities must, in order to be, exist as continually other to themselves. It is at this primordial level of alterity that one finds a conjunction between being and time, and in relation to which all forms of identity appear strictly as derivative. Harootunian attributes his central insight regarding the primacy of the present to Marx, but insofar as that present remains governed by the presence of ontology, it is essentially beholden to an earlier, more elusive movement of alterity. This is of course not to suggest that Marx cannot be read otherwise, that his thought can only be understood as confirming Harootunian's thesis concerning the privileging of the present. While it is beyond the scope of the present chapter to demonstrate this point, it can nevertheless be stated that such a claim must take as its point of departure the question of ontology, for it is at this originary level where the presence of the present begins to break down.[13]

Harootunian's decision to privilege the present lies at the heart of his thinking of time, but I believe that similar difficulties can be found in other aspects of his notion of temporality. As we witnessed in his treatment of the dyadic relation between past and present, a choice is made to accord priority to *one* of these terms at the expense of the *other* rather than to seek a more general or fundamental ground (or, more precisely, nonground) within which these oppositional terms may be said to first arise. In the philosophical tradition, the concept of time invariably appears together with the concept of space. Their basic difference can be understood in terms of the notion of sameness: whereas time in the movement of succession involves the immediate negation of an earlier moment in its passage to the next, thereby rendering sameness impossible, space enables a plurality of points to exist simultaneously, hence ensuring the possibility of sameness. It is on account of this distinction that space is typically associated with the notion of positivity while time is identified as negativity. Harootunian inherits this opposition from the philosophical tradition and chooses not to contest its representation of time as successional difference and space as simultaneous sameness. Here it is not difficult to see how this notion of time in its pure nonspatiality informs Harootunian's conception of historical time, which in its flux and heterogeneity is contrasted to the unity of capitalist time.

Thus, Harootunian confirms the classical representation of difference that obtains between temporal difference on the one hand and spatial sameness on the other. Difference is not conceived as *general* but rather strictly as regional, for the decision to posit difference (time) in its distinction from sameness (space) effectively restricts the range of difference. Already an important question arises here as to the possibility of delimiting difference if the very relation between temporal difference and spatial sameness is to be thought in terms of their mutual *difference*. Regrettably, Harootunian doesn't pursue this problem. Despite the fact that he wishes to go beyond the "claims of identity to the place of radical difference," as he declares at one point,[14] this radical difference will be forced to yield to the apparently more radical or general logic of oppositionality. If difference were to be truly radical, then it would be impossible to pose it absolutely outside of the nondifferential medium of space; on the contrary, the difference between time (difference) and space (sameness) would demand a basic reconceptualization of difference, one that now does not simply oppose itself to spatial sameness but rather acts as the general milieu in which the time-space relation can take place. Failure to expand the argument to this scale of generality condemns one to remain at the level of binarity: pure time ceases to be upon the emergence of pure space and vice versa. Harootunian clearly does not wish to subject time to the apparently greater logic of binarity or oppositionality, but his argument concerning the regional or limited nature of time inevitably leads to that conclusion.

Before proceeding with my argument, let me now turn to those passages in Harootunian's text where this privileging of time to the disadvantage of space appears most plainly. Already in *Things Seen and Unseen*, despite the warning (in the specific context of his critique of Tokugawa nativism) that the "juxtaposition of space to time resulted in a ceaseless contradiction between the two poles,"[15] these twin notions of time and space are consistently organized according to a fixed hierarchy that places the former term above the latter. Thus: "One of the consequences of reducing life to a binary system of visible and invisible realms was the *dissolution of historical time into a timeless spatial order* of enduring relationships and activities"[16]; "Among nativists, secession from the center was validated by the promise to find a cultural order in a timeless and self-sufficient community devoted both to reproducing the conditions of its social existence and to *balancing the claims of spatial atemporality . . . with the incursions of contemporary history*";[17] and "Dehistoricization . . . was the necessary precondition for *devaluing time in favor of space and place and elevating the static over the dynamic*. Just as there was no time in nature, so in folk life there was only interminable repetition."[18]

Things Seen and Unseen is a relatively early work in Harootunian's oeuvre, but this celebration of time and concomitant demonization of space appears as a constant feature throughout the wide range of his publications. Let me provide some further examples as proof of this point. From his essay

"Japan's Long Postwar: The Trick of Memory and the Ruse of History": "As a category for classifying and organizing the memory of the nation, the postwar has become an empowering trope that *condenses the temporality of a duration into an endless spatial scape and present*. In fact, I think it is precisely *this spatialization of the postwar and its refusal of temporality* that reveals its wider complicity with the forces of global capital."[19] From *Overcome by Modernity*: "This folding back and retracing ultimately made the discourse on the social ideological, inasmuch as its purpose was to remove, conceal divisions, naturalize historical relationships, and eternalize them by attributing to them coherence based on an essence outside of time. Instead of attending to the place of production, it resorted to the production of place. *The temporal process was incorporated into space.*" Considerably later in this text he writes, "It was, in any case, *the transmutation of the dimension of time into space* that explained how modern life is transported from its historical embeddedness to the timeless precincts of poetics, art, and myth."[20] From *Marx After Marx*: "Here is the meaning of Ernst Bloch's observation that *there is no time in national history, only space*"; and "This has been especially true when the nation was confronted by global conjunctures and *the threat that time would overtake space*."[21] And finally from the recent essay, "Philosophy and Answerability: The Kyoto School and the Epiphanic Moment of World History," in reference to the philosopher Miki Kiyoshi: "As a result, he risked *forfeiting the force of temporal form for the static countenance supplied by space*, ultimately embodied in the epochal figure of the imperium."[22]

How are we to understand these statements in the context of the empirical history that Harootunian is attempting to analyze? To answer this, it must immediately be recalled that no pure time nor pure space has ever appeared in history. And the reason why they *have not* appeared is because they *cannot* appear. History itself (and not merely this or that particular event in history) can only be conceived on the basis of an originary synthesis between time and space. In order for there to exist, as Harootunian described earlier, a "passage from a 'before' to an 'after' "—without which, of course, history in its most elemental sense would be inconceivable—there must be temporal succession. Far from occurring in isolation from spatiality, however, temporal succession in fact requires the medium of space in order to take place at all. In its negativity, the emergence of a moment in time coincides immediately with its extinction. Because being is not reducible to the pure force of negativity, however, the temporal moment in its passing must somehow mark itself or leave behind a trace or remainder of itself for the future. Only space is capable of remaining, that is, of surviving the negativity intrinsic to temporalization. Yet this spatial remainder, while allowing for a relation or continuity to be established between a before and an after, remains itself entirely exposed to the negativity of time. This exposure means that the remainder may at any time be destroyed, thereby introducing the possibility of discontinuity. In other words, the condition of temporal succession is *space* while the condition of remaining (i.e., spatial continuity) is *time*. At each moment, depending upon the unpredictable contingency of time, the possibility of remaining may or may not be realized.[23]

It is not my aim in this chapter to explore the consequences of Harootunian's flawed understanding of the time-space relation for his historical analyses. The above critiques of such varied phenomena as Tokugawa nativism, postwar Japanese ideology, global capitalism, the discourse on the social in interwar Japan, and national history represent, without exception, some of the most incisive work in Japanese historical scholarship. While the historiographical and, especially, political value of Harootunian's interventions is considerable, it must nevertheless be said that judgment regarding his contributions at the level of philosophy remains somewhat less certain. Harootunian's double call to philosophize history and historicize philosophy undoubtedly merits attention. But the decision to regionalize difference in opposing time and space, as well as his demand that the present be privileged above both past and future, point to serious problems that his work does not seem prepared to address.

Let us, for example, consider the problem of what Harootunian often calls "different temporalities." As we observed in the earlier quotation from *Marx After Marx*, Harootunian aims to reveal how the putative unity of capitalist time in fact contains a multiplicity of other times irreducible to itself. Or as he writes, "The supposed unity of time projected by capital and nation-state is a masquerade that invariably fails to conceal the ceaseless confrontation of different times. For Marx, these were instances of how time, or temporality, temporalized itself in the present." A similar insight appears throughout the pages of *Overcome by Modernity*, as for instance in the following passage:

> What this entailed was the construction of a temporality of the market and of commodities that circulate through it to generate an experience of time as quantitative and as flowing in a single direction. . . . This means that the temporality associated with

the market and the process of exchange inhibits the possibility that there might coexist qualitatively distinguishable times, temporalities that represented different registers of time like profane and sacred separate from each other and corresponding to different orders that cannot comingle and be reduced to each other. To be sure, we have seen the coexistence of different historical temporalities embodied in practices stemming from differing modes of production and ways of life that belonged to quantitatively different times.[24]

Once again, I am entirely in agreement with Harootunian's contestation of capitalism and the nation-state in their complicit attempt to suppress the essential heterogeneity of time through quantification. Nonetheless, I wish to signal my divergence from his claims at the point where the precise nature of such temporal disunity comes to light. For Harootunian, the historical time that has come to be violently usurped by capitalist time is regarded as purely or absolutely nonspatial. This time is not unified or quantifiable, he asserts, but rather represents a site in which different times reside, or what he terms here a "coexistence of different historical temporalities." Yet what is the precise meaning of this notion of "coexistence"? As I have discussed, the fundamental difference between time and space consists in the allowance that the latter makes for simultaneity, in which a plurality of points is able to coexist (whereas time, given the immediate disappearance of each appearing moment, strictly prohibits such coexistence). As soon as there is coexistence, in other words, there is space. This point holds true even if one is describing the coexistence of plural times, for the notion of coexistence presupposes that each individual time *remains* itself while *remaining* together with others. And all remaining, as we saw, is necessarily (although not exclusively) spatial. From a logical point of view, such coexistence of different times appears to be premised upon the individual existence of each time. If this point were to be granted, however, then Harootunian would be forced to concede that his otherwise liberatory notion of historical time is in fact informed by the "unity" of capitalist time, since any gathering of disparate entities must assume the individual identity or unified nature of each. This point, in turn, leads quickly to another: if the "co-" of coexistence signifies the presence of more than one, as does of course the appearance of *different* entities, then is not at least some degree of quantification already underway within the otherwise pure negativity of historical time?

Ethicopolitical Questions

Let me pause here in order to more comprehensively consider some of the difficulties thus far encountered in Harootunian's methodology. These difficulties, I believe, have the effect of producing a kind of gap or contradiction between the stated aims of his project and the logical consequences of his argument. Seeking to escape the trap of ideological abstraction and return to the material concreteness of history as it is lived and experienced, Harootunian is nevertheless forced to appeal to an a priori judgment whose universality and necessity are not derivable from experience itself. Insofar as all concreteness can be said to be grounded in experience, Harootunian discovers that an essentially abstract judgment that is *not* grounded in experience is paradoxically necessary to effectuate this return to experience. Hence the desired return to concreteness must take place through abstraction (thereby contaminating that concreteness). Similarly, the claim regarding the priority of the present is illustrated by the fact that the past must first pass through this present and receive its mediation in order to then lay hold of its historical identity as past. Because the identity of the present is *itself* mediated by the past, however, Harootunian's goal of directing all historical inquiry to the present must remain unrealized, since the privileged endpoint or destination of the present reveals itself to be nothing more than a temporary way station that subsequently leads on to the past (and which then, to follow this dialectical movement, leads back to the present ad infinitum). Finally, the desire to think the present as a unique site of temporal heterogeneity appears alongside Harootunian's decision to purify time of all remnants of spatiality. Like the return of the repressed, however, the medium of space that Harootunian attempts to exclude as both politically and ethically objectionable will come to silently inform his notion of "different temporalities." In order for these different temporalities to coexist, they must be spatial, and this means that they must also contain elements of the same unity and quantification that Harootunian otherwise wishes to restrict to the mode of capitalist time. If temporalities are said to be *different* from one another, then this difference cannot simply name the absence of identity between one thing and other. Nor can it name, at a deeper level, simply the absence of identity between time and space. Conceived in its most radical manner, difference would also have to name the absence of identity between time and *itself*, between space and *itself*.

It seems evident that Harootunian devalues space because of its apparently fixed, static quality. As the foregoing quotations reveal, the problem of space is treated less in philosophical terms than in the specific context of politics and ethics. The identity of such historical phenomena as the nation-state, imperialism, and global capitalism is at least partly determined on the basis of a spatiality that is itself defined as a kind of evil. Time, by contrast, appears in Harootunian's text as an unalloyed good that preexists space and whose being is threatened by the incursion or intrusion that is space's emergence. My point here is that Harootunian does not simply privilege time over space, for their relationship is not only hierarchical but also, significantly, temporal. Time is conceived as more originary than space, but the later emergence of space carries the danger of violently usurping or replacing the time that rightfully precedes it. Hence such expressions as "the dissolution of historical time into a timeless spatial order of enduring relationships and activities"; "devaluing time in favor of space"; "condenses the temporality of a duration into an endless spatial scape and present"; "[t]he temporal process was incorporated into space"; "the transmutation of the dimension of time into space"; and finally, "he risked forfeiting the force of temporal form for the static countenance supplied by space." (The single exception to this pattern appears in the phrase "the threat that time would overtake space," but in fact what is under discussion in this passage is the nation-state, which is seen as having already effectuated a spatial usurpation of time.) This temporal ordering of the time-space relation is not accidental. On the contrary, this decision is instrumental in allowing Harootunian to effectively politicize and ethicize these interrelated philosophical concepts. If space is regarded strictly as intruding upon a time that preexists it, then this is because the site of politics and ethics is determined as one in which evil can only supervene upon a more originary good.

Let me clarify that I am not contesting Harootunian's attempt to apply philosophical conceptuality to historical phenomena in such a way as to consolidate the political and ethical force of his argument. More than any other scholar in Japan studies, Harootunian has taught us that *all* forms of human practice, even or perhaps especially philosophy, are ineluctably historical and thus also charged with political and ethical elements. My claim, rather, is that the particular manner in which these concepts are applied to history is revealing of Harootunian's ethicopolitical thinking, and that this thinking runs the risk of a certain prelapsarianism. Structurally, the supervening of space upon time is equivalent in his text to the supervening of capitalist time upon historical time as well as the supervening of such negative historical phenomena (all in some way characteristic of modernity) as the nation-state system, imperialism, and global capitalism, etc., upon an earlier, premodern period characterized by the apparent lack of such evils. Harootunian is certainly correct to draw attention to the historical devastation wrought by these modern institutions, but my concern is whether political and ethical issues are not in some way misrecognized when one determines time as an originary good, one that is moreover absolutely exterior to the later evil that is space.

In light of the considerable ethicopolitical weight that Harootunian brings to bear upon the notions of time and space, it is interesting to observe a certain hesitation or inconsistency on his part when he discusses the precise nature of their relation. In *Things Seen and Unseen*, for example, one finds the following footnote:

> By chronotope Bakhtin meant the "intrinsic connectedness of temporal and spatial relationships that are artistically expressed in literature." Acknowledging its metaphoric value, Bakhtin argued in this brilliant essay ("Forms of Time and Chronotope in the Novel") that the term "expresses *the inseparability of space and time* (time as a fourth dimension of space)' as it is articulated in certain narratives. . . . The concept of chronotope *has the advantage of not privileging either space or time but seeing them always as relational and functional.*[25]

A similar formulation appears in *Overcome by Modernity* in the context of Harootunian's discussion of the philosopher Watsuji Tetsurō:

> *Temporality and spatiality are inseparable*, leading to a "double life," he asserted, and any "intention" to grasp only the dimension of time as the structuring agency and structure of human existence will collapse into a view that detects human existence simply at the level of individual consciousness. "When the double structure is grasped as the essence of humanity, then *it is immediately clear that spatiality must at the same time correspond to temporality*" . . . By the same measure, the double structure of temporality and spatiality are transformed into "climatic and cultural historicality." *The inseparability of time and space* is registered in the inseparable relationship between history and climate/culture.[26]

And finally in *Marx After Marx* we witness the return of the chronotope:

This brings us back to taking into account the conditions explaining how Marx envisioned the historical process involved in capitalism's 'becoming' and why historical time embodied in antecedents was deposited 'behind' the system, occupying *both a spatial and temporal registers* [sic] *to form a new chronotope.*[27]

Certainly these three passages are very different from one another. In the second passage, in particular, it is difficult to discern the precise tone of Harootunian's presentation of Watsuji and how far he is willing to endorse the philosopher's description of the indivisibility between time and space. Nevertheless, both his affirmative reference to Bakhtin and the fact that he continues to make use of the notion of chronotope even in the much later book on Marx clearly suggests that the nature of this relation between time and space remains at some level unresolved. Furthermore, just as the figure of the chronotope returns from the text of 1988 to that of 2015, so too does the Bakhtin quotation of "the inseparability of space and time" strikingly repeat itself in Harootunian's own expression of "[t]he inseparability of time and space" that appears in his analysis of Watsuji.

Why are these details important? At stake here, I believe, is the complicated question of the status of ethics and politics in Harootunian's thinking. Two distinct interpretations of the time-space relation reveal themselves in his text. What might be called the dominant conception consists of positing time (good) as necessarily prior to space (evil). As I have noted, this understanding brings Harootunian very close to a prelapsarian position in which the emergence of evil can only be explained as a *fall* from a more originary good. In contrast, a more marginal or peripheral conception appears in the thinking of time and space as fundamentally "inseparable," a determination whose possible range of meanings is considerably narrowed by the qualification that this view possesses "the advantage of not privileging either space or time but seeing them always as relational and functional." To be sure, significant questions arise in this description regarding the exact nature of the "inseparability" and "relationality" between time and space. If we were to draw out the consequences of this claim of "not privileging either" in the form of something like an essential (rather than merely accidental or empirical) co-implication, however, then the effects of such redetermination for an understanding of ethics and politics should be evident. The above movement of *supervening*—space upon a prior time, evil upon a prior good—would now yield to a general milieu in which all binaries can be seen to not disappear but rather to contaminate and interweave with one another at an originary level. Here it must be remarked that the major difficulty with Harootunian's treatment of ethics and politics appears in his tendency to conceive of these issues in an excessively oppositional manner. Following the tradition of ethicopolitical thought, found as much in religion as in philosophy, that which is represented as good is perceived to be absolutely exterior to that which appears as evil. This absolute exteriority, however, is not conceived in exclusively spatial terms, for otherwise the privileging of one term over the other would run the risk of appearing unduly arbitrary and subjective. It is in order to avoid this trap and ground one's ethicopolitical act of decision on putatively objective criteria that the relation between good and evil (or what is ethically and politically desirable and what is not) must be temporalized, that is, incorporated within a sequential framework of before and after. In accordance with the long history of ethicopolitical thought, then, the binarization of good and evil comes to be further consolidated or in some sense secured by their temporal organization in terms of primacy and derivativeness.

Let me state this more concretely: the various historical phenomena that Harootunian attacks as ethically and politically wrong—the nation-state system, imperialism, global capitalism, etc.—are determined along the lines of spatiality and thus assigned, either implicitly or explicitly, a temporal ordering of derivativeness. Just as space interrupts a prior time, or just as capitalist time interrupts a prior historical time, so too do these modern institutions appear to wreak their violence upon a preexisting period of good. The attribution of a specifically spatial character to nation-states, empires, and global capital unequivocally announces this message. As goes without saying, the point here is not to cast doubt on these particular ethicopolitical determinations—Harootunian's challenge to the diverse and mutually mediating institutions of modernity is as forceful as it is admirable. Rather, questions must be asked regarding whether these instances of historical evil exist purely outside of their opposite and whether their relation to these opposites is to be conceived strictly on the basis of supervention. If, in marked contrast to this standpoint, such oppositionality can be shown to first emerge from a more general milieu of difference and alterity, then what sort of ethicopolitical consequences might be drawn from this insight? The challenge posed to this attempt to think ethics and politics *otherwise* lies in retaining the force and value of these terms while nevertheless resisting their traditional appeal to identity.

Confronted with the general movement of difference and alterity, an ethicopolitical thinking centered on oppositionality and sequentiality will invariably be forced to reckon with the constant threat of time, now understood not as the binary contrast of space but rather as that which is always already spatialized "in itself." To the degree that ethicopolitical thought fails to consider the radical difference that is time—that is to say, historically, nearly always—it runs the risk of complacency and self-righteousness. In the context of ethics and politics, the tremendous challenge posed to the interrelated notions of oppositionality and sequentiality is that temporal difference never leaves these logics undisturbed. At each moment, what previously appeared as (i.e., what had been retroactively determined as) instances of good and evil must now be reconceptualized anew. In his various historical analyses, Harootunian sets forth robust critiques of such modern phenomena as, for example, nationalism, imperialism, and global capitalism. What we must bear in mind, however, is that these phenomena never appear in the world as such. In other words, they fundamentally lack any *present* identity. It would be a mistake, I believe, to claim that a correct ethicopolitical stance resides in opposing, at all times, any given or predetermined historical instance. Once such a universal ethicopolitical rule is established, its mere application to each singular case results in what can only be called an effacement of historical difference. In wishing to be absolutely ethical by adhering to fixed ethicopolitical standards, then, one ironically ends up sacrificing the very flexibility and responsiveness required for ethical judgment. The failure of the concept of application lies in its reduction of historical events to the level of particularity as subsumed by the universal rule. Here we can observe how the practice of ethicopolitical prescription—literally, a "writing before"—so easily harbors a notion of subjective mastery that effectively relieves us from the task of encountering the world each time differently, thereby opening up the possibility of responding to its singularity. Neither historical phenomena nor our ethicopolitical responses to them ever reveal their identity in the time of the present: if they did, ethics would simply be a matter of knowledge. If the possibility for any response to be ethical rests upon its resistance to the present, this is because ethics can only be determined qua ethics from the perspective of a future that can never be known in advance.

My reservation concerning Harootunian's thinking of ethics and politics centers on what Jean-François Lyotard famously described as the problem of the "grand narrative."[28] Certainly the various historical evils that Harootunian condemns in his work are ethically and politically egregious. Nevertheless, a trap must be recognized in conceiving of these historical phenomena in a manner that is excessively comprehensive or totalizing. Failure to heed this trap exposes one to the risk of emphasizing structure at the expense of genesis, or rather of forgetting that genesis is that which both allows and disallows structure to continually operate qua structure. For example, while the primary thrust of Harootunian's criticisms of modernity and capitalism brooks no disagreement, is it credible that the fundamental experience of time in modern society is, as he claims, one of "repetition of the ever new in the ever same?"[29] At issue here, then, is "the problem of time, the market's capacity to effectively freeze the moment of history, replacing lived time with the procession of the timeless commodity."[30] Following this logic, history itself is divided into two major epochs: a modernity in which time has been violently deprived of its difference, resulting in the pure circularity of repetition in which what may appear to be new is really only a superficial or inauthentic form of novelty that testifies to the global domination of sameness; and an era prior to the modern that is characterized by time still remaining close to itself, true to itself, such that the multiplicity of what is called "lived time" opens up a fuller and more authentic experience of existence. From this ethicopolitical standpoint, the future appears as that which might overcome the suppression of time that has long impoverished us moderns, and this emancipation from an unjust modernity can be enacted by returning to the pure ("lived") temporality of the past. In this narrative, it is the present that must be privileged because it informs us, in the clarity of the here and now, that modernity *is* unethical. This *is* that is the present identity of modernity represents the punctuality of a time in which unethicality reveals itself to me in its immediacy and transparency, and this presence between the historical phenomenon and myself effectively assures me that my ethical judgment is correct.

In order to more clearly shed light on some of the limitations of this conception of the present, let me now turn to an instance in which Harootunian's analysis of historical phenomena leads to a gesture of more or less unqualified ethicopolitical affirmation. It should be noted that such expressions of approbation are quite rare in his text, which is otherwise marked by the uninterrupted force of his critique. For this very reason, however, I believe that the following example of ethical and political integrity merits attention. In this passage, Harootunian directs focus to what he calls a "history of the present" as it appears in the filmmaker Imamura Shōhei's work, *History of Postwar Japan as Told by a Barmaid*:

> History, if this term has any sense, is the history of the present and is thus necessarily politicized. It is, I believe, only history if the interventions force moments of critique and make possible

the realization of promises transmitted and recovered by tradition. Something of this possibility was disclosed by Imamura Shōhei in his extraordinary *History of Postwar Japan as Told by a Barmaid* [Nippon sengoshi: Madamu Onboro no seikatsu] (1971). In this brilliant documentary, now a missed moment, Imamura lays hold of a history of the present, the immediate postwar years as lived and experienced by his interlocutor, Onboro, who gradually shows that her everyday life reveals a history vastly different from the publicly evolving narrative of political events marking Japan's recovery in the 1950s and 1960s. The history of Imamura's Madam Junky within the postwar era is entirely different from the postwar history of Katō [Norihiro] and the revisionist historians. Her life is one of neither disavowal nor denial but is governed simply by the problem of getting on as best she can, given her circumstances. . . . Early in the film Imamura juxtaposes her view concerning the war, defeat, and the immediate postwar against a stunning public scene in which people are shown praying at a shrine, undoubtedly imploring the gods for good fortune in this dark moment of Japan's history. He asks her how she feels about the war and its ending, whether she is saddened and suffers grief and remorse, against a backdrop of people expressing regret and pleading for godly intercession. Onboro responds cheerfully, saying how glad she is that the war has ended and what a nuisance it had been and expressing the necessity of now getting on with her life . . . Imamura emphasizes both her optimism and her energy, expressed continuously by behavior that is both autonomous and independent, despite the obvious fact that she is deriving her livelihood from the Americans. By contrast, Imamura's portrayal of a kind of "sanctioned" and "public" history centered on the Occupation and Japan's subsequent recovery under obvious US direction suggests simply a narrative of dependence that will lead to the nightmare of the long postwar . . . Onboro is living off the page, as it were, outside the official narrative of postwar Japan and postwar as Japan, recounting her experiences to the director's questions, so that her everyday life cumulatively writes a different history.[31]

This discussion of the film and its protagonist Onboro eventually leads to the celebration of this figure's *seikatsu*, or "everyday life":

With Onboro there is no sense of a deception, of living a lie and not seeing it as such, or of the recognition of a true reality that somehow has been buried by the military occupation. There is no need to insist that this unhappy state can be terminated if only the distortion and deception are acknowledged. The appearance of *honne* is a signification that announces this necessity. For her, however, and presumably for Imamura, continuing the postwar has a reality for the rich and the powerful, both Japanese and Americans, while she has seen its beginning as something of a blessing whose end comes when she leaves Japan for San Diego, married to an American sailor. Yet we cannot help thinking that this decision finally frees her from an environment that had held her hostage to both class and gender, even if it was somewhat ameliorated by the presence of U.S. lifestyles and material culture. Leaving Japan meant ending the postwar for Imamura and, for Onboro, a liberation from the social constraints she had so resourcefully exploited. . . . What the director manages to orchestrate is the coexistence of different narratives and temporalities—and especially the experience of everyday life writing its own history that marks a radical difference. Imamura's barmaid is mercifully free from the fetishized structure of repetitive disavowal that represents Japan as successfully modern while it seeks to portray Japanese as essentially unchanged.[32]

In these lines it is Japan's ideology of the postwar that Harootunian attacks for its attempt to dissimulate the threat that modernity poses to notions of national identity. While Harootunian raises important points regarding the orchestrated rituals of national interpolation as well as US-Japan complicity during the postwar era, it must be recognized that the larger framework within which his critique is articulated is one of fairly straightforward opposition. Here Onboro appears as a lone figure of resistance through whom the battle lines are clearly drawn. Time and again, ethicopolitical thought can be seen to commence with a single cut or incision, and this marking produces two distinct entities whose relation is depicted as one of absolute exteriority. On one side, we find postwar Japanese ideology in its various manifestations, including the contemporary critic Katō Norihiro and his project of restoring Japan to its "true reality that somehow has been buried by the military occupation." On the opposing side, we are introduced to Onboro, whose indifference to Japan's postwar status determines her existence as strictly outside of this ideology. The language employed by Harootunian reinforces the purity of this binary: Onboro's history is "vastly different" from that of postwar ideology and "entirely different" from the narrative constructed by Katō; shots of her appear as "juxtapose[d]" to those of people who participate in this ideology; while her overall depiction can be understood "by contrast" to the official images proffered by the state. This ethicopolitical duality is further consolidated through the use of certain codes presented by Imamura and then repeated by Harootunian: Onboro is female, *burakumin* ("her pariah class status"),[33] associated with "everyday life," and visually foregrounded in the film as a single individual, whereas Japan's postwar ideologues are described as male, elite, committed to the task of national representation, and cinematically framed as a public collective.

My aim here is not to call into question the real ethical and political differences that motivate both Imamura's film and Harootunian's commentary. In the absence of a thinking of differential time within which all ethicopolitical decisions must take place, however, there is the considerable danger of simplifying the complexity that *at each moment* inheres in ethical practice. If ethics consisted merely of confirming the value (what is good, what is evil) of historical phenomena by reference to the codes or standards that have already been determined in advance, then the ongoing movement of history would be unnecessary. What concerns me here is a certain orthodoxy, or even dogmatism—found equally on the "left" and "right" of the political spectrum—that comes to strip the moment of ethicopolitical decision of its intrinsic undecidability.[34] Following Imamura, Harootunian's depiction of ethical and political issues on the restricted basis of a *two*—either *for* or *against*—has the unfortunate effect of reducing the multiplicity and heterogeneity that he otherwise wishes to think on the basis of historical time. In this regard, I believe that we can discern in the above passages a further temptation to bypass the various complications of ethical practice by appealing to something like a notion of simplicity. Unlike the ideologues with their subtle machinations, Onboro is portrayed as being in touch with something basic or unadulterated about social existence: "Her life is one of neither disavowal nor denial but is governed simply by the problem of getting on as best she can, given her circumstances." Now this word "simply" must give one pause, for there is nothing ever simple about ethicopolitical issues given the general milieu of alterity in which they necessarily unfold. In direct contrast to the postwar bureaucrats Harootunian denounces, Onboro is identified through the lens of "everyday life," which is implicitly determined on the basis of a concreteness and authenticity that confirms her positive ethicopolitical status.

In analyzing power relations on the basis of an oppositional framework, the use of such overdetermined terms as "life" and "simple" to signal one's ethical intent risks summoning the classical divide between nature and culture. According to this reading, Onboro, whose simplicity of everyday life is illustrated by the fact that she need think of nothing more than "the problem of getting on as best she can, given her circumstances," represents something like a child of nature, one whose primal innocence (regardless of her sexualization as a bar hostess near a US military base) removes her from any taint of nationalist ideology. Here let us recall Harootunian's critique of modernity with its circular repetition and inauthentic newness in favor of what appears to be a prior historical period characterized by the still vibrant multiplicity of "lived time." My point is that there exists in this conceptual system a danger of nostalgia, one that directly contradicts Harootunian's largely exceptional analyses of this structure.[35] This danger appears most clearly in the notion of return: what is posited as an originary good comes to be corrupted by an evil that is determined to exist completely outside of it, and the only way to advance beyond the scope of this evil is to return to the good that may yet be reborn in the future. As I have remarked, this is precisely the manner in which the time-space relation is conceived, and this fundamental relation informs the antagonism between historical time and capitalist time as well as between premodernity and modernity. In this regard, it is important to note a significant difference between Onboro's simplicity (a simplicity that derives from the authentic concreteness of "everyday life") and the multiplicity that Harootunian, following Marx, finds to be characteristic of the time of the present. Yet this difference can be seen to conceal a deeper level of identity, I believe, for both are determined as in some sense primary or originary vis-à-vis the derivatively unethical (postwar ideology, the temporal circularity of capitalism). The natural state that joins together, in very distinct contexts, Onboro and the heterogeneous present gives itself as a site of ethicopolitical plenitude. This is contrasted to the evil that is *organization* or manipulation (culture), which links the otherwise apparently dissimilar acts of interpolation of national identity and the quantification of time.

The question of return hinges on the presence of the border. Just as the current state of ethicopolitical evil can ideally be overcome by returning to a past good as it manifests itself in the future, so too does Harootunian locate in his reading of Imamura's film a decisive break that separates the postwar present from a period that is both temporally beyond and ethicopolitically superior to it. Whereas "the rich and the powerful, both Japanese and Americans" wish to continue the postwar and its vision of Japan as economically modern and yet culturally unchanged, Onboro makes the heroic decision to leave Japan, thus symbolically rising above the ethicopolitical depravity that is postwar ideology. "Leaving Japan meant ending the postwar for Imamura," as Harootunian concludes. Even before her departure, Onboro is distinguished from the ideologues on the basis of the value of autonomy, a trait that is counterposed to the openly negative quality of dependence: "Imamura emphasizes both her optimism and her energy, expressed continuously by behavior that is both *autonomous and independent*, despite the obvious fact that she is deriving her livelihood from the Americans. By contrast, Imamura's portrayal of a kind of 'sanctioned' and 'public' history centered on the Occupation and Japan's subsequent recovery under obvious U.S. direction suggests simply a *narrative of dependence* that will lead to the nightmare of the long postwar." With her decision to leave behind the spatiotemporal border of postwar Japan, however, Onboro experiences in Harootunian's treatment a critical elevation of moral status from the level of autonomy to that of freedom. From his standpoint, this severance from postwar society is to be regarded unambiguously as one of emancipation. As he remarks, repeating this notion of emancipation thrice in order to drive home the point: "Yet we cannot help thinking that this decision finally *frees* her from an environment that had held her hostage to both class and gender. . . . Leaving Japan meant ending the postwar for Imamura and, for Onboro, a *liberation* from the social constraints she had so resourcefully exploited . . . Imamura's barmaid is mercifully *free* from the fetishized structure of repetitive disavowal that represents Japan as successfully modern while it seeks to portray Japanese as essentially unchanged."

In his analysis of Imamura's work, Harootunian determines the value of dependence as ethically and politically negative. Its negativity derives from its distance from authentic freedom at both the individual and national level. Central to this determination is a notion of normativity according to which undesirable actions and properties are to be excluded from the site of what is held to be the ideal society. As we saw previously, the medium of space must be posited as an ethicopolitical evil because of its fixed, static quality. However, a close examination of space reveals that not only are the concepts of history and society logically unthinkable without it, but that indeed space functions as a necessary condition for the otherwise positive value of temporal succession. This originary contamination (or co-implication) of time and space, I believe, creates a powerful tremor throughout the ethicopolitical surface of Harootunian's text. My claim here is that similar problems beset his decision to stigmatize the notion of dependence in favor of that which appears to be "autonomous and independent."

In the context of the individual, Onboro is praised because of her refusal to participate in the collective hysteria that is national identification. She is her own woman, as one says, and this notion of "ownness," never sufficiently interrogated in Harootunian's text,[36] indicates how comfortably images of heroic individualism are encapsulated within a metaphysics of subjectivity. The subject can only be a subject insofar as it maintains its own "autonomous and independent" existence in relation to not only other individuals but ultimately to the world itself. In the context of the nation, Harootunian denounces Japan because its postwar recovery was not achieved by this nation alone but rather largely through American support. Hence Japan's revival in the 1950s and 1960s reveals itself to be "simply a narrative of dependence," as he states. This criticism is a disturbing one partially because it seems to posit a state of national autonomy or sovereignty as a form of geopolitical normativity. Certainly Harootunian is correct to draw attention to the essentially imperialist relation that the United States has maintained with Japan in the postwar era, but any endorsement of Japanese autonomy or independence as a desirable national goal is deeply problematic.[37] More fundamentally, however, the notion of dependence is attacked because it reveals an insufficiency or deficiency—some type of abnormality—at the basic level of the self. The difficulty with this criticism, however, is that dependence is conceived commonsensically as a failure that occurs strictly at the empirical level. That is to say, the integrity of the self is accepted as an original, normative state that can, however, come to be threatened by certain circumstances—afflicting either the personal or individual (Onboro) or the nation (postwar Japan)—that either may or may not take place. What is overlooked in this empirical understanding of dependence is a more general conception that determines dependence to be an essential condition of any selfhood. The self, then, is in and of itself inadequate, at all times dependent upon that which is irreducibly other to it in order to remain itself. Dependence is not merely an accidental failing that detracts from what is otherwise seen to be a full presence or plenitude; on the contrary, it is a general condition of existence for all entities, one that fundamentally exposes them, in all fragility, to the constant movement that is spatiotemporal difference.

Corresponding to this opposition between dependence and independence or autonomy is the duality between freedom and unfreedom. Onboro, it is suggested, is already freer than the postwar ideologues because of her personal sense of independence as well as her modest needs for survival, of merely "getting on as best she can, given her circumstances." Harootunian, here again closely following Imamura, establishes a connection between Onboro's positive ethicopolitical existence and her current state of happiness: she is described as "cheerful" and "glad," full of "optimism and . . . energy," and this personal exuberance is directly contrasted to the crowd of people who have been interpolated by postwar ideology, and who appear "saddened and suffer[ing] grief and remorse" while "expressing regret" for their collective misfortune. In the tradition of ethicopolitical thought, as can be seen most plainly in certain religious discourses, what is affirmed as a positive ethical stance typically appears linked to the personal benefits that can be enjoyed by its practitioners (either immediately or ultimately) through observance of the prescribed codes and standards. In hastily conjoining a position of ethical good with personal happiness in the case of Onboro, and then juxtaposing this to the ethical evil and personal suffering found among the ideologues and their disciples, Harootunian comes perilously close to repeating this tradition.

However, it is with the notion of freedom or emancipation that he appears to confirm a view of ethics and politics grounded upon the value of simplicity. In the inherent complexity that is the ethicopolitical decision, can there ever be an absolute break with that which is held to be evil? In departing from the spatiotemporal site that is postwar Japan, can Onboro now truly be regarded as "free" and "liberated," as Harootunian suggests? Let me reiterate that, without exception, *all* ethicopolitical decisions can only take place within the general milieu that is spatiotemporal difference. In this milieu, every instance of ethical good, just as every instance of freedom, occurs instantaneously. That is to say, the instance qua instant appears only to disappear immediately, thereby opening the way for new and other instances of ethicopolitical decision making. My point here is that the discourse of emancipation can easily seem to imply some type of finality or resolution—Onboro's decision to leave postwar Japan now decisively frees her from any risk of contamination with Japanese ideology—but that it is precisely the difference that is (spatialized) time that *at all times* (because at each and every time, i.e., time in its singularity) forbids such freedom.

I would like now to conclude my reading of Harootunian's ethicopolitical analysis of Imamura's film with a brief glance at his notion of writing. As the foregoing passage reveals, Harootunian refers to this notion in two separate instances: "Onboro is living off the page, as it were, outside the official narrative of postwar Japan and postwar as Japan, recounting her experiences to the director's questions, so that *her everyday life cumulatively writes a different history*" and "What the director manages to orchestrate is the coexistence of different narratives and temporalities—and especially *the experience of everyday life writing its own history that marks a radical difference.*" In line with our suspicion of a certain appeal to the value of simplicity in Harootunian's treatment of ethicopolitical issues, it is important to note that writing, in and of itself, is nothing. Writing, in Hegelian terms, is an entity that has yet to be awakened to itself, for this awakening can only take place through the medium of reading. The valuation of writing, in which life is said to transcribe "its *own* history," is motivated by the presence that putatively obtains between history as it is immediately lived and experienced and the marked history of that history. History thus doubles itself: the first time as it is concretely lived by Onboro and the second time as it is cinematically recorded in Imamura's film. For Harootunian, this writing must be determined as one of "difference" because it is entirely unlike the homogeneous nationalist narratives of postwar Japanese ideology. Onboro is "living off the page" because her marginal existence can only be excluded from those more conventional, less authentic representations of Japan that are sanctioned by the state. Yet this ethicopolitical difference that Harootunian wishes to think in terms of writing gives itself in the present, since that is the time in which the putative lack of difference characteristic of postwar ideology is identified in its difference from the "radical difference" associated with Onboro's everyday life experiences. In this mediated passage from Onboro to Imamura's Onboro to Harootunian's interpretation of Imamura's Onboro, however, writing is inexorably forced to concede ground to reading. The reason why there can be no writing of the present, in other words, is that such writing remains constantly exposed to (or dependent upon) the reading of the future. Only through reading, which must take place in the displaced future of writing, can writing then be retroactively constituted as having signified what it originally appeared to signify in the immediacy of its present. If that is the case, however, then the framework of more or less straightforward ethicopolitical opposition within which Harootunian examines Imamura's film necessarily breaks down. This tension that holds together the difference between the postwar suppression of difference and Onboro's "radical difference" is now loosened to reveal that it is the future, or rather the future of reading—the future that *is* reading—that at any moment threatens to unravel all oppositions by pointing beyond present identity.

Heidegger: Temporality and Presence

This dismantling of the present brings us now to Heidegger, who likewise devoted himself to issues of time and history, as well as to the complex relation between history and philosophy, but in a manner quite unlike that of Harootunian. Indeed, Harootunian explicitly touches on Heidegger's thought at various points in his work. What is interesting here is that the unreserved approbation we see Harootunian express for Imamura (and for Imamura's protagonist Onboro) is now drastically reversed in his treatment of Heidegger. Virtually without exception, the discussion of the German philosopher is striking for the uniform harshness of its tone. Certainly there exist ethical and political reasons for this hostility, not simply given the fact of Heidegger's involvement with National Socialism in the 1930s but also because of the attitude of dismissal and even contempt that Harootunian finds to be characteristic of Heidegger's view of everydayness. In this regard, it must be noted that Harootunian's opinion of philosophers as a whole is consistently low. He refers with approval to the Marxist thinker Tosaka Jun's judgment that, in Harootunian's gloss, "philosophers were separated from the 'actualities' of everyday life by their confusing metaphysics with reality."[38] In this line already we can glimpse a certain logic of Harootunian's sympathies and antipathies with regard to conceptual thought. In accordance with his central methodological gesture of conceiving difference through the lens of oppositionality, Harootunian accepts the traditional distinction between physics (i.e., physical reality) and metaphysics and reinforces it through appeal to the related duality between concrete presence and abstract absence. What is real is the here and now of everydayness, and philosophy errs in misrecognizing that its main responsibility lies in remaining close to this presence rather than straying into the empty and sterile terrain that is "metaphysics." If philosophy is to be viable, then, it must ground itself in the concrete "actualities" of what is empirically and temporally present.

It is thus not surprising that Harootunian's critique of Heideggerian philosophy departs from the question of the material reality of everyday existence. If philosophers in general, given "their confusing metaphysics with reality," tend to lose sight of what appears most immediately before them, then Heidegger will be denounced as especially guilty of this offense. The charge against Heidegger arises because of the philosopher's inattention to the particularities of the daily life that surrounds him. As Harootunian declares, "Heidegger is too abstract, uninterested in analyzing social forms or concrete historical existence."³⁹ From Harootunian's perspective, this unwillingness to theoretically engage with social phenomena must be traced back not to the disciplinary distinction between philosophy and sociology but rather to the specific nature of Heidegger's ontological project: "Heidegger, it should be remembered, imagined everyday life as the least differentiated and determinate expression of Being's existence, which accounts for his lack of sociological specificity."⁴⁰ Harootunian more fully elaborates on his dissatisfactions with Heidegger through negative comparison with Walter Benjamin:

> Heidegger's formulation of everydayness . . . also carefully avoided the specificity of social form. Yet its frequent appeals to "idle talk," "chatter," "alienation," "averageness," and the like identified it with a world already being lived and experienced in the modern, mass societies of the great metropolitan centers. . . . It was, in fact, this return to the concrete of what was immediately given as a historical formation rather than the flight to primordial identification, a conception of the construction of life akin to political action rather than the absence of a theory of repetition, that accounts for the real difference between Benjamin and Heidegger and their political positions. Benjamin was as socially specific and sensitive to historical forms in his writings as Heidegger was indefinite and indeterminate.⁴¹

An important point needs to be emphasized here concerning the totality of the object of inquiry. For Harootunian, clearly, this object is society. For Heidegger, on the other hand, the totality whose dynamics and structure he undertakes to think is that of Being. Fundamental differences emerge from this division, as can be seen especially clearly in Harootunian's conviction that the true task of philosophy consists in attending to the multiple nature of quotidian existence. His argument, significantly, is not that philosophy *should not* make its home in the pure and lofty heights of ideation, but rather that, in a strict sense, it *cannot*, for such environment will always contain elements that testify to the concreteness and particularity of social being. Hence his reminder to Heidegger that, regardless of the thinker's aims, the practice of philosophy remains inescapably a *practice* and so has no choice but to draw its resources from the immediate world around it: "Yet its frequent appeals to 'idle talk,' 'chatter,' 'alienation,' 'averageness,' and the like identified it with a world already being lived and experienced in the modern, mass societies of the great metropolitan centers." Harootunian's point is a strong one, and his suggestion that philosophy, in its tendency towards abstraction, runs the risk of apoliticality certainly merits consideration. At the same time, however, we must recognize that the valuation of society over Being is motivated at its core by a privileging of the notion of presence and its ancillary notions of nearness, concreteness, and immediacy. The real, as I remarked, is determined in Harootunian's text as the centrifugal here and now, and this determination sanctions the theoretical and political directive to "return to the concrete of what was immediately given," as he writes.

Harootunian is referring specifically to Benjamin in this phrase, but the appeal to "the concrete" to which one must "return," a concreteness that presents itself in what is "immediately given," crucially informs his affirmative reading of Imamura and Onboro as well. Heidegger, by contrast, is attacked for his failure to consider this concreteness and immediacy—two cornerstones of the notion of society in its distinction from Being—as the departure point of his thinking. In this regard, the privileging of society for the nearness, concreteness, and immediacy of presence that it affords nevertheless can be seen to exclude (or at the very least insufficiently consider) the criterion of generality. If, that is to say, society and Being must both be understood as totalities, their relation is by no means symmetrical. By definition, the generality of Being is uniquely unsurpassable, a truth that Heidegger recalls in the opening pages of *Being and Time* when he writes, "The 'universality' of Being '*transcends*' any universality of genus."[42] The question, then, is what comes to be lost in this inattention to the generality of Being, for this generality contains within itself even the totality of society. Whereas society occupies only a part of Being and is thus unable to unilaterally determine the general dynamics according to which Being occurs or unfolds, Being "itself" dictates its general structure to every aspect of society. My claim is that despite the considerable political import of Harootunian's privileging of society, the concomitant neglect of the question of Being in its generality exposes one to the risk of accepting (i.e., unconsciously repeating) the dominant conception of ontology as it has been historically handed down to us from the philosophical tradition. According to this tradition, Being is to be grasped as *substance*, or that which in its objective and material presence appears to exist in and of itself in an already complete state. Given Harootunian's determination of reality on the basis of a present presence that gives itself proximately, concretely, and immediately, the suspicion arises that the otherwise forcefully politicized notion of society that he introduces remains silently hostage to a conservative conception of ontology.[43]

This question of ontology leads directly to the problematic of time. Harootunian contends that "Heidegger 'resacralized' time as Being's destiny toward death,"[44] but this description truly fails to do justice to the radicality of Heidegger's insight into the manner in which a certain interpretation of time has come to determine the philosophical understanding of Being. As Heidegger asserts:

> In other words, in our process of destruction we find ourselves faced with the task of Interpreting the basis of the ancient ontology in the light of the problematic of Temporality. When this is done, it will be manifest that the ancient way of interpreting the Being of entities is oriented towards the "world" or "Nature" in the widest sense, and that it is indeed in terms of "time" that its understanding of Being is obtained. . . . Entities are grasped in their Being as "presence"; this means that they are understood with regard to a definite mode of time—the *"Present."*[45]

For Heidegger, the ontological tradition—from ancient Greece to modern philosophy—developed by unwittingly allowing the time of the present to govern the determination of beings as present. To say that a present being "is," then, is to say that it possesses an objectivity and reality that testifies to its status as substance. It is this tradition that Heidegger sets out to "destruct" by posing the general question of the Being of all beings, an inquiry that aims to loosen the powerful hold of the interrelated concepts of the present and presence. If, as Heidegger implies, the effects of the ontological tradition can be seen to continue even today in the privileging of the present and presence, then how might we understand Harootunian's position not only with regard to Heidegger but, much more urgently, in connection with his commitment to uphold the values of present temporality and concrete and immediate being? I wish to underline here that my interest lies less in Harootunian's particular engagement with Heidegger as such than in what this engagement reveals about Harootunian's broader conceptions of time and ontology—conceptions that, moreover, can be seen to function as the very framework of his thinking.

In *History's Disquiet*, Harootunian provides a summary of Heidegger's notion of ecstatic temporality:

> Inauthentic time was steeped in inauthentic understanding that did not recognize Being's finitude and so diverted Dasein as being for death. According to Heidegger, this diversion from

true destiny is accomplished through a triple inauthenticity of future, present, and past: "waiting for" and the "ecstasy" that anticipates the next moment that will succeed and take the place of the preceding; the "now" that presupposes the constancy and permanence of the present, its eternity; and the "memory" of the past that supposes that each present moment is deposited and thus stored up in memory. By the same measure, authentic temporality knows only the "ecstasy" of Dasein in time, of being's "thrownness"—projected to go out and meet itself. . . . Thus there is a corresponding triple ecstasy—"anticipation," the "instant," and the "repetition." A genuinely authentic history in this scheme is possible only with this understanding of time, as opposed to its reverse which is posited on a continual succession, representing only the artificiality of clock time.[46]

What is noteworthy in this description is Harootunian's strong emphasis on the opposition Heidegger draws between authenticity and inauthenticity. The terms Heidegger uses for these concepts are *Eigentlichkeit* and *Uneigentlichkeit*, which derive from the adjective *eigen*, meaning "own." At issue, then, is a kind of ownness or propriety, and this sense is aptly conveyed in the English "authentic," which originates in the Greek *autos* for "self." For Heidegger, this distinction between authenticity and inauthenticity depends upon Dasein's self-relation: whether Dasein remains close to itself in its proper mineness or whether, on the contrary, it loses itself in its absorption in the world, a state that is typically associated with the They. Following a line of attack typically associated with Adorno,[47] Harootunian responds sharply to Heidegger by returning to the point of philosophy's disregard for concrete sociality and history, which is tacitly seen as responsible for the excessively isolated and abstract nature of its concepts: "Heidegger had reduced *alltagslichkeit* [sic] ["everydayness"] to the mediocre world of the They (*das Man*)—the domain of complete negativity—and insisted on returning to the temporality of Being's 'authentic historicality.' Heidegger's conception of inauthenticity was thoroughly deshistoricized."[48]

It is important to note here a certain deflection of the question of ecstatic temporality so as to focus critical attention more directly on the notion of inauthenticity. Heidegger's concept of time represents a decisive contribution to the history of philosophy, one without which some of the most radical elements of contemporary thought would be unimaginable, and yet Harootunian decides to restrict his discussion of Heideggerian time to the question of inauthenticity. Certain advantages appear in this interpretive strategy but also certain disadvantages. I would like to make two points in this connection:

(1) What initially appears purely as an advantage gradually reveals itself to be more complicated. Harootunian's dissatisfaction with Heidegger's notion of inauthenticity stems from its association with everydayness as a negative value. Whereas Heidegger views everydayness as a site of homogeneity, one that is opposed to philosophy and is typically dominated by inauthenticity and the They, Harootunian celebrates the everyday for its constant flux and diversity. Harootunian sees Heidegger's contempt for everyday life in its link to inauthenticity as part of a long, elitist tradition in philosophy that judges the everyday to be an unworthy object of philosophical reflection. From this perspective, it is the ownness or mineness of authenticity that represents, contra Heidegger, the real domain of homogeneity, since Dasein comes into its solipsistic self-relation precisely by excluding the variety of concrete, material differences that make up history and sociality. To the degree that Dasein discovers its authenticity, then, it falls into the classical philosophical trap of rejecting what it denigrates as the vulgar multiplicity of the world in favor of the true and pure realm of ideation. If inauthenticity is to be understood in terms of the common, the daily, the habitual, etc., then Harootunian will seek to reverse Heidegger's negative evaluation of these traits and embrace this excluded sphere. The valuable insight that Harootunian presents here can be summarized as follows: only in what resists the interiorization of authentic ownness can one find the politicized sphere of history and the social.[49]

This advantage, however, contains within it a core element of the authenticity/inauthenticity binary that cannot be so easily controlled. Earlier I called attention to Harootunian's insufficient interrogation of the notion of ownness. Given that the distinction between Heideggerian authenticity and inauthenticity hinges upon the question of what is and is not properly my own, Harootunian's challenge to Heidegger can be seen to create effects that threaten to overwhelm crucial aspects of his own argument. Harootunian aims to reverse Heidegger and privilege the notion of inauthenticity in such a way as to redirect attention to the radical alterity that he finds to be characteristic of history and sociality. Yet the exteriority of ownness that Harootunian attempts to think functions rather like a Pandora's box. If one unleashes a logic of negativity vis-à-vis the various received concepts of ownness, then one will invariably be forced to rethink certain fundamental aspects of one's "own" discourse.

This can be seen especially clearly with regard to the problem of subjectivity. Harootunian treats this problem in nearly all of his works, but for convenience sake let us return to his discussion of Imamura's protagonist Onboro so as to better understand why the attack on Heideggerian ownness risks jeopardizing important facets of his own historical-political project. As we saw, Harootunian privileges Onboro as an exemplar of concrete everydayness and political resistance because of her "behavior that is both autonomous and independent." It is precisely this quality of autonomy that leads her ultimately to emancipation from the various bonds that had unfairly restricted her existence in Japan. My claim here is that the logic of ownness covertly informs Harootunian's affirmative reading of Onboro. At one and the same time, authentic Dasein is contested for its self-containment and flight from exteriority while the figure of Onboro—free, autonomous, and independent—is celebrated for exactly the same reasons. Certainly these two discussions take place in utterly different contexts, but such difference must not obscure the fact that Harootunian is appealing to what is in effect the same structure of subjectivity.

I agree with the general thrust of Harootunian's criticism of Heideggerian authenticity, for such recourse to an isolated sphere of ownness or mineness threatens to exclude vital forms of difference. But if one is to then reconceive inauthenticity as the site of a repressed exteriority or alterity, one that will return to overwhelm the restricted domain of what is otherwise authentically my own, then *all* forms of subjectivity must suffer its effects. To privilege Onboro because she is seen to represent a politically progressive form of subjectivity while condemning Heidegger's authentic Dasein because it is judged to be politically conservative (or elitist, depoliticized, etc.) appears to be an arbitrary decision. Harootunian provides a valuable hint regarding the limitations of subjectivity by displacing emphasis from authenticity to inauthenticity, as he presents the latter as a kind of return of the historically and socially repressed. In so doing, however, he can be seen to set loose a general force of disappropriation (exteriority, alterity: that which poses an essential threat to the proper) that calls into question important features of his own argument.

(2) The primary disadvantage of deflecting the issue of Heidegger's concept of time so as to draw attention instead to the dyad of authenticity/inauthenticity consists in underestimating the foundational nature of this concept. By "foundational" I mean that the question of ecstatic temporality possesses an unparalleled level of generality that by definition

affects any and all forms of being, including those of history and sociality. The most immediate consequence of this rethinking of time is that the traditional valuation of ontological presence and the temporally present now finds itself irretrievably disturbed. I wish to stress here that one of the principal difficulties with Harootunian's methodology lies in his aim to think difference—what he calls alternately "radical difference" or "genuine difference"[50]—on the basis of present presence. From Heidegger's standpoint, this appeal to presence in the *now* time of the present places Harootunian squarely in the same tradition of metaphysics that he otherwise wishes to contest. This tradition is characterized by the desire to find exemption from difference—the "fact" of difference is recognized only to then be disavowed through the positing of a putatively higher and more original instance of unity and identity—and so the nature of Harootunian's intervention is cause for some puzzlement. As I mentioned previously, in reading Harootunian one must be sensitive to the gap opened up between the expressed aims of his project and the underlying logic or structure of his argument. The creditable attempt to think difference could, I believe, benefit greatly from a serious consideration of Heidegger's notion of ecstatic temporality. Indeed, Harootunian's sustained interest in Heidegger as well as the constancy of his commitment to the problematic of time might well suggest a certain degree of influence of Heideggerian time on Harootunian's own thinking. The intense antipathy shown to Heidegger's philosophy, however, discourages such a reading. What comes to be lost in this attitude—an attitude that is also a reading strategy—is an insight into the way in which ecstatic time fundamentally incapacitates any project of presence.

In *Being and Time*, Heidegger develops his notion of ecstatic temporality as follows:

> *Temporality is the primordial "outside-of-itself" in and for itself.* We therefore call the phenomena of the future, the character of having been, and the Present, the *"ecstases"* of temporality. Temporality is not, prior to this, an entity which first emerges from *itself*; its essence is a process of temporalizing in the unity of the ecstases. What is characteristic of the 'time' which is accessible to the ordinary understanding, consists, among other things, precisely in the fact that it is a pure sequence of "nows," without beginning and without end, in which the ecstatical character of primordial temporality has been levelled off.[51]

It is instructive to consider the profound difference between time in its ecstasy and what Heidegger calls here the "ordinary understanding" of time. If the latter has traditionally viewed time in such a way as to "level off" its ecstatic movement, this is because time has been subordinated to the presence of punctuality. Hence one regards time as "a pure sequence of 'nows'" in which the passage or line of time appears to be constituted by a series of discrete, individual points (or instants), each different from one another while remaining identical to itself. In this sense, it is difficult to reconcile Harootunian's representation of Heideggerian time, which he characterizes as "a succession and accumulation of presents,"[52] with Heidegger's own conception, since this view is precisely the one that *Being and Time* dismisses as inauthentic. Time resists comprehension as a present point because it *is* not; at each moment, the presence of its identity is forced to stand ecstatically outside of itself, thereby rendering any present or presence nothing more than a derivative effect. In order for there to be time, there must be a before and after. Metaphysics will conceive of the presence of the present *now* as a way to stabilize this otherwise disappropriating movement (i.e., the double pull away from presence). Again, difference (past [the before], future [the after]) is acknowledged strictly on the condition that it ultimately yield to a higher instance of identity, and this is the role assigned to the present. If time consisted only of a series of discrete instants, however, there could be no movement. It is precisely in order to think a kind of negativity of time, one that opens up the possibility of relationality between such present instants, that the insufficiency of presence and the present reveals itself.

As far as Harootunian's own project is concerned, the desire to think time as both qualitatively superior and temporally prior to space would appear to be substantially aided by appeal to Heidegger's notion of ecstatic temporality. While I have demonstrated that this desire is ultimately a vain one—that time and space must on the contrary be thought in terms of an originary synthesis—it is nonetheless the case that time determined on the basis of presence falls into the very trap of fixed and static spatiality that Harootunian otherwise wishes to avoid. The present can be understood as that central point of unity and self-identity that serves to anchor time amid the thoroughly dispersive force that is the past and future. In its "*primordial 'outside-of-itself,'*" ecstatic temporality can be said to release that negativity that enables each instant to open onto the next, thereby raising time to its genuine level of movement. If negativity is not taken into account and temporality not determined as incessant self-exteriorization, then one is left with a series of present points that seem unable to make way for one another through an originary dynamic of appearing and disappearing. Regardless of the laudable intent to ground ethics and politics on the present as a site of "radical difference," the very presence of the present remains constituted by its logical exclusion of the absence of both the past that is no longer and the future that is not yet. If radical difference is to be conceived, then, one must first of all acknowledge that it undermines all attempts to privilege the particular form of the present.

Yet Heidegger's understanding of time contains an additional aspect that speaks directly to Harootunian's project. As Heidegger claims, "Temporality is not, prior to this, an entity which first emerges from *itself*; its essence is a process of temporalizing in the unity of the ecstases."[53] At stake here is a certain ruse of metaphysics that attempts to think movement and difference strictly from the departure point of self-identical presence. The essence of temporality is temporalization, Heidegger declares, and this conception is contrasted with the more traditional notion of temporality as a being or entity whose experience of ecstasy takes place only *after* it has *first* been constituted as itself. Ecstatic temporality is "primordial": its essence is to be other to itself in an unceasing movement of self-differentiation. If essence is classically understood to signify a thing's interiority—that which allows it to be identified as itself in distinction from those things that are unlike it—then the radicality of Heidegger's thinking of time comes properly into view. In the tradition of philosophy that Heidegger is here contesting, the essential identity of something only appears insofar as it marks its difference from other things. With the notion of time ecstatically standing outside of itself, however, we are now given to think something like an essential difference, one that precedes even the basic opposition between identity and difference.

The difference between Harootunian's notion of radical or genuine difference and the Heideggerian thought of essential difference as opened up by the notion of ecstatic temporality consists in the profoundly asymmetrical levels of generality to which they make appeal. For Harootunian, difference is to be conceived strictly as the opposite of identity. This kernel of opposition is grasped in the ethical and political terms of good and evil. The good that is difference, temporality, and multiplicity, etc. thus comes to be directly contrasted to the evil that is identity, spatiality, and unity, etc. As I have indicated, this framework of oppositionality invariably appears in Harootunian's text together with that of sequentiality. As a result, the opposition between good and evil is configured according to a relation of primacy: *first* there is good, but this good is *afterward* somehow overtaken and corrupted by evil. Heidegger's thinking of temporality forcefully addresses this difficulty by conceiving of corruption or contamination—the originary exteriorization of the self, the exposure to alterity that is suffered not empirically or accidentally but essentially—as structurally enfolded within the "entity" itself. In its displacement of the traditional dualities of identity versus difference and interiority versus exteriority, the concept of ecstasy (i.e., essential difference) reveals itself to be infinitely more general since it no longer operates according to the logic of opposition.

Conclusion

In the discourse of ethics, a prelapsarian ideology frequently asserts itself by claiming that present evil came to appear through its supervention upon, or usurpation of, an earlier instance of good. This discourse teleologically envisions a future end to the present evil, and this can be achieved by returning to a past moment or period that is seen to preexist the initial emergence of that evil. Such prelapsarianism can be found equally in philosophy and religion, but in all cases it makes covert appeal to a notion of time and presence that Heidegger's ecstatic temporality severely places in doubt. If presence and absence can no longer be regarded as oppositional but instead as strangely interwoven, then one is forced to think questions of ethics and politics (and history, sociality, etc.) at a level of conceptuality that is more fundamental than this division. At this level, difference must be understood to name that which never presents itself, that which never appears in the full light that is the time of the present. As soon as difference is cognized, it will have already dissembled itself and assumed a more simple or straightforward form as the mere opposite of identity.

In the opening pages of *Things Seen and Unseen*, Harootunian speaks of the writings of the past as "texts that come to us as traces or inscriptions of losses, as reminders of absent presences."[54] This description contains an elegant and, I believe, entirely appropriate sense of pathos, and certainly it seems apt to conceive of the gap between the present and the past as one of unrecoverable loss. At the same time, however, presence again appears to be insistently conceived as that which first gives itself immediately and concretely in the time of the present. For a fleeting moment something is there; it possesses an original here and now that functions as the key to reclaiming it after it has inevitably slipped away from us into the past. The problem, however, is that this present moment itself is at every instant pulled outside of itself into the past that is no longer and the future that is not yet. As Heidegger realized, this violent rending or division of the instant does not take place, however minimally, merely *after* its appearance. In Harootunian's terms, such a conception would have to be regarded as an excessive and unjust spatialization of time, that is, it attempts to fix that which by its nature eludes all capture. The immediate movement of exteriorization named in the *ec-* of ecstasy means that there can be no purity of presence in either the past, present, or future. If the present is seen to uniquely possess a real, concrete presence that serves to justify its elevation above the past and future, this is because the past and future are both modes of absence. As Harootunian has so convincingly argued throughout his work, however—and this is, I believe, one of the central paradoxes of his thinking—the present is what it is because the past has partly formed it as such. (As of course the future has as well, but Harootunian is far less interested in that relation.) But what this means is that the present, given its essential debt to the past, is not entirely present in either sense of this term: the present cannot be fully *there* or identical to itself because it exists partially elsewhere, and the present never simply *is* because it is also, and at every moment, a *was* (or, even more precisely, a *will have been*, but again this brings us to the question of the future).

Despite these methodological differences, however, the fact remains that Harootunian's work represents some of the most powerful thinking in the field of Japan studies. Within this field, the very insight that scholarship must first attend to fundamental questions of methodology before grasping on to this or that particular research object comes directly from Harootunian's thinking. It is precisely because of this insight that he was able to recognize the immense fetishization of Japan, and sought to counteract this tendency of fascination with the strange Asian object by reflecting upon the far deeper and more disturbing strangeness of the Japan studies scholar becoming fascinated by the strange Asian object. For Harootunian, this metacritical move is inseparable from the move to ethics, politics, history, and sociality. In this regard, Harootunian's response to the disciplines of both Japan studies and historiography can be seen to derive from a profound dissatisfaction with the traditional scholarly convention of posing a subject of knowledge directly before a corresponding object of knowledge. The metacritical move was instrumental in releasing the subject from the artificial fixity of this position, and through this release the various unseen minutiae and, indeed, *messiness* of history could begin to gradually come into view. Several decades after Harootunian first began writing, the urgency and necessity of this move still remain with us today.

Chapter 3

The Question of Subjectivity in North American Japanese Literary Studies

> Even if writers strip a character naked, they must leave on the final layer of clothing, for the character would disappear if they removed it.
>
> —Takeuchi Yoshimi[1]

Introduction

It would be difficult to overestimate the prodigious changes that have occurred in the field of Japanese literary studies in North America. Scholars who pioneered the field were forced to reckon with the fact that Japanese literary works were virtually unknown at the time. Following the end of World War II, lingering anti-Japanese sentiment produced a variety of racist images of the Japanese as a barbaric, warmongering people whose cultural impoverishment was but one aspect of the country's larger civilizational backwardness. A generation of scholars of Japanese literature, many of whom had received their initial language training while serving in the US military, sought to counteract this racism by calling attention to the remarkable aesthetic sensitivity and refinement found in the works of Japanese fiction. This dramatic shift in focus required, first of all, the extensive labor of translation: in the decades following the war, much of what came to be regarded as the Japanese literary canon appeared for the first time in English. Translations of "premodern" works, such as the plays of Chikamatsu and the poetry of Bashō, were published together with the novels of such twentieth-century authors as Kawabata Yasunari and Tanizaki Jun'ichirō. This work was supplemented by literary anthologies and studies of individual writers as well as, beyond the walls of the academy, more general books on Japanese culture intended for a public curious to learn more about its former enemy.

If this presentation of the various riches of Japanese literature helped bring about a newfound appreciation of Japanese culture and a concomitant decline in racist attitudes, however, it did so at a price. For the image of Japan that gradually began to rise up in its place was one of Oriental exoticism. Rather than a discourse centered on the irrational militarism and aggression that was seen to exist throughout Japanese history, one could now discover a tradition characterized by harmonious relations with nature and a profound awareness of the transience of existence. This transition, significantly, coincided with a symbolic regendering of Japanese identity from male to female. The iconic image of the warrior, in which the premodern samurai with his sword seamlessly evolved into the modern soldier with his gun, was now replaced by a young kimono-clad woman gazing tranquilly at the surrounding cherry blossoms.[2] Anxious to promote the idea of a peaceful Japan that could serve as the newly trusted partner of the United States in the context of Cold War Asia, scholars of Japanese literature played a decisive role in reracializing Japan in terms of passivity and subservience. In this way, the desired overcoming of racism led directly to the formation of another racism, this one ideally suited to a dangerous Cold War environment in which Japanese security was assured through participating in the larger project of American hegemony.

Much of the scholarship of that earlier generation of Japanologists was divorced from the concerns of social critique, but this tendency must be understood on the basis of the institutional desire to demarcate a more or less pure space of aesthetics and cultural appreciation outside of the entanglements of politics, and this was particularly the case in light of the painful memories of the war that still remained from the not-so-distant past. Theoretical research, moreover, was limited to the lessons gleaned from New Criticism, which promoted a view of the literary text as a largely self-contained entity whose various levels of meaning could be deciphered with the tools of formalist analysis. If, from our present standpoint, the Japanese literary scholarship of the past appears excessively insular, this is due to both a general tendency to regard fiction as essentially apolitical and the desire to treat individual literary works as autonomous and hence approachable in dehistoricized terms.

These two mutually reinforcing views continued to inform Japanese literary studies until the emergence of the various "culture wars" in US academia during the 1980s and 1990s. At that time, the privileged status of Western canonical literature was perceived to be under attack, and the resulting debates, at times ferocious, could not but affect the field of Japanese literary studies. At issue was the tenuous positionality of the West during this era of growing multiculturalism, but also actively contested was the idea of literature as an autonomous realm of aesthetics that existed in some sense apart from social and political forces. Departments of Japanese literature, having long occupied their own distinct if somewhat isolated space within the humanities, now came under increasing pressure to participate in the broader debates about literary theory that were already roiling the departments of English and comparative literature. Predictably, this pressure initially met with a powerful wave of resistance: given Japan's Asian identity as well as the historical uniqueness of its culture, as the argument ran, of what use could new theories and methodologies of literature be when these latter derived so clearly from the West? In this way, attempts were made to shield the study of Japanese literature from foreign methodologies, thereby evincing a historical forgetfulness of the fact that "literary theory" had already been abundantly present at the dawn of modern fiction in Japan.[3]

The increasing engagement with the various texts of literary theory throughout the humanities led to a quandary in Japanese literary studies. Outright rejection of its use meant risking further ghettoization vis-à-vis the scholarship of other national literatures. In addition to the suspicion that "Western theory" was by nature inapplicable to non-Western texts, one could discern a forceful desire to safeguard the singularity and inherent elusiveness of literature from the threat of theoretical reductivism. Thus, the battle against literary theory was typically fought under the banner of close reading. On the other hand, however, what was seen as an excessive commitment to literary theory raised doubts as to both one's linguistic competency and familiarity with the basic empirical information required for expertise in the field. By opening the study of Japanese literature beyond the hitherto closed field of Japan, incorporating foreign methodologies so as to better interpret Japanese texts, the very framework of Japanese national literature was implicitly called into question. In many cases, this predicament as to the relevance of "Western theory" to Japanese literary scholarship was resolved in such a way that both extremes were safely averted. What emerged were studies of Japanese literature that continued to rely on the same forms of empirical information (with, of course, new developments and additions at the level of content) while nevertheless making intermittent, strategic references to the various thinkers and texts of literary theory.

It is striking, when comparing earlier generations of Japanese literary scholarship with more recent examples, how different the theoretical frameworks and methodological approaches appear at first glance. One can only conclude that the assimilation of literary theory in the field of Japanese literary studies has been successful. Rather than receding into further ghettoization, the widespread acceptance and active employment of theoretical research seem to have greatly invigorated the discipline. With few exceptions, graduate training now requires (or at the very least encourages) some level of engagement with theoretical ideas in order to more firmly grasp the various Japanese objects of study. Likewise, essays and monographs on Japanese literature invariably include reference to concepts generally associated with, for example, feminism, Marxism, deconstruction, cultural studies, and postcolonial studies. When seen against the work of such pioneering scholars in the field as Donald Keene, Edward Seidensticker, and Edwin McClellan, for example, all signs appear to point in the direction of theoretical progress.

My aim in this chapter is to more closely examine these signs and evaluate the degree of success of this incorporation of literary theory within the field of Japanese literary studies. I take as my key the notion of subjectivity, as this notion has been used widely in works that have sought to grapple with the demands of conceptual rigor and philosophical abstraction imposed by certain types of literary theory. The notion of subjectivity is indeed crucial. Given that the field of Japan studies presupposes the existence of a people identified as Japanese, the question of the formation of national identity must be regarded as inseparable from the question of subjectivity itself. In other words, if one engages in the study of Japanese literary texts as written by recognizably Japanese authors, then one is already committed to a certain view of subjectivity, regardless of whether one is explicitly aware of this or not. In my investigation of the question of the subject as it appears in the research on Japanese literature, I undertake readings of the work of three specific scholars: Tomi Suzuki, author of *Narrating the Self: Fictions of Japanese Modernity* (1996); Alan Tansman, author of *The Writings of Kōda Aya, a Japanese Literary Daughter* (1993) and *The Aesthetics of Japanese Fascism* (2009); and Dennis Washburn, author of *The Dilemma of the Modern in Japanese Fiction* (1995) and *Translating Mount Fuji: Modern Japanese Fiction and the Ethics of Identity* (2007). These texts were chosen less for their valuable archival contributions than for the exemplary intelligence they demonstrate at the level of engagement with their respective research objects. Graduate students and scholars alike must refer to these works in order to better comprehend such important objects of inquiry as, respectively, the I-novel, Japanese fascism, and Japanese literary modernity. However, it is precisely this question of the objectivity of the object that I seek to raise in my analysis of these scholars' treatment of subjectivity. My contention is that attentive readings of these individual works will help shed light on more general or structural problems that beset the field of Japanese literary studies as a whole. By deepening the level of conceptual reflection on the notion of subjectivity, I believe, one gains clearer insight into the distinct manner in which Japanese objects come to be constituted. In this way, I aim to broaden my inquiry beyond the limits of the particular object so as to open up the general and, I believe, considerably more urgent question of methodology.

Subjectivity and Retroactivity

In *Narrating the Self: Fictions of Japanese Modernity*, Tomi Suzuki argues that critical reflection on the notion of subjectivity is essential to help us better understand not only the various texts that make up the particular field of Japanese literature, but indeed the phenomenon of Japanese modernity as a whole. Here Suzuki takes as her object of study the so-called I-novel, the *watakushi shōsetsu* or *shi shōsetsu*, what Donald Keene describes as "perhaps the most striking feature of modern Japanese literature."[4] The striking quality of this genre lies in the widespread assumption that the experiences and thoughts of the fictional protagonist are to be recognized as ultimately a reflection of the author himself. In this sense, the mediation of fiction comes to collapse under the weight of the real. Suzuki responds to this traditional mode of reading the I-novel by insisting upon the importance of mediation: whereas standard interpretations seek to derive fictional mediation from the primacy and immediacy of lived experience, she boldly reverses this order by arguing that such immediacy must be grasped as strictly an *effect* of mediation. The text of the I-novel cannot be understood as a mere expression of the author's individual self, but must first of all be read as a text in all of its heterogeneity, inconsistency, and indirection. The desire to overcome such textual qualities so as to arrive at the extra- or pretextual self as origin, Suzuki declares, is finally to do violence to the richness of this unique branch of Japanese literature.

In order to effectuate this fundamental shift from author to text, Suzuki appeals to the notion of reading. Reading, understood as an act that takes place of necessity *after* the time of writing, produces retroactive effects that shape our understanding of reality. If the traditional interpretation of the I-novel posits the empirical author as cause, then Suzuki intervenes in this literary history by arguing that such cause can only be located retroactively through the delayed act of reading. The identity of writing is nothing in and of itself; on the contrary, it awaits creation by readings that seek to return to it through or despite this temporal lag. Retroactive reading is set forth as the methodological crux of Suzuki's engagement with the tradition of I-novel interpretation, and accounts for her attack on such Japanese literary scholars as Edward Fowler and Iremela Hijiya-Kirschnereit. For these scholars, as Suzuki writes, the I-novel is regarded as "an inherent literary genre with identifiable textual features and an essential meaning that can be correctly decoded and interpreted."[5] In their refusal to consider the retroactive nature of reading, Fowler and Hijiya-Kirschnereit, regardless of their divergent methodological perspectives (which Suzuki describes as a "textual" approach and "sociological" approach, respectively), equally fall prey to the trap of identity. Such appeal to identity can be seen in their determination of the various properties or qualities of the I-novel as "inherent" in the texts themselves. What allows an I-novel to be recognized as itself, in other words, are the internal—or, quoting Fowler, "intrinsic"—features of the work. An I-novel is an I-novel because it contains the requisite I-novel properties within itself. In a crucial move, Suzuki then links this claim of interiority at the level of individual Japanese literary texts with that of the entirety of Japanese culture. Fowler and Hijiya-Kirschnereit, she charges, both posit a continuity between these I-novel texts and what is imagined to be—here Suzuki again quotes Fowler—the "indigenous linguistic and epistemological tradition."[6]

In order to appreciate the argument that Suzuki articulates against Fowler and Hijiya-Kirschnereit, it is imperative that one recognize the different spatiotemporal borders involved. From Suzuki's standpoint, the texts and tradition of the I-novel are, in the work of these scholars, reductively grasped on the basis of an interiority that establishes the identity of this particular object of inquiry. The I-novel is temporally self-sufficient in that its properties are seen to be present within the writing itself. In this view, the time of reading can do nothing but *repeat* those features already contained within the writing. Spatially, moreover, reading must hold itself within the contours already determined by the I-novel texts and tradition. It is this underlying notion of interiority that ensures that this discourse remains close to itself, such that the "intrinsic" qualities of the individual

I-novel text are broadened at the national cultural level in the collective formation of an "indigenous" tradition. For Suzuki, such interiority can only be maintained by dismissing the consequences of a retroactive reading that incessantly wrenches open any enclosure of these texts. If, as Suzuki asserts, the I-novel only comes to its identity retroactively through the act of reading, then the time of the I-novel must be recognized as outside of it. This temporal excess of the I-novel vis-à-vis itself means that any spatial demarcation of its borders must end in failure, since any delineation of itself in its identity can ultimately be understood as a singular act of reading, one that awaits confirmation through future readings that may always possibly determine the I-novel otherwise.

In her critical response to Fowler and Hijiya-Kirschnereit, and indeed to the entire tradition of I-novel interpretation, Suzuki is keen to stake out for herself the position of exteriority. The attack against these scholars is not motivated, in the first instance, by claims of insufficient empirical information or an inability to comprehend the various individual texts contained within this genre. On the contrary, Suzuki condemns Fowler and Hijiya-Kirschnereit for their theoretical shortcomings. The tradition of I-novel scholarship, as represented by these scholars, asserts that this genre can be identified as present in itself, within its proper interiority. Such an unexamined notion of presence, Suzuki emphasizes, gives way to problems at both the literary and cultural level, for a regarding of fictional texts in their "intrinsic" characteristics is replicated in the insistence on viewing Japanese culture as "indigenous" and thus uniquely closed off from its outside. By introducing the notion of retroactive reading, Suzuki aims to open up this tradition by identifying a temporal and spatial exteriority as primary, and only through which literary texts and cultural traditions may come to be constituted in their retroactivity. In this way, the success of Suzuki's project can be evaluated on the basis of the theoretical and conceptual claims that she sets forth as necessary for a more sophisticated and rigorous understanding of the I-novel, one that goes beyond the precritical dogmatism of past readings.

Here a powerful tension can be discerned in Suzuki's intervention. On the one hand, she faults I-novel scholarship for its conceptual naiveté, its failure to interrogate such central notions as mediation, reflection, and authorial identity. On the other hand, however, her own theoretical reflections remain brief and undeveloped. Apart from her attack on Fowler and Hijiya-Kirschnereit that appears in the opening pages of *Narrating the Self*, the analyses Suzuki offers throughout the book in fact reveal a great many similarities with conventional I-novel scholarship. How is one to make sense of this tension? One possible answer to this question involves the notion of continuity, a notion that Suzuki associates with the unexamined concept of identity characteristic of nearly all previous I-novel scholarship. One must take care, she warns, against "creating a historical continuity between the I-novel and the 'indigenous Japanese tradition.'"[7] This raises the question of how far Suzuki herself avoids this trap of identity in her thinking of discontinuity, or that which *interrupts* what appears to be an otherwise seamless historical linkage. The unity and interiority of Japanese tradition come to be reinforced by situating the I-novel within its borders, thereby establishing a continuous chain of Japanese literary texts that extends from the past to the present. Suzuki attempts to disrupt this tradition and its enabling notion of continuity by calling attention to a certain contingency at work in the very identification of the I-novel as such. As she writes:

> Contrary to the arguments of previous studies, the so-called I-novel is not a genre that can be defined by certain referential, thematic, or formal characteristics. Instead, as I shall argue, the reader's expectations concerning, and belief in, the single identity of the protagonist, the narrator, and the author of a given text ultimately make a text an I-novel. The I-novel is best defined as a mode of reading that assumes that the I-novel is a single-voiced, "direct" expression of the author's "self" and that its written language is "transparent"—characteristics hitherto regarded as "intrinsic" features of the I-novel. The I-novel, instead of being a particular literary form or genre, was a literary and ideological paradigm by which a vast majority of literary works were judged and described. *Any text can become an I-novel if read in this mode.*[8]

Rather than being present to itself in its own interiority, as in the case of previous scholarship, the I-novel must now be seen as dependent upon future readings, beyond the time and place of its original writing, in order to belatedly become what it is. Now this notion of retroactive reading that Suzuki introduces must be recognized in all its force, for it involves a reconceptualization of identity beyond any given or established parameters in its turn toward an outside that remains, precisely, always ahead of or in excess of itself. This is the threat that exteriority, when conceived radically as movement rather than as a simple outside, poses to interiority. Suzuki stresses the elemental displacement of identity at work here when she concludes, "*Any text* can become an I-novel if read in this mode."

It is curious, then, that Suzuki goes on to present in her study many of the most conventional examples of I-novel discourse, texts that are also given extensive treatment in the work of such scholars as Keene, Fowler, and Hijiya-Kirschnereit. Given the disappropriating force of retroactive reading, which can, once certain generic conditions are satisfied, make of "any text" an I-novel, it is revealing that Suzuki's determination of this literary form broadly follows that of the I-novel tradition. Temporally, works that Suzuki identifies as part of I-novel discourse center on the early twentieth century, which accords with the standard interpretation. And spatially, Suzuki appears content to remain entirely within the confines of Japan. Despite her reconceptualization of this genre, which, devoid of any specific geographical markers, aims to expose these texts to the contingency of their outside, Suzuki nonetheless confirms the tradition in her exclusive focus on works she identifies as "Japanese." If, to follow Suzuki's redefinition of this genre, these texts must now be regarded as "a mode of reading that assumes that the I-novel is a single-voiced, 'direct' expression of the author's 'self' and that its written language is 'transparent,'" then, as she rightly concludes, "any text" whatsoever that comes to be read in this manner can be identified as an I-novel. Yet the literary texts that actually appear in *Narrating the Self* are exclusively "Japanese." Despite Suzuki's opposition to the notion of Japanese tradition as "indigenous"—an opposition that she repeats in various places throughout her book—her methodological shift in emphasis from originary author and writing to retroactive reading appears to leave entirely in place the attachment to Japanese cultural interiority. How then are we to account for this contradiction?

The repetition of tradition in the very gesture by which one attempts to depart from it possesses, of course, a long history. In order to understand the lure of tradition, one must go beyond analysis of discrete empirical examples that already form part of a continuing practice or institution and examine the underlying logic that governs that continuity itself. Failure to confront the dominant logic or principles of a tradition condemns one to look strictly at objects within that tradition, objects that appear to exist outside of oneself as subject. In this way, one risks disavowing one's own silent complicity with the tradition that one otherwise wishes to contest. By scrutinizing the general logic that accounts for the insistent force wielded by tradition to diachronically bind its members to itself, however, one no longer operates according to the epistemological distance of the subject-object relation but instead creates for oneself *the chance to understand tradition differently through recognition of one's very relation to it.* At stake here is something that the philosopher Michael Naas has felicitously called "taking on the tradition."⁹ In preceding me, tradition already lays claim to my identity, placing me in the position to "take it on" as I internalize this particular historical practice and become shaped by its dictates in my formation as subject. In that very act of reception, however, the possibility always exists for me to actively "take on" the tradition, to challenge it and negotiate its logic of capture so that it may henceforth be transformed or deformed.

Suzuki's relation with the tradition of the I-novel can be more clearly understood by examining her criticism of the major concept of binarity. For Suzuki, such binarity appears as one of the constitutive factors in the formation of this tradition: "The notion of the I-novel was always formulated on a polar axis that contrasted the Western novel with its Japanese counterpart. . . . [T]he I-novel meta-narrative was premised on a binary, polar opposition between the Western novel, which was seen as a fictional, imaginative construct, and the Japanese I-novel, which was characterized as a factual, direct expression of the author's lived experience."¹⁰ It is not difficult to confirm Suzuki's analysis of the unexamined oppositionality between Japan and the West that has often been posited in I-novel discourse. We can observe this feature, for example, in Keene: "The 'I-novels,' as such examples of autobiographical fiction came to be called, had their roots in a romantic discovery but developed in terms of naturalistic descriptions of ordinary life led by ordinary men. . . . In the West Naturalism had been a reaction to Romanticism, but in Japan, where European literary developments that had occurred over a period of many years were sometimes introduced and adopted within a single decade, Naturalism and Romanticism might be found in the same work."¹¹ Fowler, in his *Rhetoric of Confession*, echoes Keene and the I-novel tradition by maintaining this same opposition: "Unlike 'pure literature' in the west, which calls to mind an author aloof from his writing after the manner of Flaubert or Joyce, 'pure literature' in Japan (a category to which the *shishōsetsu* belongs) is considered inherently referential in nature: its meaning derives from an extraliterary source, namely, the author's life."¹²

Given Suzuki's attack on the I-novel tradition, from which she attempts to theoretically distance herself, one might expect a refusal of this binary logic in her textual analysis. According to the notion of retroactive reading, in which identity is found to exist not within an entity but rather outside of it, incessantly beyond itself in its spatiotemporal exposure to futurity, the very formation of interiority is understood to take place on the basis of an exteriority that, for structural reasons, resists unity with the object that it nevertheless constitutes. Despite appearances, the relation between interiority and exteriority cannot be regarded as oppositional or dualistic given that the latter, understood in all rigor as a movement of spatiotemporal difference, functions as the very milieu in which the former comes into being. The difficulty here is that Suzuki wishes to make use of this notion of retroactive reading without appearing to grasp the extent of its unsettling implications. Indeed, she first presents this notion in the introduction of *Narrating the Self* through the very framework of East-West oppositionality that she otherwise appears to condemn. Drawing on the work of the critic Philippe Lejeune, Suzuki asserts that the genre of autobiography must be identified strictly through textual elements rather than by naively appealing to the extratextual, empirical reality of the author's individual self. Suzuki warns, however, that Lejeune's insights have only limited applicability to I-novel scholarship given the fundamental difference between the entities Japan and the West (Europe): "For Lejeune, the 'meaning' of a text depends on how it is read. Ultimately, however, Lejeune stresses the author's initiative in establishing this mutual contract. . . . Modern Japanese literature, however, did not have the kind of codified epistemological and literary consensus (such as the distinction between fiction and autobiography) that Lejeune finds in modern European literature. The referential, autobiographical reading of these texts was not necessarily the result of a contract proposed by the author. In the case of the I-novel, it is ultimately the reader who assumes a 'hidden contract' in the text."[13]

The act of reading is deceptively complex, for it involves at its core a notion of temporality that powerfully undermines any commonsensical, precritical understanding of time. Suzuki is correct to link the act of reading with the movement of retroactivity, but unless one grasps the radical threat to identity posed by an understanding of time as ecstatically outside of itself—always both ahead of and before itself in the complex interweaving of past and future—then one risks falling back into the same dogmatism that one otherwise wishes to denounce. Reading is necessarily a reading *of* writing, but the temporal difference that separates these two acts can only be reconciled or overcome by returning to the past from one's standpoint in the present, a present that at every moment slips irrevocably outside of itself into the future. Reading, in its futurity, returns to the past scene of writing, but because such return is in principle impossible given the fact that the past is now lost or dead, we are forced to acknowledge that reading never quite arrives at its destination. A double bind can be seen to emerge here: on the one hand, reading is inescapably a reading of writing, but on the other hand the impossibility of return implies that reading never purely apprehends writing in its identity, that the original writing remains to some degree inaccessible to a reading that nevertheless derives from it. The complex relation between reading and writing defies any reduction to oppositionality since each of these acts draws its identity strictly through relationality with its other: reading cannot be posed against writing because writing can only be determined as itself through being read, just as reading can only take place through a kind of inscriptive retracing or remarking of what is written. As soon as one sets forth this relation in binary terms, a hidden communication between these two acts will already have taken place, thereby unravelling that binarity.

For Suzuki, however, the "binary, polar opposition" that she finds to exist between the entities Japan and the West in previous I-novel scholarship is not merely repeated in her own work; it is repeated through the very concept of reading that otherwise reveals the fallacy of binary thinking. Despite its capacity to undermine all binarity, reading is presented in Suzuki's work in straightforwardly binaristic terms. Signaling her departure from Lejeune, she poses the Western figure of the writing author against the Japanese figure of the reader in order to illustrate the failure of Western criticism to comprehend the unique features of Japanese texts. This determination of Japan and the West as oppositional is in no way an isolated example, an instance limited solely to her dialogue with Lejeune. Throughout the pages of *Narrating the Self*, Suzuki refers time and again to such entities as "Western writers," "Western histories," "Western sources," "Western novels," the "Western discourse on truth and sex," and the "modern Western distinction between 'fiction' and 'nonfiction,' " etc., without defining this governing term "West" beyond the determination of its status as in some way opposite to Japan. Suzuki presents her methodological approach as historical—"my study emphasizes the historical formation of a discursive field in which the corpus of the I-novel was retroactively created and defined," as she writes[14]—but this claim raises the troubling question of why she declines to historicize the notion of the West and instead merely accepts its meaning at face value in the manner of Keene, Fowler, and Hijiya-Kirschnereit. If binary thought is essentially inimical to the movement of history, then the tacit reliance upon the concept of binarity to explain historical relations points to a certain unexamined ahistoricality at work in one's methodology.

One of the powerful ironies operative in Suzuki's project is that the notion of retroactive reading that she deploys contains precisely the resources to disturb the "binary, polar opposition" that she nevertheless endorses. This can be seen even in her treatment of "the West," as her examination of I-novel literature at one point discloses that the notion of Western identity to which she is otherwise committed necessarily yields to the more general logic of retroactivity. She uncovers this insight in Tanizaki Jun'ichirō's celebrated 1924 novel *Chijin no ai* ("A Fool's Love," translated into English as *Naomi*). In the beginning of this work, the protagonist and narrator Jōji meets a young woman named Naomi and is immediately captivated by her name. As Jōji relates, "Strangely enough, once I knew that she had such a sophisticated name, she began to take on an intelligent, Western look. I started to think what a shame it would be to let her go on as a hostess in a place like that."[15] Tanizaki clearly marks the unusual temporality of Jōji's experience, for the typical development from the immediacy of sensory perception to mediated reflection is here reversed in the fact that the protagonist's gaze upon Naomi is already shaped by his knowledge of her name. Because she possesses a name that sounds Western, her very physical appearance comes to be perceived by him as Western. Focusing on this notion of the West, Suzuki provides the following reading of these lines:

> Jōji goes on to recall how his life, particularly his sexual life, was shaped by what we could call a single, magical signifier: that of the West. Jōji is initially attracted to Naomi not by her character or even by her appearance but by her name, which sounds Western to him. (Jōji visualizes her name in Roman letters, as NAOMI.) The magical signifier calls for a corresponding "substance"; once Jōji is attracted to her Western name, he notices that she indeed looks like a Westerner.[16]

This analysis reveals a surprising difference between Tanizaki and Suzuki, one that calls attention to significant limitations in the latter's understanding of retroactivity. Suzuki is certainly correct to underline the enormous force wielded by the West in Jōji's thinking. Her interpretation of this passage in terms of the ability of the *signifier* "West" to produce the effect of what she calls the *substance* "West" aptly conveys the power of linguistic representation to actively form and give shape to the empirical reality that it otherwise claims merely to reflect. Nonetheless, Tanizaki shows that the relation between language and perception contains at its core a temporal aspect that ensures that we never receive the world as such, in its objective identity. When Jōji remarks, "Strangely enough, once I knew that she had such a sophisticated name (*namae ga haikara da to naru to*), she began to take on an intelligent, Western look," the true strangeness at issue here concerns the movement of time. Whereas language is conventionally understood to duplicate a preexisting reality, Tanizaki shows that it in fact doubles no fixed object that precedes it but rather actively creates that origin as a delayed, retroactive effect. In other words, Tanizaki's description of Jōji makes appeal to the same notion of retroactive reading that Suzuki presents as the central methodological tool of *Narrating the Self*. The traces of Naomi's physical features are retraced by Jōji in such a way as to attribute meaning to them from a position of spatiotemporal exteriority. Naomi is not seen as resembling a Westerner on account of any "intrinsic" characteristics she might possess, but rather strictly because of the retroactive projection that is enacted by the male protagonist and narrator.[17]

It is noteworthy, then, that Suzuki's reading of this passage avoids any analysis based on the notion of retroactivity. The great achievement of retroactive reading lies in its recognition of a kind of lacuna found at the heart of all presence. No entity can be fully self-sufficient or present to itself because the time of identity is radically dislocated from itself. A thing is unable to exist purely as itself, as it *is* in its quiddity or whatness, because the movement most essential to it is that of the future anterior, in which it strictly *will have been*. Retroactivity takes as its point of departure the insight that the traditional privileging of the present is unsustainable, and that a shift to futurity is necessary to account for the multiple, constantly changing determinations of identity. Such futurity, however, does not disrupt present identity merely to relocate it at some fixed later moment, however distantly that may be envisioned. On the contrary, what is at issue here is precisely the self-negating movement of time, according to which the appearance of an entity takes place too early for it to be properly identified while the determination of that entity as itself takes place too late given the entity's subsequent alteration, its ceasing to be identically what it previously was. For structural reasons, all retroactive determinations must fail given their incommensurability with the past entity, but in this failure they paradoxically open up the possibility of returning to that entity anew. In this way, an entity's identity can be seen to experience constant disruption in its spatial parameters as well, for each attempt to demarcate its borders comes inevitably to be negated with all subsequent remarkings.

Throughout the pages of *Narrating the Self*, Suzuki time and again unleashes the force of retroactive reading only to draw it back once it threatens to disturb the claims of identity. In *Chijin no ai*, Tanizaki discovers a certain defect in the notion of Western identity, for it is forced to depend on spatiotemporal elements that exist outside of it in order to then constitute itself in delayed, ricochet fashion. One could rightly conclude from Tanizaki's work that no Western identity can be found to exist as such, in its original propriety. Suzuki refuses to draw this conclusion, however, and this might well appear surprising in light of her commitment to the notion of retroactivity. In her critical response to traditional I-novel scholarship, Suzuki insists that the identity of the I-novel, in terms of both individual texts and its relation to Japanese culture as a whole, does not exist in and of itself. There is no I-novel, in other words, for its identity is already compromised or to some degree negotiated by the movement of time. However, the notion of the West, despite the clue offered in Tanizaki's novel, appears to fall outside the scope of Suzuki's retroactive reading. Restricting her object of analysis to *Japanese* literary phenomena as these have been shaped by the omnipresent *West*, Suzuki ensures that the only form of identity threatened by retroactive reading is that of the I-novel. Cultural identity, as it appears in the entities "Japan" and "the West," is accepted as such.

Given that the notion of retroactivity is in principle capable of undermining *all* forms of identity, it is revealing that Suzuki limits its force exclusively to Japanese literary texts whose own national cultural affiliation remains unquestioned. Contra Keene, Fowler, and Hijiya-Kirschnereit, Suzuki vigorously contests the notion of an I-novel identity; following Keene, Fowler, and Hijiya-Kirschnereit, however, she no less vigorously confirms the notion of Japanese and Western identity. As Suzuki reminds us, the tradition of I-novel discourse repeatedly situates its object of inquiry within the framework of East-West binarity. In order to challenge the theoretically naïve recourse to identity that informs this tradition, however, one must broaden the range allowed the notion of retroactivity so that its destabilizing effects may appear not only at the level of discrete objects but also, and especially, at that of the general logic that structures the field and gives support to its many dogmatic assumptions. Nevertheless, it would be a mistake to regard the restrictions imposed upon retroactivity as a mere oversight, an accidental incompleteness in what is otherwise a comprehensive and theoretically responsible reexamination of the I-novel genre. Ultimately, what is at issue here is subjective desire, a desire that must be recognized before all else as institutional and conceptual rather than merely individual. Placed securely beyond the scope of retroactivity, the presence of the entities Japan and the West structures *Narrating the West* just as firmly as it does the most conventional I-novel scholarship. Only by first accepting what appears to be the fixed identity of these geopolitical coordinates can analysis of literary phenomena then take place in their national specificity.

In this regard, it is worth considering the question of what discourse on the I-novel might look like were it to resist simply affirming these notions of cultural identity. If the notions of "Japan" and "the West" were not merely accepted as self-evident, what kind of general framework might be employed to better understand I-novel texts? At a certain point in *Narrating the Self*, Suzuki finds herself confronted by the possible disappearance of any fixed or given Japanese identity. As she writes, "For Mushakōji and the Shirakaba group, *there were no Japanese*: there existed only Humanity (*ningen*), or Mankind (*jinrui*), together with such universals as Love, Art, Nature, Justice, Beauty, and Life. All of these were defined in relation to Humanity, a universal reality directly represented by each of their individual selves. This absolute acceptance of Western discourse, the uncritical universalism and internationalism . . ."[18]

Here I am not interested in the empirical question of whether the Shirakaba group actually were or were not in "absolute acceptance of Western discourse." Rather, what concerns me is, given the sustained commitment to Japanese and Western identity, Suzuki's reaction to the possibility that the former might somehow disappear. This possibility must be vigorously denounced, and indeed the attack on the Shirakaba group for their "uncritical universalism and internationalism" appears no less severe than the earlier condemnation of Fowler and Hijiya-Kirschnereit. Japanese identity must by all means be safeguarded from such threat. If Suzuki criticizes previous I-novel scholarship for its naïve positing of Japanese tradition as "indigenous," then the failure to grasp the various implications of such culturalism leads all the more surely to its unwitting repetition. Against any threat to Japanese identity, Suzuki at one point asserts that comprehension of the I-novel must be linked with what she calls "Japan's cultural identity and tradition": "This study reveals that I-novel discourse cannot be reduced to the so-called liberal-humanist or romantic view of the self and language—the self viewed as an autonomous entity and the source of its own language—but always involves the (hi)story of Japan's cultural identity and tradition."[19]

In light of the long history of cultural nationalism, how does one avoid merely repeating this discourse? Given the political dynamics involved, it appears rather fruitless to call attention to the problem of identity formation in the context of this or that particular literary genre if the very framing device through which national cultural identity is confirmed remains unexamined. Here let me clarify the stakes of my argument. It is ultimately of minor importance that Suzuki's conceptual or theoretical understanding represents little advance over that of Keene, Fowler, and Hijiya-Kirschnereit.

Suzuki discovers an extremely powerful resource that can be used to disrupt the claims of identity, and yet, following the tradition of I-novel scholarship that she otherwise attacks, this resource comes to be employed in the service of a conservative culturalist politics, one that reinforces the capacity of the nation-state to remain close to itself in its aesthetic dimension. I want to emphasize that this is not a question of discipline. Suzuki's failure to interrogate the notion of Japanese cultural interiority does not simply follow from the fact that her work is situated in the field of literary studies, a failure that would conceivably be rectified through more rigorous application of the tools she borrows from the discipline of philosophy. The truth of the matter is that nationalism and culturalism can be found extensively throughout the disciplines of both literature and philosophy. Nevertheless, the desire to conceive of literary texts as *either* Japanese *or* Western reveals a thinking that remains in thrall to the unexamined notions of binarity and identity. It is at this point that the hidden link between a certain kind of literary and philosophical discourse begins to come into view.

These discourses converge, I believe, at the philosophical notion of presence. In Suzuki's literary history, this notion manifests itself most pervasively in the form of geopolitical identity. This presence somehow resists the dislocating effects of retroactivity, for otherwise I-novel texts could no longer be seen as exclusively Japanese in their negotiation with those political and cultural forces that derive from the putative West. Suzuki's indebtedness to a certain philosophical vocabulary bears remarking for the following reason: if concepts are merely used cosmetically, then not only is their critical force diminished, but one also risks reproducing the very dogmatism that these concepts are designed to attack. Ample evidence of such usage can be found in Suzuki's appeal to the notion of the trace. In *Narrating the Self*, the importance of this term is signaled to the reader by its appearance in the title of Part III, "Traces of the Self." Unfortunately, as with the notion of retroactivity, this term is never adequately explained or developed. It seems clear that Suzuki is intent to employ this term or concept as a means to distance herself from the theoretical unsophistication of past I-novel scholarship. "Traces," in Suzuki's account, appears to mean something like "pieces" or "fragments," that which in its partiality cannot be understood as fully real. However, this reading of the notion of trace leaves disappointingly intact the concept of presence that it is in fact fully equipped to confront.

At its most general level, the notion of the trace must be situated at the level of ontology. Here there can be found a complex interweaving between time and space that reveals the impossibility of presence, whether in the form of identity or binarity. In order for anything to exist in time, it must reckon with a movement of negativity that at each moment introduces loss and alteration to all entities. Such change does not merely take place *after* an entity has been constituted as itself; on the contrary, an entity's exposure to temporal difference is originary, occurring from the moment it first appears in the world, thereby prohibiting any consolidation of identity as such. The only way for something to resist this absolute negativity of time and continue on as itself is for it to leave behind a material or spatial trace of itself for the future. In order for anything to remain in time, in other words, there must appear a spatial trace of itself that survives despite the loss and alteration of itself as effected by negativity. Nevertheless, such spatialization of time is incapable of ever purely bringing about an exemption from time, which means that the spatial trace remains constantly subject to the threat of its own negation or destruction. This fundamental relation between time and space indicates that an entity's being in the world is above all marked by finitude, and hence by an ineradicable sense of fragility or precariousness.

If Suzuki never explores the strange logic of the trace, this does not prevent her from thematizing the question of time as it appears in I-novel discourse. For Suzuki, the concept of time holds the key to a deeper understanding of the problematic of subjectivity as depicted by I-novel writers. Again, the appeal to a philosophical discourse is necessitated by the desire to introduce greater rigor to our understanding of these literary texts. The notion of trace and the problems of time and subjectivity emerge as an attempt to overcome the persistent trap of interiority, for, as we have seen, such interiority can only be constituted derivatively or belatedly, through a kind of return movement that takes its bearings from the notion of spatio-temporal exteriority. Whereas I-novel discourse traditionally insists on seeing the fictional protagonist as a direct reflection of the individual author himself, Suzuki aims to challenge this underlying assumption of subjective unity by raising the question of time. As she writes in her analysis of Shiga Naoya's 1912 work *Ōtsu Junkichi*, "The widespread assumption about the immediacy and directness of Shiga's writing has, however, led to the ignoring of the significance of the temporal distancing between past and present."[20] Here the notion of temporal distance should be recognized as part of Suzuki's ongoing attempt to emphasize the importance of exteriority. The traditional stress on the values of "immediacy" and "directness" allows writing to remain close to the writer as origin, thereby limiting the dispersive effects of the text that are otherwise released through an underlining of temporal distance.

Shiga's novel focuses on what Suzuki calls "the space and time of recollection." The narrator Junkichi recalls the actions of his younger, past self from the perspective of the narrative present. Suzuki calls attention to this temporal difference by quoting two passages in which Junkichi uses the same expression *sono toki no genzai ni oite*: "In other words, at that time [*sono toki no genzai ni oite*], I had not yet achieved work that could give me a sense of self-confidence" and "I had rarely experienced such violent and sudden anger. But I was clearly aware *at that time* [*sono toki no genzai ni oite*] that I was not forced to act in such a desperate fashion."[21] Suzuki offers the following reading of these lines:

> But the very act of distancing, in which the narrator "I" suddenly starts using the plural pronoun "we" (*watakushidomo*) to describe the young Junkichi's confrontation with his father, as if to support the young Junkichi's otherwise vulnerable position, undermines the declared distance and instead reveals the "I"'s strong need, even now, to assert his "achievement" and "self-confidence." Instead of being a distanced, objective self-portrayal, as suggested in the beginning, the recollection of the "past" becomes an effort to assert Junkichi's identity and independence from the father by deliberately making a distinction between the past and the present.
>
> For the narrating "I," recollecting becomes a process by which he attempts to overcome his past by demonstrating that his present self is more mature, by placing his past in an ironic perspective, and by showing a deeper and more comprehensive understanding of his past self.[22]

Once again a troubling gap appears between Suzuki's desire to think exteriority and her own repetition of that interiority that she otherwise condemns. The enormously complex issue of time and subjectivity comes in her reading to be reduced to a mere question of character psychology. Suzuki foregrounds the temporal division opened up in the act of recollection, for the actively writing "I" of the narrative present cannot be immediately equated with the passively written "I" of the narrative past. In her account, however, this division does nothing but reveal, as she writes, "Junkichi's identity and independence from the father," for "he attempts to overcome his past by demonstrating that this present self is more mature." By focusing on the excessively narrow issue of individual psychology, Suzuki demonstrates that her own thinking of the self or subject remains caught up in the conventional understanding of subjectivity as a site of interiority. What this means is that *time*, which is presented in *Narrating the Self* as holding a key to unlocking the secret of subjectivity, *is kept vigilantly outside the subject*. Suzuki fails to grasp the complexity of Shiga's expression *sono toki no genzai ni oite* because this phrase doesn't simply mean "at that time." More literally, these words can be translated as "in the present of that time." By thinking of the present as located in another time of the past, one quickly realizes that such present cannot remain purely as itself but is instead contaminated or infiltrated by the past in which it now finds itself. However, the present is not, in this instance, under siege solely from the past. Shiga's narrator attempts to identify a "present of that (past) time," and this desire can only be realized because that past present is already directed toward the future in order to be recollected at all. Here we touch upon the radical dislocation of time at work in all acts of recollection. One thinks recollection inadequately, strictly within the parameters of subjective interiority, if one grounds the return to the past merely upon man's individual faculty of memory. Even prior to such recall, recollection takes place most essentially through the movement of the trace: time in its flow ceaselessly passes away, but in its passing leaves behind a residual inscription of itself that has a chance of surviving into the future. The event that is remembered or recollected thus exists as strangely contorted from itself, for only by sending itself into the future can it possibly be determined as the past event that it retroactively will have been.

When confronted with the various analytic resources of philosophical discourse, a traditional literary criticism that has already determined its object of inquiry along the most particularistic national cultural lines runs the risk of utilizing those resources so as to better consolidate the claims of culturalism. Yet cultural identity does not simply make use of such indexes as language and aesthetic tradition; it also employs the historical discourse of race in its identification of difference among discrete geopolitical entities. When one speaks about the distinction between Japan and the West, for example, one often locates that difference beyond the division between the Japanese language and those multiple languages that are reflexively grouped together under the collective heading of "the West" or, alternatively, the disparity in the modes of reception of such schools as Romanticism and Naturalism in their influence on literary works. In modernity, the notion of race presents itself as a tool used to more accurately distinguish geopolitical formations and the movement of populations. This notion informs us that the opposition between Japan and the West manifests itself in the identity of the latter as "white" in contrast to the former's determination strictly as "yellow" or nonwhite. No less than philosophical conceptuality, the notion of race exerts considerable pressure on conventional literary criticism in its ability to examine and make sense of the complexities of the modern world. In nearly all cases, the discipline of literature takes as its most proper realm the individual texts and schools of thought that together form the accepted category of literature, as well as those larger sociohistorical forces that constantly shape and reshape literature in its myriad instantiations. In literary studies in general, and in the field of Japanese literature more specifically, the notion of race is invariably considered external to literary phenomena.

In *Narrating the Self*, Suzuki confirms this tradition by omitting any discussion of race that might cast doubt on what appears to be its self-evident nature. This is a curious decision given that the full title of the book, *Narrating the Self: Fictions of Japanese Modernity*, suggests that the author aims to confront not only the problem of subjectivity but also the topic of modernity in the context of Japan. A vast amount of space is devoted in this work to the minutiae of I-novel discourse—and, indeed, there can be little doubt that Suzuki's knowledge of the various dates, authors, and texts that make up this discourse exceeds even that of Keene, Fowler, and Hijiya-Kirschnereit—but such meticulous attention raises the question of what might be called a distribution of resources: if one wishes to seriously examine the issue of subjectivity in its relation to the discourse of Japanese modernity, is it sufficient to avoid any theoretical examination of the notion of race and instead provide vast amounts of empirical information on the I-novel? When one considers the historical question of how "subjects" living on the Japanese archipelago in the modern era thought about themselves in their putative collective identity and thus relative difference from others who lived elsewhere in the world, was the topic of race truly so inconsequential when compared with what appears in these pages to be the urgent issue of the I-novel?

At this point, let me emphasize that Suzuki's *Narrating the Self* can in no way be understood as an isolated example—as a text that emerged purely in and of itself, as if in a historical vacuum. This book presents itself in the larger context of Japanese literary scholarship, and its manner of positing its object of inquiry as well as its adoption of certain methodological positions must be seen as in some sense reflective of that field as a whole. Rather than evaluating Suzuki's work in individual terms, then, I want to argue that it is necessary to consider it *symptomatically* in the specifically Freudian sense of this term as linked to a kind of repression. As Freud writes in a well-known passage, "A symptom is a sign of, and a substitute for, an instinctual satisfaction which has remained in abeyance; it is a consequence of the process of repression."[23] Ultimately, the treatment of race in *Narrating the Self* is of interest because it reveals what I believe is an institutional desire to displace the complex question of racial identity in such a way as to conceal its centrality to Japan studies. In Freud, the failure of repression to fully negate its object leads to the substitution of this latter; in other words, the object of repression can appear strictly on the condition that it *not appear as itself.* Japanese literary scholarship has traditionally identified the question of race as existing beyond the borders of literature. Only the most cursory attention is paid to this subject, even in works that claim to address the issue of modernity in Japan and are forced to acknowledge the implicit presence of race as it informs the discourse of East-West oppositionality. This is all the more remarkable when one considers the enormous resources devoted to unearthing the most arcane, molecular elements of literary phenomena. It is difficult to conceive of the notions of East and West without recognizing the racial elements at play in these terms. At one and the same time, the question of race is addressed and averted in the gesture by which one approaches the topic of subjectivity through the coordinates of East-West identity.

How, then, are we to respond when this otherwise repressed question of race appears not merely *outside* but rather already *within* those texts that constitute the objects of literary research? One of the most fascinating encounters in *Narrating the Self* is that which takes place between Suzuki in her role as subject of knowledge and Tanizaki Jun'ichirō in his position as epistemological object. Earlier I examined how Suzuki, despite her deployment of the notion of retroactive reading, strangely exempts the identity of the West from all retroactivity, in contradistinction to Tanizaki and his clue that such identity can only arrive at itself belatedly, strictly through the navigation of temporal difference. The appearance of the issue of race in this same novel, *Chijin no ai*, is no accident. Tanizaki grasps that the signifier "West" refers to more than a geographical region, for it contains certain fixed racial associations as well. In this work, the narrator and protagonist Jōji are attracted to the young Naomi because of her Western name and the whiteness of her skin. Tanizaki time and again calls attention to this link between the West and whiteness. Upon gazing at the sleeping Naomi, for instance, Jōji recounts: "Taking care not to awaken her, I sat by her pillow, held my breath, and stealthily gazed at her sleeping form. . . . My eyes moved back and forth between the pure white (*junpaku*) Western paper in the book and the whiteness (*shirosa*) of her breast."²⁴ Significantly, Jōji's desire to view Naomi in terms of whiteness is only challenged when the couple encounters a Russian woman. As Jōji reflects:

> What set [the Russian woman] apart from Naomi most of all was the extraordinary whiteness of her skin. Her pale lavender veins, faintly visible beneath the white surface like speckles on marble, were weirdly beautiful. I'd often complimented Naomi on her hands as I toyed with them. "What exquisite hands you have. As white as a Westerner's." But now, to my regret, I could see that there was a difference. Naomi's hands weren't a vivid white—indeed, seen after the countess's hand (*ittan kono te wo mita ato deha*), her skin looked murky.²⁵

Upon quoting this long passage, Suzuki offers the following reading:

> Juxtaposed to that of a "true Western lady," a Russian dance teacher, Naomi's glossy "Western" beauty is here degraded to an imperfect imitation of a "true Westerner," whose "pure white skin" dazzles Jōji. What is beneath this "white skin"—the "substance" of the "true Westerner"—is unattainable or even irrelevant for Jōji, since it is the strong radiance of the pure white surface that enraptures and blinds him. The absolute hierarchy constructed here between the true Westerner and the fake . . . Jōji's "West" can be reduced, in the final analysis, to the "white skin" of a Western woman. It is literally no more than skin deep.²⁶

Exactly as with Suzuki's interpretation of Tanizaki's representation of the West, the element of retroactivity comes once again to be effaced. Tanizaki's description of Jōji's sudden realization that Naomi is actually less white than he had originally imagined centers on this unusual folding back of time in order to confirm identity. For Jōji, Naomi's whiteness is belatedly revealed to be something other than and indeed inferior to white: it is *dosuguroi*, meaning "murky," "darkish," or "dusky." The same skin that at one moment in time appeared to him as comparable to the "pure white" of Western paper now, when revisited or returned to at a later moment in time after glimpsing what appears to be the even whiter skin of a "Westerner," reappears as *dosu*, meaning "turbid" or "muddy." However, Suzuki says nothing about this retroactive formation of identity. It seems clear that Tanizaki employs this device of retroactivity in order to show that the narrator-protagonist actively creates Naomi's Western identity in precisely the same way that he later withdraws it from her. In the first instance, Naomi's physical appearance becomes Western (and hence white) through Jōji's foreknowledge of her name, whereas in the second instance her physical appearance becomes nonwhite and hence non-Western or Japanese through his encounter with the Russian woman. Suzuki neglects to see how Tanizaki exposes the instability of the notion of Western or white identity by linking its appearance or creation at a certain point in time with its disappearance or withdrawal at a later point.

Rather than investigate the strange fluidity of race, which is linked to what Etienne Balibar calls "the necessary polymorphism of racism,"[27] Suzuki attempts to determine the source of the Eurocentrism that pervades *Chijin no ai* through recourse to the various biographical details from Tanizaki's own life. As she writes, "In 1921 Tanizaki moved to a Western-style house in Yokohama, a district inhabited by many foreigners. He sported Western-style clothes, wore shoes even inside his house, started to take English lessons, and learned dancing from a Russian lady. Indeed many of the episodes described in *Chijin no ai* appear to be based on Tanizaki's personal experience."[28] In this turn to authorial biography, Suzuki can be seen to repeat the tradition of Japanese literary scholarship in its most conservative aspects. Despite her desire to contest this tradition and place the study of Japanese literature on more sophisticated theoretical footing, she comes to reinscribe a certain disavowal at work by screening out the racial elements that subtend the notion of East-West identity. In his analysis of this same novel, for example, Donald Keene also focuses on the biographical elements present in the work: "Tanizaki's fascination with his sister-in-law, Seiko, seems to have been much like Jōji's for Naomi; Seiko had un-Japanese features, un-Japanese gaiety, and un-Japanese waywardness."[29] Such details as Tanizaki's habit of wearing shoes in his house or his personal attraction for his sister-in-law might well be of interest to certain readers, but the question remains as to why the invitation to pursue the implications of the destabilization of cultural identity that appear in the pages of *Chijin no ai* is so easily declined.

Symptomatically, traditional literary scholarship comes to reveal its narrowness when a forceful unsettling of accepted notions and values that takes place at the level of the *object* of knowledge is ignored by the *subject* of knowledge for fear that such unsettling might threaten the solidity of certain methodological frameworks already in place and that have been widely sanctioned by the institution. If Suzuki were to heed the message in Tanizaki that identity, whether in its national, cultural, or racial forms, can only be constituted retroactively, then it would no longer be possible to uncritically refer to such entities as "Western writers," "Western histories," "Western sources," or "Western novels," etc. Suzuki employs the notion of retroactive reading as a tool with which to address the conceptual laxity that she still finds within the tradition of Japanese literary research. Yet the use of this tool comes to be restricted to those specific literary phenomena that have already been determined as "Japanese" in this nation's distinction from "the West," for otherwise the entire methodological edifice that structures the research might begin to collapse. As a result, Suzuki is able to quote long passages in which Tanizaki explicitly calls into question the notion of identity as immediate or self-evident without, however, recognizing the implications of what she is quoting. This feature of Suzuki's work produces a noticeable gap between Tanizaki's act of disturbing identity and Suzuki's attempt to restabilize it.

Following Tanizaki, we can more clearly discern the underlying presence of race in the notions of Western and Japanese (or Eastern, Asian) identity. *Chijin no ai* calls attention to the vastly unequal geopolitical relations that have given shape to the modern world. This world is dominated by the West, which insists on regarding itself as white, at the expense of the remainder of the globe, whose lack or deficiency can be seen in its derivative identity as merely non-Western and nonwhite.[30] Yet Tanizaki also shows that the difference between the white West and the nonwhite non-West, as appears concretely in the novel in the figure of the murky or dark Japanese, also comes to inform the difference between the human and the animal. This can be seen in a conversation that takes place between Naomi and her friends at a Ginza dance hall when they glimpse a young Japanese woman named Kikuko who strikes them as gaudy and uncouth. Let us again quote Suzuki quoting Tanizaki:

> "And look at the way she's dressed. I don't mind if somebody tries to look like a Westerner, but she doesn't look like one at all. Pathetic. She's a monkey." . . .
> "A monkey? That's good. She's a monkey, all right."
> "You're a fine one to talk. Didn't you bring her? Really, Ma-chan, she looks just awful and you ought to tell her so. She'll never look Western with that face. It has 'Japan,' 'Pure Japan' written all over it."
> "In other words, a pitiful effort."[31]

In response to this association drawn by Tanizaki between the nonwhite Japanese and the animal, Suzuki provides the following reading:

> Naomi's blunt criticism of the 'monkey's pitiful effort' makes its point, but the ironical effect of the passage derives from Naomi's unwitting revelation of her own coarseness and superficial understanding of things Western. Kikuko is indeed unaware of her comic appearance or the others' ridicule. But the same is true of Naomi. Those who laugh at other people's superficial and comical imitation of Western manners immediately become the object of their own biting criticism.[32]

Suzuki's avoidance of the question of race is entirely consistent here. This avoidance is challenged repeatedly by Tanizaki, but the discomfiting problems he poses regarding the nature of cultural identity are firmly swept aside by an insular mode of literary criticism that never strays too far from analysis of character psychology. Suzuki grasps that Naomi's denigration of Kikuko as a "monkey" is unwittingly a form of self-denigration, but she utterly fails to comprehend the more general message conveyed by Tanizaki that to be associated in the modern world with " 'Japan,' 'Pure Japan' " is effectively to be racialized and animalized as a monkey. From the perspective of Naomi and her friends, to be Western is to be fully human. The development from animality to humanity is one in which man gradually arrives at himself by actualizing the faculty of reason that otherwise exists merely latently or dormantly within him. As Hegel understood, this course of man's self-actualization as the privileged embodiment of reason must be grasped as the very movement of history. As he declares in *The Philosophy of History*, "The History of the World travels from East to West, for Europe is absolutely the end of History, Asia the beginning."[33] In this historical schema, the beginning is marked by an animality whose status derives from the fact that reason, existing merely embryonically, has yet to appear to itself. Humanity only truly announces itself once the animal recognizes itself as animal, and that initial moment of self-consciousness represents an inchoate reason that will teleologically evolve over time into a fully achieved modernity that appears at history's end. In contrast to history's beginning, where man is as yet dark, bestial, and Eastern, the end of history will signal the triumph of an authentic humanity and the overcoming of all vestigial animality.

In concluding our reading of Suzuki's *Narrating the Self*, it bears asking whether subjectivity ever purely instantiates itself as "Eastern" (Japanese) or

"Western" and, if so, what does this mean? It is certainly true that the modern world, in its overlapping levels of mediation, insists that the individual subject be determined according to those social formations with which he or she is seen to be most closely affiliated. Hence the subject can appear without contradiction as, for example, Eastern, Japanese, "colored" (*yūshoku jinshu*), and simian or only imperfectly human because such formations as geopolitical region, nation-state, race, and humanity all exist as mutually mediating. These determinations must be recognized as an intrinsic part of modernity, but one poorly contests the inequality of the modern world by simply identifying with these positions in the aim of challenging the West and its position of global dominance. On the contrary, a rigorous examination of the notion of subjectivity must take as its point of departure the questioning of such forms of identity.

Subjectivity and Binding

Alan Tansman's *The Aesthetics of Japanese Fascism* represents a significant intervention in the study of Japanese fascism. In the field of Japan studies, research of fascism has traditionally been undertaken from the disciplinary perspectives of history and political science. Once it was granted that the concept of fascism was not limited to Europe but could also productively be used as an analytical tool in the context of Japan, a series of valuable works appeared that sought to link the rise of fascism to the global phenomenon of modernity. These works took as their point of departure the insight that fascist elements must be grasped with regard to the nature of modern society itself. With the development of the nation-state system, the unifying ideologies of language, race, and ethnicity worked to create homogenous populations through the violent eradication of difference, thereby providing the conditions in certain areas for fascist formations to thrive. In the case of Japan, much of our understanding of the historical and political dimensions of fascist violence can be credited to recent scholarship. Tansman's contribution lies in helping us conceive of Japanese fascism even more broadly by shedding light on its aesthetic aspects. While the main focus of his book is literature and literary criticism, he also turns his attention to investigating fascist strands in Japanese cinema, music, and folklore.

It is noteworthy, however, that *The Aesthetics of Japanese Fascism* equally commits itself to the task of exploring Japanese fascism from the standpoint of philosophy. Beyond the occasional remarks on individual philosophers, some of which are quite critical, Tansman sets forth arguments regarding the status of such classical concepts as subjectivity, time, language, repetition, and the sublime. These latter discussions can be said to form the theoretical scaffolding that structures and lends substance to the close readings of a variety of thinkers, some of whom, as in the case of Kobayashi Hideo and Yasuda Yojūrō, developed sophisticated and highly elusive arguments that reflect their own engagement with philosophical discourse. In this regard, Tansman's presentation of philosophy is articulated at the distinct, if overlapping, levels of research object and research methodology. In order to evaluate the overall success of his project of determining the nature of Japanese fascist aesthetics, one must first examine the status of the conceptual tools and methods he uses to constitute the particular objects of that aesthetics. As goes without saying, such objects in their objectivity do not exist in any natural or given state. If, from our own vantage point of the present, the historical phenomenon of Japanese fascism remains yet historically recent, then the general consensus as to the validity of this notion or determination of Japanese fascism must be recognized as more recent still. Such a gap between the initial appearance of a phenomenon and its subsequent, retroactive determination *as itself* testifies to the irreducible contingency inherent in any act by which objects come to be constituted. It is imperative that we keep this point in mind in order to better assess the subject's own investment in this epistemological operation.

Early in his discussion, Tansman attempts to uncover the meaning of the concept of fascism by explicitly drawing it back to its etymological root. In this way, fascism reveals itself to be above all a question of binding:

> Japanese fascism shared with its European cognates the desire to bind. Their common yearning is inscribed in the coincidence between the etymology of *fascism* (the 'binding' of the Roman fasces) and the connotations of the Japanese term for binding then being used in propaganda: *musubi*. Rife with state religious implications, *musubi* suggests the harmonizing powers of the gods and, by extension, the binding powers of the state. But if in Italy binding was conceived as explicitly 'political,' in Japan it was decidedly not so. It was 'religious' and therefore beyond all politics and ideology, including fascism itself.[34]

Throughout the book Tansman refers to a number of different historical manifestations of fascism. Beyond the fascist regimes of Germany, Italy, and

Japan, mention is also made of Spanish, French, and Irish fascisms as well as of fascist thinkers in England and the United States. What ties all of the different varieties of state fascism together, however, is the mechanism of binding. Here it is essential that we understand why Tansman attaches so much weight to this process of binding. By translating *fasces* as *musubi*, he seeks to establish the underlying commonality between Japanese fascism and other forms of fascism. This commonality consists in the ideological operation by which individual subjects come to lose their identity in being appropriated for the political ends of the state. Individuals are forced to submit to the brutal violence of fascist forms of government, which strips them of their personal will and autonomy such that their identity comes to be defined strictly in accordance with state dictates. In this manner, fascist ideology takes as its aim the transformation of individual citizens into a collectivity that is bound together as an anonymous, undifferentiated mass where all march in lockstep and speak in one voice. Tansman elaborates this point in his discussion of the 1937 government tract *Kokutai no hongi* [The essence of the national polity]:

> As if aware of its own disavowals and its own textual repressions, *The Essence of the National Polity* repeatedly speaks of a *musubi*—a knot, tie, or bond that fastens things together, like the Roman symbol of authority that Mussolini adopted for this style of fascism, axes bundled together by rods. All the book's rhetorical force has as its goal this "binding" or "fastening," though this is not the mechanical conjoining of independent, equal individuals based in reason and logic. Rather, it is the organic binding that harmonizes the parts within the whole and that, finally, stirs the whole to action.[35]

The term *musubi* thus names the mechanism through which originally discrete entities come to be bound together and assimilated as one. Let us note, however, that two different types of binding are here identified. On the one hand, there exists what Tansman calls "the mechanical conjoining of independent, equal individuals," and this conjoining apparently takes place on the basis of "reason and logic." On the other hand, we find an "organic binding that harmonizes the parts within the whole and that . . . stirs the whole to action." It becomes clear in these lines that the political problem of binding contains at its core the question of subjectivity, and particularly how individual subjectivity comes to be transformed into collective subjectivity.

This partly explains why Tansman is at times forced to adopt a philosophical or conceptual vocabulary: if the historical phenomenon of fascism depended for its emergence on the ideological binding of individual subjects, then one must directly confront and take into account the otherwise abstract notion of subjectivity. Nevertheless, a certain inconsistency in his argument already appears regarding the precise status of binding. Following its etymological root, Tansman wishes to determine fascism as fundamentally a problem of binding. He is soon forced to acknowledge, however, that there exists not one but rather two forms of binding: organic binding and mechanical binding, or what he refers to in this passage as "conjoining."

The concept of binding, in other words, reveals itself to be more general than Tansman initially allows. This generality of binding should come as no surprise, for all political questions in a sense stem from the site of the polis, where a plurality of individuals engages with one another in a mode of relationality that is rife with tensions and antagonisms. There can be no collective existence without the presence of such differential forces, and this difference testifies to the need to create various technologies of binding. In his desire to set forth a critique of fascism, however, Tansman is at pains to separate out a "good" or positive binding from a "bad," negative binding. Although both of these forms function by bridging together individual parts in the service of a whole, the former seems able to avoid the trap of fascism by grounding its operation in "independent, equal individuals." Because these individuals are each autonomous entities, their existence cannot be reduced to mere "organic" parts that do nothing more than "harmonize" with other parts in carrying out the aims of the whole. On the contrary, their very nature as independent requires that any process of collectivization take place in accordance with the principles of "reason and logic." Tansman does not explain the relation between the qualities of independence and equality as characteristic of these nonfascist individuals and those of reason and logic that mark their nonfascist binding or conjoining—it is unclear whether individuals become independent and equal strictly through this linking together or whether, inversely, the linking becomes reasonable and logical on account of the individuals' original status as independent and equal. But what must in any event be recognized is the importance for Tansman of establishing this normative model of intersubjectivity. In order to avoid the dangerous binding of fascism, another type of binding must be sought, one that is marked by the putatively nonfascist qualities of independence, equality, reason, and logic.

The normal, nonfascist subject thus resists the trap of fascism by insisting on his own independence or autonomy as a sovereign individual, immune to the lure of bindings that do not satisfy the demands of reason and logic. This normative conception of subjectivity informs the main argument presented in *The Aesthetics of Japanese Fascism*, but its articulation can in fact be found most explicitly in the opening pages of Tansman's earlier work, *The Writings of Kōda Aya, a Japanese Literary Daughter:*

> The dichotomy [between the social and the personal] is refuted by a basic assumption guiding this study. While individuals are to a great degree shaped by social norms and pressures, a part of each individual resists invasion from the outside and represents a "residual area of inner freedom." The self is never fully exhausted by socially defined roles; and literature, as an act of power, allows individuals to explore the ways they have been socially constructed and to discover an inner, private zone. . . . Such ideas may seem old-fashioned in light of structuralist and post-structuralist attacks on the concept of a self existing outside the framework of society or language. Underlying the premise of this study, however, is the assumption that Kōda Aya brought a creative intelligence to her writing, that she grappled with socially imposed values and structures and attempted to write within social and literary categories without being swallowed up by them. The word *self*, then, designates the writer's imagination as it works to write itself onto the complex social and linguistic map of its time."[36]

Prior to the fascist binding that otherwise compromises its independence, the individual subject here reveals itself to be originally present to itself in its interiority and privacy. Indeed, Tansman effectively demonstrates in these lines how it is possible for individuals to resist entanglement in fascist ideology. While external forces are always at work in shaping the self, nevertheless "a part of each individual resists invasion from the outside and represents a 'residual area of inner freedom.'" Fascism can be rejected, then, because it belongs first and foremost to the external world, safely beyond the "inner, private zone" that marks the self in its sovereign enclosure. In this sense, we can begin to see how *any* binding, fascist or otherwise, can in principle be refused by the individual subject. Doubtless there exist ethically "good" bindings and "bad" bindings, but even prior to this question of content Tansman insists on the subject's ontological difference from all bindings in general. If the subject were originally bound by the world, he could not be determined as independent. This is an important distinction: it is not simply that Tansman asserts that the individual subject *should be* independent from external forces, as this would be tantamount to acknowledging that the subject originally lacks such independence, that he is essentially exposed or vulnerable to all bindings—which can thus no longer be determined as existing purely outside of himself. On the contrary, the claim is a much more fundamental (if traditional, metaphysical) one. In Tansman's account, to be an individual subject is to be an entity that *is* or *exists* as ultimately independent from the binding forces of the outside world.

In *The Aesthetics of Japanese Fascism*, the individual's rejection of fascism takes place in the first instance through his insistence on his own proper individuality. He recognizes himself as different from other individuals because no one else can possess that "residual area of inner freedom," that "inner, private zone" that belongs to him alone. For Tansman, the attack against fascism finds its main support in the force of subjectivism. Whatever other evils it may contain, fascism essentially poses itself as a threat to the integrity of the individual subject. Here it is worthwhile recalling that the notion of "individual" signifies an indivisibility; it designates the minimal unit that in its identity cannot be split or rendered from itself without thereby losing that identity. Binding operates by drawing the individual self outside of itself and attaching it to another. It is this exposure to the difference of the nonself that robs the individual of his or her integrity and as-suchness. Fascism seeks to negate individual identity in order to reconstitute it in the form of collective identity, and Tansman responds to this threat by calling for the return of identity to the sphere of the individual subject.

The Aesthetics of Japanese Fascism can be read above all as a defense of individual subjectivity against the collective subjectivity associated with fascism. Collective existence is made possible through an ideological binding of individuals, whereas these individuals themselves are determined to exist prior to all binding and ideology. So it is that Tansman condemns Japanese "writers and intellectuals [who] became entranced by new myths that had the power to seem not to be myths and by beautiful objects into which one might submerge one's subjectivity and thereby heal the fracture between self and the world."[37] This "fracture between self and the world" is assumed to be self-evident; it represents the original state that Japanese fascists attempt to disavow in their desire to expunge individual identity through attachment to forces that exist externally, beyond the proper realm of the self. In this context, the individual must be determined as a subject because he exists in a manner that is opposed to the world, which thereby comes to be reduced to the status of object. In this dualist ontology, the indivisibility of individuals appears at an ultimate remove from the world from which they are divided. This division, or "fracturing," functions as the condition for all relations between self and world to take place, but this relationality can at no time jeopardize the undivided nature of the individual himself.

If fascism made use of the technology of binding in order to negate individual subjectivity and reconstitute it in the form of collective subjectivity, as Tansman argues, then Japanese fascism must be seen as especially guilty of this offense because of its historical antagonism with the West. As he writes in the case of Japan:

> Intellectuals argued for, and creative artists made attractive, the abandonment of individuality—an abstract modern notion, seen as perniciously Western, festering at the core of the crisis—and searched for an identity grounded in native culture and life, mediated through absolute identification with "the people" (*minzoku*) and the state. The individual came to be viewed not only as selfish but also as an inadequate source of meaning, while "the people" and the state became idealized as sources of authentic action and identity.[38]

In this account, the emergence of Japanese fascism and its emphasis on collective identity is attributed in part to a certain sense of *ressentiment* harbored by Japanese intellectuals against Western culture. Given their opposition to the West, any privileging of the value of individuality must be rejected as foreign and countered by a return to the putatively more traditional Japanese notion of collectivism. Tansman shows himself to be quite critical of this response, but nowhere does he challenge the terms that frame this confrontation. That is to say, the simple dichotomy between individuality and collectivity comes to be remarked or repeated, and with it of course the binary between Japan and "the West." If Japanese intellectuals sought to overcome Western modernity and its emphasis on the individual through recourse to a nativist conception of a communal people, then Tansman's project consists in overcoming that overcoming, or reactively negating that negation, by appealing to the enduring truth of the individual. In this regard, the association of the people with the concept of mediation as expressed in the foregoing passage ("an identity . . . mediated through absolute identification with 'the people' (*minzoku*) and the state") is by no means coincidental. Here the mediated quality of collective existence is implicitly contrasted with the putative immediacy of the individual. The underlying argument is that Western modernity must be credited with recognizing the rightful priority and centrality of the individual but that, due to historical antagonisms and their own cultural *ressentiment*, the Japanese betrayed this legacy by seeking to negate the individual in the form of collectivism.

This attitude can be seen quite clearly in the explanation Tansman provides concerning the emergence among Japanese intellectuals of this notion of collectivism. This notion was a belated one, entirely dependent on the very concept of the individual that it sought to negate. In this narrative, modern Japanese culture was unilaterally bound to the West, and its various ideological products must be seen in that light. However, nowhere in this narrative does one find an analogous historicization of the so-called Western concept of individuality. On the contrary, such historicization is avoided because the primacy of the individual is accepted as natural. As we have seen, Tansman insists on the centrality of the individual self, that "inner, private zone" that above all serves to anchor one's identity in an otherwise contingent world. All ties or binding to this world, fascist or otherwise, must therefore be condemned as derivative and unnatural. Fascism may be regarded as a political evil for any number of reasons, but one of its greatest sins against civilization lies in its attempt to displace the individual. Following this logic, the defeat of Japanese fascism may be regarded in global terms as the restoration of the individual to its rightful place, but here Tansman's discourse encounters another inconsistency. If Japanese fascism in fact betrayed the legacy of "Western" modernity by seeking to replace the individual with the collective, then how can one account for the historical fact that this legacy was already betrayed from "within" by the fascism that developed in "the West" itself?

Such questioning must be rigorously avoided in order to preserve the pure oppositionality that is held to exist between the geopolitical entities of "the West" and Japan as well as between a normative conception of individuality and the latently fascist quality of collectivism. Tansman's commitment to such dualism can be found throughout the pages of *The Aesthetics of Japanese Fascism*. This framework transcends any particular object of analysis and must instead be recognized as a guiding methodological feature of the work. One characteristic example of this can be seen in the distinction he draws between German fascism and Japanese fascism:

> The German aesthetic solution to fallenness was what Susan Sontag called the "fascinating fascism" of sublime grandeur, as evoked, for example, in the films of Leni Riefenstahl. In contrast,

> the readings in this book show that the aesthetics of Japanese fascism manifest a melancholy tonality. Stamped by popular Buddhist sensibility, this . . . pervasive melancholy is also often troped by writers (and filmmakers) as feminine. . . . We will see that the native content many Japanese called on was the traditionally sanctioned aesthetics of the pathos of melancholy loss, revolving around the affective pull of a feminine figure.[39]

Here the otherwise formal or abstract opposition between Japan and "the West" is filled in with the content of their mutual cultural differences. Such difference is grounded upon the presence of the unit, which is ultimately self-identical. Just as the individual human being constitutes a unity or selfsame identity that shields it from the contingency of the outside world—failing which it could no longer exist as itself—so too do individual cultural entities adhere to precisely this same logic. Once again, individuality names an indivisibility, and it is this ultimately undivided quality, its as-suchness, that serves to distinguish the particular unit from all others. In the historically specific context of fascism, Tansman comes to determine the German model as male ("This is in sharp contrast to Klaus Theweleit's discussion of the German fascist aesthetic, which reveals a cult of masculinity and misogyny"),[40] endowed with "sublime grandeur," and presumably Christian, whereas the Japanese fascist aesthetic is described as female, informed by a "pervasive melancholy tonality," and Buddhist. All the readings of Japanese texts, whether literary, cinematic, philosophical, musical, etc., are governed by the methodological *decision* Tansman makes at the outset of his work that these materials, whatever their generic differences, must be treated as both the logical opposite of German texts and as uniquely expressive of the female, Buddhist, melancholic essence of what he calls the "distinctively Japanese cultural imagination."[41]

Yet the simplistic dualism that informs this work appears in its most concentrated form with regard to the question of subjectivity. Here we begin to understand why the concept of binding must be identified as politically evil, for given the assumption that self and world exist in a strictly antithetical or oppositional relation, any connection (tying, binding, etc.) between them risks disturbing the self-identity of each. In order to problematize this dualist framework, I believe, we must attempt to think the concept of binding or relationality as ontologically *prior* to the constitution of anything as itself. From this perspective, neither the subject nor the various objects of the world can ever purely give or present themselves as such. Self-identity is necessarily mediated because it takes place belatedly, only *after* the "subject" or "object" in question has been exposed to that which is irreducibly other than themselves. Now there can be no argument concerning the grave dangers of fascist collectivism, but the binding that draws the individual subject away from itself toward something beyond it must be recognized as originary—that is to say, such binding exists even before the individual self constitutes itself as itself. Tansman's commitment to a dualist ontology takes as its point of departure the assumption that the self must be initially posited as self-identical: only because the self is *first* itself can it *then* be drawn into binding relations with the world. Here, it should be noted, the resulting opposition between selfsame interiority and differential exteriority illustrates through exactly the same logic both the sovereign domain of the individual subject and the pure Japaneseness of Japan—but this is, of course, merely to show that culturalism remains essentially a subjectivism.

In contrast to this dualism, a concept of originary binding testifies to a certain structural corruption or lack of purity at the very heart of the self. For Tansman, binding is that which violates the self's primal integrity, and he can therefore only conceive of it in terms of the violence of fascism. Far from being inherently fascist, however, the notion of binding demonstrates that the self exists as essentially exposed to an alterity that it cannot master and over which it ultimately has no control. Rather than being limited to the historical phenomenon of fascism, such alterity instead names the differential force of the world in general. It is precisely this alterity in its inextricable binding of the self to the world that Freud tried to think in his major work "Beyond the Pleasure Principle," as when he declares that "binding [*Bindung*] is a preparatory act which introduces and assures the dominance of the pleasure principle."[42] Freud's text was published in 1920, which makes it contemporary not only with elements of German fascism but also with the Japanese fascism whose origins Tansman seeks in this same decade. Must we then, following Tansman's suggestion, suspect Freud and his notion of binding as somehow complicit with fascism? Or is it rather the case that binding is a *general* concept that seeks to account for the original lack of self-identity and so radical openness to the world and its alterity?

In the opening decades of the twentieth century, certain philosophers crucially recognized the need to go beyond the traditional subject-object opposition and think this originary exposure of the self. Most famously, Heidegger set forth the notion of "Being-towards-death" in order to show that man's (*Dasein*'s) existence, far from being that of a self-grounding subject or substratum, was above all a matter of finitude. As he writes in *Being and Time*, it is in *Dasein*'s essential mortality that it becomes "[f]ree for its ownmost possibilities, which are determined by the *end* and so are understood as *finite* [*endliche*]."⁴³ Given the serious threat that such a conception poses to the idea of a stable, self-present identity, however, it is hardly surprising that Tansman dismisses Heidegger out of hand. Although he shows little evidence of having actually read the Heideggerian text (we are informed in a footnote that his interpretation of Heidegger in fact derives from George Steiner), his judgment of Heidegger could not be more withering: "Heidegger's urgent desire to locate authenticity in a language that eschewed ratiocination and logical argumentation and proceeded, instead, through intense etymological probing, hypnotic repetitions, cadences, and tautologies in order to approximate that original state of rapture and astonishment in which poet and god were one."⁴⁴ Similar treatment is reserved for the Kyoto School philosopher Nishida Kitarō. Like Heidegger, Nishida revealed that man does not exist as a disembodied subject whose consciousness and faculty of reason allow him to stand apart from the world. On the contrary, man is in the first instance materially bound to the world through what Nishida called "pure experience" (*junsui keiken*): "Over time I came to realize that it is not that experience exists because there is an individual (*kojin*), but that an individual exists because there is experience."⁴⁵ These words appear in Nishida's most well-known work, *Zen no kenkyū* (1911). Despite Tansman's belief that this is a book about Zen Buddhism (he translates this work's title as "Research on zen" rather than "An inquiry into the good") and despite his reliance on a single essay by Ieaki Kenichi that serves to replace any actual engagement with Nishida, the philosopher is nevertheless condemned for his critique of the notion of individual will, as this apparently helped pave the path to fascist collectivism: "Nishida, whose goal of 'pure experience' and the development of 'absolute will' through the mediation of the 'act' promises a 'place' where 'even free will disappears.'"⁴⁶

Nishida and, above all, Heidegger may certainly be attacked for their complicity with fascist ideology, but such criticisms cannot take refuge behind a simple and theoretically naïve return to the sanctity of the individual. Nevertheless, one of the astonishing features of *The Aesthetics of Japanese Fascism* is its argument that all attempts to dismantle subjectivity, no matter how philosophically sophisticated, may be soundly rebutted by the notion of the individual self as "an inner, private zone." This phrase appears in Tansman's reading of Kōda Aya, but the valuation of privacy as a site of interiority can be seen to centrally inform his reading of Japanese aesthetic fascist texts as well. For example, in response to the question of how one might resist fascism, Tansman effectively recommends that one keep a private diary: "The very existence of private diaries suggests the persistence of an interiority never fully appropriated by government authorities, one that may not have recognized the proprietary summons of the state and that may have thus managed to slip through—or resist—the net of ideology."[47] Here, the extremely complex operation of ideology, as Althusser showed, appearing in the very formation of the individual subject as such (and hence eludes identification on the basis of any duality between inside and outside), is dealt with by Tansman through the positing of a pure domain of "interiority" that lies beyond the reach of the state. Because it reveals the individual in his or her most natural or original condition, privacy is marked as a site of immediacy. This holds true even for the language uttered by the private individual: "Such words, written in private moments, have a *directness* altogether lacking in the highly troped language of professional writers."[48] Finally, following the rigid binarism that governs the various readings of "fascist" texts, the notion of the private is presented as a simple opposition to the public. "Another form of resistance, that of refusing to write in the public sphere in order to safeguard the privacy of the imagination."[49]

The private realm must be "safeguarded" in order to ensure the integrity of the individual remains intact. Any form of alterity that threatens the identity of this realm must therefore be violently excluded. If Tansman, following the critic Isoda Kōichi, determines one of the aims of fascism to be the attainment of a "state of repose (*ansoku jōtai*)," that is, "a calm, cocooning respite from modern life,"[50] then it is hard to see how the logic of his argument avoids repeating this same fascist trap. Of course, Tansman intends to formulate a critique of fascism, but his consistent appeal to a notion of subjectivism reveals an underlying commonality with the fascist project *as defined by his own terms*. Early in *The Aesthetics of Japanese Fascism*, for example, we are told that fascism "provided the possibility for an experience of immediacy and unity . . . by promoting the myth of a nation unified by the natural bonds of its blood and spirit."[51] Thus fascism is determined on the basis of a notion of collective subjectivity that violently eradicates difference in its aim to create an "experience of immediacy and unity." What Tansman fails to recognize is that both collective subjectivity and individual subjectivity are necessarily grounded on the concept of the subject, and that this subject inaugurates and maintains itself in its identity by eliminating that which is determined to be other to itself. In wishing to preserve the unique oneness of an *individual human being* against the anonymizing effects of fascist collectivism, Tansman ignores how this same collectivity in turn forms an *individual national culture*. In each case, the formation of the individual as an ultimately undivided and self-present unit—which is the condition for any "experience of immediacy and unity"—takes place through the violent reduction of alterity.

Because the individual is never fully equal or consonant with itself, relationality with the world can begin to take place. Tansman's desire to safeguard "an inner, private zone"—where the individual self can exist purely as itself in, for example, its act of keeping diaries, in issuing language that "directly" reflects itself in its original identity—implies in its logic that the political evil he calls "fascism" initially emerges in the loss or violation of this realm. *The Aesthetics of Japanese Fascism* surveys various instances in which individual identity comes to suffer loss. In some cases, Japanese intellectuals are condemned for their putative desire to sacrifice that identity in "merging" with state collectivism, whereas in other instances they are denounced for "merging" with other individuals as well as with aesthetic or everyday objects. (A typical example: "The ecstatic moment when individuals merge through violence at the end of *Snow Country* uncomfortably resembles the orgiastic vision of war that the Japanese state offered its citizens from the 1930s through the end of the war in 1945.")[52] Even prior to reaching its destination in its fusion with the state, other individuals, or various objects, however, the self must first transgress the border that marks its own proper interiority and separates it from the outside. If, following Tansman's argument, "fascism" is what takes place upon the individual's *arrival* at that which is other than itself, then the very moment of *departure* from that border already signals the beginning of "fascism." Again, we see here how the desire to "safeguard" borders can easily lead to an espousal of the same type of violence one otherwise wishes to criticize.

In simple mathematic terms, an individual's relation with another individual or thing can never purely be formulated as $1 + 1 = 2$. If an individual were strictly "independent" or self-present, no relationality could ever take place at all. In this regard, the paradoxical condition for an individual's worldly or material existence is that he or she *not* be an individual, if we are to understand this term in its "original" sense as a unit that in its identity remains absolutely undivided from itself. The 1 with which Tansman wishes to equate the individual is both *less than* and *more than* 1: it is less than 1 because it can never be purely constituted as itself, but it is at the same time (and precisely for the same reason) more than 1, since the alterity or difference that affects it and irrevocably draws it outside of itself takes place most originally from the moment of its appearance. Certain intellectuals that Tansman discusses in his book sought to explore this primal absence of identity, as for example the literary critics Kobayashi Hideo and Yasuda Yojūrō. Predictably, however, their efforts come to be harshly denounced as complicit with fascist ideology. As Tansman asserts with regard to Kobayashi's questioning of the primacy of the self, "It may be that Kobayashi's debunking of the self as a source of conscious action and reflection was so thorough that it disinclined him to make ethical judgments about the actions of the self. It should be clear by now that this disinclination is of a piece with his aesthetic attitudes."[53] Much the same impatience can be seen with regard to Yasuda's project of challenging the purity of binary logic: "The fascist moments, those instances in Yasuda's writing that blur distinctions between art and life and between subject and object, contributed to a poetics of sorrow that extolled the virtues of frailty and defeat, while colluding with a fascist ideology of violence and coercion."[54]

In order to avoid any possible misunderstanding, let me stress that I am *not* arguing that Kobayashi and Yasuda should be seen as in any way innocent of collusion with Japanese fascist politics. There can be no question that each sought to serve the wartime project of the Japanese state.[55] However, any castigation of the attempt to "blur distinctions between subject and object" as inherently a "fascist moment" is to reveal an inability to understand either philosophy or fascism itself. The dismantling of the traditional subject-object dichotomy, and with it a critique of the power of consciousness and reflection as tools used by the epistemological subject to reduce the material alterity of the world, appear in the thought of some of the most important philosophers and writers in the modern era. From Tansman's perspective, however, such discourse must be seen as dangerous insofar as it threatens the centrality of the individual and casts doubt on the capacity of identity to guarantee rootedness and stability. As he declares regarding Kobayashi, "Any way out of the morass of Kobayashi's prose diminishes his own aesthetic goal, by bringing lucidity where he wanted opacity, logic where he wanted feeling, and abstraction where he wanted concreteness. The clearest way out of the traps Kobayashi set for the rational reader is to understand that his writing is a parody of the work of exegetical analysis."[56] Here the elusiveness of Kobayashi's thought is reduced to the simple duality of an either/or structure: the ideas he presents must be treated in terms of *either* lucidity, logic, and abstraction *or* opacity, feeling, and concreteness. Putatively lacking any real coherence, these ideas thus do not merit the name of "analysis" but must instead be judged a mere parody thereof. If

Tansman regards Kobayashi's attack on binary logic as a form of violence, then he responds by exercising a similar violence in protecting this logic, thereby returning Kobayashi's thought to the same sterile oppositionality from which he sought to escape.

If no type of individual entity, whether, for example, human or national-cultural, ever purely coincides with itself in its immediacy, then how is one to explain the widespread perception of individual identity in political life? In the period Tansman surveys—which stretches from the 1920s, when Japanese aesthetic fascism is said to originate with the short stories of Akutagawa Ryūnosuke, to the 1980s, when it finally disappears with the last works of the singer Misora Hibari and the novelist Nakagami Kenji—wars are, after all, fought by individual nations, individual citizens are mobilized to join the war effort, and a range of individual discourses grounded in the nation-state (as, for example, Japanese literature and Japanese philosophy) develops and comes to be reinforced. Here we encounter the pivotal question of language. In order for any individual entity to be identified as itself, a name must be used through which that act of identification can take place. Given that this name can never be absolutely proper to the entity itself (e.g., other entities might possess the same name or the name itself might vary depending upon context), however, the act of identification can always suffer disturbance. Linguistic identification occurs necessarily *after* the appearance of the individual entity to be identified, which is to say that any strict simultaneity between the individual and its own identity must be recognized as impossible. Indeed, it is only because of the temporal gap opened up between an individual's appearance and its retrospective attribution of identity that it can ever be determined as itself at all. What this reveals, however, is that every act of identification is irreducibly contingent: no referentiality between a linguistic mark and an individual entity can be fixed or guaranteed in advance.

I want to emphasize this temporal dimension of identification in order to call attention to the politicality that inheres in every linguistic act. Individual identity comes to be produced strictly as a delayed effect. In certain contexts, of course, such identification is necessary in helping us acquire a more comprehensive knowledge of the past, as for example when we refer to the "Japanese nation-state" or the "Japanese invasion of China." Yet this same process can always be used for ideological ends, as when the Japanese state together with conservative intellectuals seek to inculcate a heightened sense of Japaneseness among its citizens, thereby in effect remarking or reminding them, "You are Japanese!" Precisely because individual identity is never immediately given, it must be constantly remarked, and this remarking is directed to a reality that, no matter how minimally, is already past. Such retroactive identification may serve either "fascist" or progressive political ends, but no structure of referentiality can ever be exempt from this temporal gap.

It thus seems curious that Tansman takes Yasuda and Kobayashi to task for their skepticism concerning the pure referentiality of language. As he writes, "Yasuda rejected the clear referentiality of literature because to him the goal of literature was to express what cannot be explained."[57] No explanation is offered as to why literary referentiality must be "clear," but the reasoning behind this criticism comes to emerge in the parallel attack on Kobayashi. For Tansman, Kobayashi is

> an author who no longer believes that language functions properly, who believes that it no longer speaks concretely of real things. . . . The problem for Kobayashi, as for Yasuda, was not that language had become unclear but that in becoming too clear it had lost its texture and its ability to render the density of objects. This was an illness that needed a cure. The cure was to be found in the attenuation of the referential function of language and its renewal through paradox, obscurity, and the texture of musical rhythms.[58]

These writers must be condemned because they appear to distort what is otherwise the proper capacity of language to reflect the external world. Language, if it is to "function properly," must transparently refer back to the objects it names without the obstacles of "paradox," "obscurity," and "texture." As we saw previously in Tansman's commitment to a normative model of intersubjectivity, which operates on the basis of "reason and logic," here too language comes to be submitted to a kind of litmus test that measures its susceptibility to appropriation by fascist aesthetics. In this account, "fascist" language is that which obfuscates its relation to the objects it represents, thereby creating confusion and a lack of epistemological certitude. For Tansman, it is precisely this distortion of referentiality, communication,[59] and logic that is symptomatic of fascist ideology. Now there can be no argument that such mystification is to be found in various instances of fascist discourse. But the disruption of referentiality can be seen to haunt *all* discourse—political, aesthetic, or otherwise. The disturbance of referentiality that Tansman associates with fascist ideology is in no way limited to this latter; on the contrary, as we indicated above, it is a general feature of language itself.

The gap that separates an individual entity from the linguistic marker that identifies it as itself opens the possibility for all ideological abuses and manipulations. At the same time, however, we must recognize that this gap functions as the condition for any linguistic element to signify as such. Tansman wishes, *through language*, to foreclose the possibility of all "fascist" appropriations of language, but the absolute reduction of language to the thing that it names would result in the annihilation of language itself. Were language to "function properly" by *merging* with its represented object, then not only fascist discourse but also Tansman's own discourse would become impossible. Whatever violence Kobayashi and Yasuda may have perpetrated in their support of the Japanese state, the desire to eliminate all disturbances so as to attain an ideal referential transparency represents a greater level of violence by far.

Given that no act of language is ever neutral, that every utterance is on the contrary informed by a variety of political stakes, how are we then to conceive of Tansman's own references to the entity "Japan"? In order to answer this question, let us recall that Tansman wishes to determine fascism on the basis of the subordination of individual subjectivity (privacy, interiority) to collective subjectivity. As we have argued, such distinction between individual and collective subjectivity overlooks the common ground of subjective identity upon which each stand. If the transformation from the individual to the collective represents a potential threat to the integrity of the individual—precisely by drawing it outside of itself through the operation of binding—then we have suggested that this threat takes place most originally from the moment an individual comes into being, that is to say, even prior to its constitution as itself. The "residual area of inner freedom" that Tansman wishes to preserve from all history, materiality, and alterity reveals itself in our reading to be already bound to exteriority in general. This exteriority divides the putative indivisibility of the individual from itself. Such exposure to the world does not, contra Tansman, directly result in "fascism." Rather, it can be far more fruitfully conceived in terms of what Derrida called *mes chances*, which signifies both the futural "chances" that someone or something might have and the possibility of "cruelty" (*méchance*) that can never be entirely reduced from that chance of futurity.[60]

At one point in *The Aesthetics of Japanese Fascism*, Tansman attacks what he calls Yasuda's "glorification of native cultural forms," quoting Yasuda as follows: "I realized that the notion that Japan was to become great through

Germany was completely wrong. Germany is a country that exists after Goethe. Japan has a culture over a thousand years old."[61] At first glance, the critical aim here appears to be evident: in his desire to posit a site of pure Japaneseness over the past millennium, Yasuda disregards the historical break of modernity and the formation of the nation-state system, thereby violently merging innumerable individuals as mere parts within the organicity of this diachronic whole. In fact, however, Tansman repeats Yasuda's nativist glorification in strikingly similar terms. When writing on Akutagawa, for example, Tansman states that Yasuda "is as intimate with Rodin, Gauguin, Dante, and Ambrose Bierce as he is with the prose (*The Tale of Genji*) or poetry (*Man'yōshū*) of *his own tradition*."[62] Given that the Man'yōshū was compiled over a thousand years ago, it is worth asking whether the entity "Japan" could have existed at that time and also how it was able to survive identically as itself throughout the differential course of its "own tradition." This is in no way an isolated example. Elsewhere, Tansman describes Ki no Tsurayuki (872–945) as "the father of Japanese lyric poetry."[63] In his reading of Kōda Aya, moreover, pages are devoted to binding Aya's works to such classical texts as the *Kojiki* (712), *Tale of Genji* (early eleventh century), *Hōjōki* (1212), and *Tsurezuregusa* (1332). In this way, the "individuality" of all of these disparate writers and texts comes to be violently subsumed under the collective heading of "Japanese literature." Committed to the project of national culturalism, however—much like Kobayashi and Yasuda as well as many other figures denounced as "fascist"—Tansman finds such subsumption to be acceptable, mere collateral damage in the task of preserving the integrity of "Japan" in one of its aesthetic dimensions.

Subjectivity and Alterity

In *Translating Mount Fuji: Modern Japanese Fiction and the Ethics of Identity*, Dennis Washburn sets out to expand upon the insights regarding the specifically modern nature of Japanese literary texts first presented a dozen years earlier in his monograph, *The Dilemma of the Modern in Japanese Fiction*. Whereas this latter work sought to identify the central challenge posed to Japanese writers as that of arriving at a cultural synthesis between Japan and the West in order to secure for themselves the privileged status of modern, the former determines the phenomenon of Japanese modernity in terms of the historical transition from communal values that exist externally to the individual to those values actively created by the individual himself, on the basis of reason and moral intuition, in the realm of his subjective interiority. For Washburn, it is Western modernity that is responsible for formulating a concept of individual autonomy in which skepticism and the demand for personal verification make it possible to finally question the received, otherwise unexamined values of the cultural tradition. Yet this development of autonomy threatens to undermine the dominant beliefs and mores of the larger culture to which the individual belongs, exposing these values to a dangerous relativism. The culture responds to this threat by reinforcing the hold of a sense of collective authenticity, in effect reminding the individual that his or her identity derives most fundamentally from their status as a member of the overall community. As Washburn argues, it is this underlying tension between individual autonomy and collective authenticity that animates many of the most significant texts in modern Japanese literature. Through a series of close readings of such canonical writers as, for example, Natsume Sōseki, Mori Ōgai, Yokomitsu Riichi, Ōoka Shōhei, and Mishima Yukio, Washburn demonstrates that the conflict between the Western notion of subjective autonomy and the traditional Japanese demand for cultural authenticity must be grasped as a defining characteristic of Japanese modernity.

In his two studies on modern Japanese literature, Washburn describes his own methodological approach as one that remains independent of both literary theory and the critique of modernization theory. His reservations concerning the attack on modernization theory are expressed in the very final lines of *The Dilemma of the Modern in Japanese Fiction*:

> If it is misleading to describe Japanese literature in terms of standards that reflect Western notions of modernity, then it is equally misleading to see the problem that Meiji writers faced in defining a modern Japanese identity as simply one of trying to break free of the cultural hegemony of the West. Although the critique, or deconstruction, of modernization theory in the West seeks to free our readings of Japanese (or of any other non-Western) narratives from culturally bound assumptions in order to return us to a supposedly native reading of the Japanese tradition, in fact such a critique is itself a nativism that binds us ever more tightly to our own assumptions. The only means to break though these cultural boundaries, I believe, is an exhaustive survey of the ways in which individual authors construct a modern Japanese identity through narrative. This book is a step toward achieving that end.[64]

In *Translating Mount Fuji*, Washburn states his disagreement with the general premises and claims of literary theory in the book's opening pages:

> The suspicion that there may be no persuasive response to these questions arises from the challenge to literary studies presented by the prestige of the sciences as a knowledge-producing institution. The success of the sciences in explaining the world is seen to derive from its rigorous methodologies and its stress on observable and testable outcomes. Consequently, a near obsession with developing "literary theory" has come to dominate contemporary conceptions of reading. The very term "literary theory" strikes me as a marvelous curiosity. Theory denotes knowledge of the principles and methodologies of a discipline, which is how it is used in the phrase "literary theory," but the word also denotes a principle or set of hypotheses verified or at least potentially verifiable by their taxonomic rigor and predictive capability. The epistemological claims of the word theory seem at best inapplicable and at worst irrelevant to the knowledge that may be achieved by professing literature.[65]

I quote these passages at length in order to better assess the particular nature of Washburn's project. He determines this project in opposition to two contemporary trends that he regards negatively as promoting a false or inaccurate understanding of literary texts in the wider field of Japan studies. Washburn frames his work in terms of neither literary theory nor the critique of modernization theory. Here I have no intention of simply showing that, contra Washburn, a commitment to literary theory and an active contestation of modernization theory are in fact the most productive ways of engaging with Japanese literary texts. Rather, what interests me is the specific manner in which Washburn appears to grasp these two intellectual trends. In both cases, he is intent on establishing the parameters of knowledge that can legitimately be acquired. The critique of modernization theory fails, Washburn declares, because its denunciation of a *Western* approach to understanding Japanese modernity merely substitutes a *native Japanese* approach. It should be emphasized that Washburn's aim is not to defend modernization theory from its critics. On the contrary, he acknowledges the Western bias inherent in the attempt to survey, and indeed in certain cases actively shape, Japanese modernization according to the models of western Europe and the United States. Yet vigilance must be exercised in this critique lest one merely reverse the terms of the debate and propose instead that Japanese modernization be grasped on a purely Japanese basis in order to avoid the trap of Eurocentrism.

Washburn returns to this issue in *Translating Mount Fuji* in the context of a discussion of the notion of bildungsroman. Bildungsroman, he reminds the reader, is a specifically German—that is to say, Western—term, and the difficulty that arises concerns the applicability of this term or concept to a Japanese—that is to say, non-Western—text. Or as Washburn puts it in his reading of Mori Ōgai's *Seinen* (Youth, 1910), "*Seinen* is also a hybrid narrative, a Japanese *Bildungsroman* that transposes a German narrative model onto native conventions for representing the ideal of manly virtue."[66] He describes the quandary of this cultural transposition as follows: "Because it may be misleading to apply Western critical terminology to a work from a non-Western tradition, it is important to consider the issue of how Western expectations and critical terminologies are brought to bear on readings of Japanese fiction. . . . The cultural specificity of the values that gave rise to and found expression in the bildungsroman may make it appear inappropriate, at first sight, to apply the term to works in the Japanese tradition. Yet certain qualities of this narrative form seem relevant to developments in modern Japanese fiction, especially the growing crisis of representation of real identities that accompanied the Meiji cultural synthesis."[67]

For Washburn, it is essential that one treat this issue of cultural difference between the West and non-West with the utmost sensitivity. Here we can understand more clearly the reason for his disagreement with the critique of modernization theory. Whereas, in his view, the critique exercises a simple reversal and thus displaces the problem of Eurocentrism to that of Japanese nativism, his approach sets forth a distinct notion of hybridity that allows one to understand modern Japanese cultural products as a commingling or coexistence of *both* Japanese *and* Western elements. Neither modernization theory nor its critique appears to grasp the complex cultural and historical forces at work in modern Japanese texts that render impossible any pure presentation of identity. What Washburn refers to in these lines as the "Meiji cultural synthesis" is in fact characteristic of Japanese modernity as a whole, and therefore any analysis of this phenomenon must resist an outmoded appeal to simple or immediate identity in order to embrace a properly *synthetic* form of identity, one in which any particular cultural entity must be recognized as a composite of diverse, hybrid elements. In dialectical terms, if modernization theory in its aim to judge Japanese modernity according to Western standards must be seen as an initial thesis, then its critique, in its insistence that that modernity can only be measured by native Japanese standards, appears as an antithesis and thus a negation of that opening position; Washburn's approach is to go beyond both these mutually exclusive standpoints by developing a notion of cultural hybridity or synthesis that incorporates both Western and Japanese elements without, however, being reducible to either. Viewed in the context of literature, this complexity of cultural difference explains Washburn's hesitation in directly applying the Western notion of bildungsroman to a Japanese or non-Western text such as Ōgai's *Seinen*. Wishing to avoid the complementary traps of Eurocentrism (which would uncritically seek to understand Ōgai purely on the basis of Western methods) and Japanese nativism (which would reject this Eurocentric approach and instead read Ōgai strictly with the tools developed by the Japanese tradition), Washburn argues that the presence of certain underlying commonalities or "relevancies" between Germany and Japan ultimately legitimate this manner of cross-cultural reading.

At first glance, Washburn's attack against what he calls the recent "near obsession" with literary theory appears curious, given that he includes in his own work references to many of the same thinkers and literary theorists (e.g., Paul de Man, Roland Barthes, Walter Benjamin, Michel Foucault, Homi Bhabha, Gerard Genette, Martin Jay, Barbara Johnson, and Paul Ricoeur, among others) that are typically found in studies that draw openly upon the resources of literary theory. If Washburn is able to engage with literary theory in a nonobsessive manner, it is because he understands and respects the epistemological limits of literary analysis. In terms that recall the traditional division between scientific and cultural knowledge in neo-Kantianism, Washburn contends that literary scholarship has remained excessively in thrall to the sciences, and that, envious of their success in unlocking the secrets of the natural world in empirically verifiable ways, this scholarship has developed and granted undue privilege to the principles of literary theory as a means of comprehending literary phenomena with greater rigor. However, as Washburn argues, the "epistemological claims of the word theory seem at best inapplicable and at worst irrelevant to the knowledge that may be achieved by professing literature." Siding firmly with the humanities (cultural knowledge) in its opposition to the sciences, he appeals to the reader that literary texts cannot be reduced to "a principle or set of hypotheses verified or at least potentially verifiable by their taxonomic rigor and predictive capability," as seems to be implied by the word or concept of theory. The inherent complexity of literature, in other words, resists subsumption within any general or abstract theory whose very generality and abstraction threaten to rob these texts of their singular difference and unpredictability.

It is at this point that we can detect a possible area of convergence between Washburn's contestation of literary theory and his denunciation of the critique of modernization theory. For Washburn, let us recall, a heightened cultural sensitivity is required in order to determine the elusive ways in which Western and native Japanese elements come to be inextricably linked in the texts of modern Japanese literature. Hybridity, which he identifies in *Translating Mount Fuji* as nothing less than "the central characteristic of modern Japanese culture,"[68] demands that one rethink the concept of Japanese cultural identity beyond the more or less homogeneous confines of Japanese tradition without, however, thereby falling prey to Eurocentric biases that would otherwise dismiss or minimize the importance of these native elements. For Japan to be truly recognized as modern, Washburn suggests, is ultimately to abandon any lingering nostalgia for cultural purity and instead embrace the unique historical synthesis created by many years of Western influence. In this regard, the notions of Japan and the West may be seen to *function* in a manner akin to that which Washburn ascribes to the notion of theory, for in each case it is a question of effacing, through indiscriminate use of a master concept or narrative, the historical and cultural singularity of modern Japan. By subsuming, for example, the innumerably diverse instances of modern Japanese literature under a single master signifier—"Japan," "the West" or even, more abstractly, "theory"—that which exists originally beyond the epistemological limits of "taxonomic rigor and predictive capability" comes to be sacrificed. Literary phenomena are of an entirely different order from that of the natural world known to science, for in their singular unpredictability and difference they resist being mastered by universal concepts. Thus the need for a hybrid method that, suspicious of the reductionism inherent in various theoretical approaches (modernization theory, antimodernization theory, literary theory), remains attentive to the vast empirical diversity contained within modern Japanese literature.

Nevertheless, it seems evident at some point that Washburn's notion of hybridity conceals as much as it reveals. Hybridity refers to a mix of heterogeneous elements that in his account remain ultimately identifiable in and of themselves. Washburn carefully notes how disruptive the notion of hybridity appears to identitarian ideologies, which seek to reduce that heterogeneity to a pure, unadulterated unity. Such reductive violence can be seen, above all, in the case of Japanese nationalism. As he writes, "The discourse on modern identity in Japan discloses the hybridity of the categories of self and individual in which Western conceptions came to coexist with indigenous ideas of socially constructed selfhood. In reaction to this disclosure, the concept of authenticity worked to conceal the hybridity of modern culture under the cloak of the belief that identity could be traced to mythical or natural origins. This belief was useful to nationalist ideologies because it facilitated the construction of idealized forms—the Japanese nation, the Japanese people, even the Japanese language."[69] For Washburn, then, the ideology of Japanese national identity aims to deny the fundamental hybridity of modern Japanese culture as that hybridity was produced by the historical influx of Western elements. Introducing a distinctly modern conception of the self as based on the autonomous individual, the West immediately brought about a confrontation of ideas with the indigenous Japanese notion of the self as collective. Given that evidence of this confrontation can be found everywhere in modern Japanese society, and particularly in this society's literary works, a methodological approach centered on the notion of hybridity is needed to demonstrate the impossibility of any desired reduction to, or abstraction of, a pure Japanese essence and instead reveal the complex coexistence of Japanese and Western elements. In opposition to Japanese nationalist ideology, Washburn shows that the constitutive elements of modern identity in Japan must be openly recognized as foreign as much as domestic, for the notion of the self that appears in its literary texts is at one and the same time autonomous (or Western) and social or collective (Japanese).

By drawing modern identity back to its original difference—a difference that, as Washburn correctly notes, ideologies of cultural authenticity strive to conceal—the notion of hybridity aims to disclose the otherwise unseen complexity that lies at the heart of the simple or immediate. Nevertheless, the determination of an entity's constitutive parts as *identifiable* must be recognized as merely displacing the problematic of identity to another level. Washburn views his project as an attack against Japanese nationalism by demonstrating that modern Japan is irreducibly synthetic or hybrid in nature. Modern Japan is thus no longer purely Japanese in any strict sense since the global phenomenon of modernity indicates the shadowy presence of the West itself. Yet to conclude that modern Japan exists as a composite of recognizably Japanese and Western elements is to commit oneself to a notion of identity that, despite one's express intentions and efforts, remains still uncomfortably close to the identitarian ideology of Japanese nationalism that one otherwise wishes to condemn. Here the critique of theoretical reductivism that calls forth Washburn's notion of hybridity exposes its limitations in its understanding of the spatiotemporal boundaries of modern Japanese identity. For this understanding is inescapably theoretical; that is to say, in this case, it appeals to the concept of identity in order to show at precisely what point that identity comes to be disturbed or complicated by the difference of hybridity. In Washburn's account, the loss of pure Japanese identity occurs at a particular time and place in history, and this time and place are called by the name *modernity*. Both spatially and temporally, what is in question is an act of violence in which an otherwise self-contained realm of interiority is breached by an outside. In spatial terms, this outside is defined as the West, whereas temporally it is marked by the age of modernity. Washburn states all of this quite succinctly in the opening pages of *The Dilemma of the Modern in Japanese Fiction*: "The modern is defined by the process of Westernization, which involved the adoption of a set of social or ethical values extrinsic to the native culture."[70]

The implication is clear: Japan was able to maintain the purity of its identity as Japan until the beginning of Meiji, from which point Japan could no longer continue on strictly as itself given the presence of foreign elements within the borders of its own (violated) interior space. Methodologically, the empiricist approach that informs Washburn's notion of hybridity reveals its limitations in his very classical (i.e., theoretical, metaphysical) desire to derive difference from a prior instance of identity. That is to say, an argument is presented regarding the nature of Japanese modernity that appears at face value to rely solely on historical and cultural data. No propaedeutic reflection appears concerning the possibility of treating historical and cultural entities *as such*, for the identity that grounds these entities, enabling them to be what they are as opposed to something other, is understood strictly in empirical rather than in philosophical terms. At the outset of Washburn's inquiry, in advance even of his preliminary discussion concerning the dichotomy between self and society that appears to divide modern Japanese literature, a general question necessarily presents itself concerning the ontological status of historical and cultural entities. The question is this: Given that all entities must exist in the differential milieu that is time and space, is it possible for these entities to persist identically as themselves? Or is it rather the case that this spatiotemporal milieu incapacitates any pure identity from the beginning, such that each entity is incessantly breached or exposed by something other or in excess of itself *in order to be at all*? This would be to radicalize the notion of alterity, even beyond the limits of Washburn's call, in another context, "to recognize difference, to acknowledge and embrace otherness."[71] When confronted with the disruption of identity in the particular case of Japan, Washburn can only see this event as an empirical or historical accident, something that either may or may not have happened, rather than in more essential terms as that which inhabits identity from its very inception. The *fact* of any actual disturbance or disruption of identity necessarily rests on the *possibility* of such disruption, but Washburn's failure to interrogate this notion on a more fundamental level guarantees that his assumption of a self-evident Japanese identity remains intact, thereby resulting in a dangerous proximity to the very nationalist ideology that he otherwise seeks to attack.

Yet it would be misleading to suggest that Washburn neglects all such questions of ontology or being. In *Translating Mount Fuji*, for example, scattered remarks appear concerning what he calls "the ontological ground of Japanese identity," "the claims of deontological and consequentialist ethics," and "the ontological core of Japanese identity," etc., but the meaning of these expressions is never truly explained or developed.[72] Perhaps the most extended remarks on this issue are to be found in the reading of the intellectual historian Maruyama Masao, and in particular his essay "De aru koto to suru koto" (Being and doing) from the 1961 collection *Nihon no shisō* (Japanese thought).[73] There Washburn shows how Maruyama sought to understand the phenomenon of Japanese modernity by contrasting Tokugawa Japan to modern Japan. Whereas the former, as he writes, "was a society based on an ethics of 'being,'"[74] the latter is characterized in terms of the actions performed by an autonomous subject. For Maruyama, the notion of "being" is here restricted to the level of the individual human being and refers negatively to the premodern absence of free will and rationality. As with Washburn, Maruyama is interested in the question of being as it relates to Japan only insofar as the general being or identity of Japan is already presupposed. This identity functions as a kind of framing device that allows for a variety of empirical questions to be posed regarding the particular nature of Japanese society, thought, and literature, etc. In this way, the issue of ontology is not only reduced to the empirical level; it is also forced to submit to a simple binary opposition vis-à-vis the notion of doing, which must therefore be placed outside of being. In each case, Washburn's as well as Maruyama's, alterity is found to exist strictly outside of Japan in the West. Western forces might transgress the boundaries marking the interior space of Japan—for Maruyama, indeed, this development is seen positively as bringing about the autonomous subject of doing—but never to the point of threatening the essential identity of Japan itself.

These ontological issues, I believe, bear directly upon the manner in which Washburn conceives of the notion of loss. Let us continue following his reading of Maruyama:

> And the sentiment of loss, as Maruyama Masao has argued, was responsible for the consciousness of crisis that emerged in the nineteenth century. The effect of a sentiment of loss is seen most immediately in the idea of authenticity, which not only arose as a means to compensate for the threat of cultural relativism, but also served as a palliative for the anxiety of loss, drawing affective power from the implied, nostalgic hope of a return to a lost unity of language and identity.[75]

If Washburn devotes considerable space to discussing Maruyama in the opening sections of *Translating Mount Fuji*, this is because he shares many of Maruyama's ideas regarding the nature of Japanese modernity. In the foregoing passage, Maruyama notes how the introduction of Western ideas and technology in the nineteenth century resulted in a sense of crisis among the Japanese that their native way of life was gradually disappearing; Washburn then links this "sentiment of loss" with the reactive ideology of cultural authenticity. Here loss involves, at its core, a violence committed to the *proper*, that is to say, for Washburn as for Maruyama, the mineness or self-identity that determines the Japanese as Japanese. Maruyama views this loss of initial Japaneseness as necessary in order to arrive at a fuller, more politically modern form of Japaneseness characterized by the development of a rational and autonomous citizenry. While Washburn endeavors to be more impartial regarding this tension between individual autonomy and collective authenticity,[76] he nonetheless remains as firmly committed as Maruyama to perceiving such loss as a destruction of that which is properly or self-identically Japanese. To be sure, a variety of subjective viewpoints may be adopted regarding what one perceives as this historic loss of Japaneseness that marked the beginning of modernity: Maruyama's positive evaluation of this development as leading to greater individual autonomy is directly countered by the ideologists of authenticity, who mourn this painful loss and dream, as Washburn writes, "of a return to a lost unity of language and identity." In a more objective sense, however, Maruyama, the nationalistic ideologists of authenticity, and Washburn all agree that modernity in the context of Japan is to be determined in the specific terms of a loss of Japaneseness. Washburn denounces the ideology of authenticity for its nostalgic hope that Japan one day return to itself by recapturing its original cultural identity. And yet, no less than the proponents of authenticity, Washburn also regards that identity as having once existed in a more or less pristine state prior to the intervention of the West. If modernity in its violence signifies the objective or historical loss of Japan to itself, then—to follow the implications of this logic—premodern Japan was yet a time in which Japanese culture remained immediately close to itself, unmarked by the foreign in its pure interiority.

In order to avoid any possible misunderstanding, let me emphasize that I am in no way contesting the fact that Meiji Japan was a site of tremendous social upheaval. Such historical changes need to be comprehensively taken into account in order to arrive at a clearer understanding of the past, and in particular of the vastly unequal forces that led to the expansion into Asia of "Western" imperial powers and the no less violent formation of the Japanese nation-state. My point, rather, is that the historical and literary historical narratives to which Washburn appeals (and to which he, in turn, contributes) are informed at their root by certain philosophical presuppositions that, despite their absolute centrality to the argument presented, remain unquestioned and largely unthematized. The notion of loss cannot merely be treated in the empirical terms of history or literary history without first assuming the original presence or identity of that which is seen to have subsequently disappeared. This is above all a methodological point. Its import does not lie in calling for a shift, or even return, from empirical discourse to philosophical discourse; on the contrary, my intent is to show that a silent philosophical commitment necessarily informs all forms of empirical discourse from the moment one begins to speak about identity. For Washburn, the loss of identity can only be regarded as a violence that supervenes from a position of exteriority. This is, in effect, to fall into the trap of what might be called a first/then structure: *first* there is presence, that which gives itself as the normal or correct state of affairs; *then*, through an act of violence that appears from the outside, there occurs a traumatic loss of presence, which introduces some type of disturbance or distortion within an entity, thereby transforming the normal into the abnormal. As is well known, this structure belongs equally to metaphysics and theology, but Washburn shows that it continues to produce effects even within studies of Japanese modernity. Hence the stunning appeal to the concept of original sin: "Taishō Japan was haunted by the *original sin* of Meiji—the decision to resist the power and cultural hegemony of the West by emulating Western material culture, by embarking on its own empire building project in Asia, by acquiescing in the racial ideology that supported colonialism, and by constructing a modern myth of Japanese cultural uniqueness."[77]

Washburn of course uses this concept of original sin metaphorically, but this does not mean that the usage is innocent. His intention here appears to be that the commencement of Westernization that signaled the transition to modernity in Meiji Japan unleashed a variety of sociopolitical evils that would continue to plague the country into the Taishō period and beyond. If modern Japanese society might be seen to contain distortions or abnormalities, then one needs to trace these defects all the way back to their historical origin in Meiji. There one can discover the presence of the foreign, that which violently interrupted Japan's historical self-relation, inserting itself in such a way that that relation could henceforth only take place mediately, at a distance or remove from itself. As with the theological doctrine of original sin, the severing of this auto-affection gives rise to various debates as to its relative merits and demerits. Washburn himself largely seems to judge the phenomenon of Japanese modernity as a great success, for it gave birth to a new form of subjective identity based on the privileged attributes of reason, ethical consciousness, and autonomy. And yet, he acknowledges, such success cannot be completely divorced from those evils that have afflicted modern Japan, at least in the Taishō period.[78] Furthermore, it must not be forgotten that the theological doctrine of original sin centers on an act of disobedience that separated man from God, an act that was preceded by a prelapsarian period of innocence or oneness in which harmony yet reigned. Original sin, in other words, *itself* originated in an earlier "time" (if indeed time can be spoken of in this sense) that was characterized by absolute unity and self-identity. Following this tradition, Washburn also attempts to derive difference—what he calls, as we have seen, "hybridity"—from an earlier instance of identity in which no foreign or improper elements yet existed, elements that would, however, eventually intervene and cause Japan to fall from itself.[79]

According to the logic of original sin, Japan must henceforth be seen as internally divided. For better or worse, the forces of Western modernity created a hybridized Japan, and this entity exists in opposition to a premodern Japan in which there was as yet no need for such "cultural synthesis." Washburn, it must be said, seems untroubled by the fact that his discourse remains so deeply grounded on a series of simple dichotomies, dichotomies whose terms, it may appear at first glance, derive not from Washburn's own methodological decisions but indeed directly from the historical and cultural materials themselves. This bears remarking for at least two reasons: 1) The extensive references to literary theory, even if done nonobsessively, introduce into Washburn's text thinkers whose keen awareness of the trap of dualistic or binaristic frameworks might have alerted him to the presence of certain problems that inhere in this type of argumentation; and 2) Far more seriously, the concept of identity, which is inarguably the object that receives the most sustained attention throughout the pages of both *The Dilemma of the Modern* and *Translating Mount Fuji*, is understood strictly in the reductive, empirical sense of *positive identity*. As a result, the relation formed by two equally positive entities can only be one of binarity, if for no other reason than the fact that they are held to exist purely opposite one another. Thus, in Washburn's text (but precisely this same tendency can be found in the texts of Suzuki and Tansman, as we have demonstrated) the entity "West" is posited as the simple opposite of that which is repeatedly called the "non-West." At no point are these terms or concepts ever considered to be other than self-evident. Following a very traditional division, the West is regarded by Washburn as the site of the individual—hence the values of autonomy, "independence of spirit," etc.—whereas the non-West (Japan) becomes the locus of the nonindividual (i.e., the group or collective)—hence the reverse values of conformity, cultural authenticity, etc. Significantly, this distinction between the West and non-West involves a core opposition between the notions of interiority and exteriority, as Washburn explains. Here non-Western culture is characterized by what he calls "aretaic ethics," which come to be challenged at the dawn of Asian modernity by the "consequentialist and deontological ethics" of the West: "Aretaic ethics posit ideals, the virtues, that are largely determined and justified by social norms or religious authority *external* to the individual" whereas "[i]n contrast, the determination and justification of value in consequentialist and deontological ethics is made on the basis of factors *internal* to the individual."[80]

As Ferdinand de Saussure famously argues in the context of linguistics, the individual units that in their totality make up a language system are "purely differential and defined not by their positive content but negatively by their relations with the other terms of the system. Their most precise characteristic is in being what the others are not."[81] This insight allows us to go beyond a substantialist or essentialist conception of identity, in which an entity is seen as capable of presenting itself as such. Once again, Washburn may appear to suggest that an empiricist method of hybridity is best equipped to gather and interpret the variety of historical and cultural data available in the texts of modern Japanese literature. The difficulty, however, is that this method is tacitly informed by an essentialist conception of identity that its own empiricist concerns prevent it from recognizing and critically calling into question. As soon as Washburn speaks of the relation between the West and non-West, in fact, positive identity has already vanished and secretly yielded to a negative or differential conception of identity. If the non-West can be defined as that which the West is not, then the West, too, can be defined as the negation of the non-West. In this way, both the West and non-West may be seen to be what they are not in any immediate or positive sense but rather strictly by virtue of being what the other is not, as Saussure contends.[82] Here it must be emphasized that positive identity and negative identity do not present themselves simply as two distinct forms of identity. In principle, negative identity always inheres within positive entities, however defined. This negativity or differentiality does not merely allow for a fixed dialectical relation to take place between things, however. On the contrary, the incessant disruption of any positive (substantialist, essentialist) notion of identity prevents the entity from ever fully or purely inhabiting itself. Once identity comes to be rethought in this more radical manner, then the opposition between the internal (domestic) and external (foreign) itself can be seen to be grounded on a more general foreignness or alterity.

If binarity is a delusion that always risks exposure, this is not because of some hidden ethical rule that states that one must not fall into dualistic modes of thinking, as is sometimes misunderstood. Rather, it is far more accurate to say that binary frameworks collapse because of the unyielding weight or pressure of spatiotemporal difference. Time, in its ecstatic movement, only gives itself as that which is no longer, for the past has already vanished, and that which is not yet, for the future is still to come. I mention this point because Washburn displays an abiding interest in the notion of time, an interest that appears at significant moments in his work, but whose implications are never rigorously pursued. *Dilemma of the Modern*, for instance, begins with a reflection on several lines from T. S. Eliot's poem "Burnt Norton": "Words move, music moves/Only in time; but that which is only living/Can only die. Words, after speech, reach/Into the silence."[83] In the opening pages of *Translating Mount Fuji*, Washburn shifts his attention from Eliot to Borges and Cervantes. In question is a passage from *Don Quixote* that appears in Borges's short story, "Pierre Menard, Author of the *Quixote*": "truth, whose mother is history, rival of time, depository of deeds, witness of the past, exemplar and adviser to the present, and the future's counselor." The narrator of this text, as Washburn reminds us in his summary, judges these words to be inferior to those of Pierre Menard, who from his very different historical and personal perspective repeats Cervantes's passage identically: "truth, whose mother is history, rival of time, depository of deeds, witness of the past, exemplar and adviser to the present, and the future's counselor."[84]

Despite the quite diverse contexts of Washburn's two books, published more than a decade apart, the shared concern with the notion of time certainly gives one pause. In the Eliot poem, the strange movement of time that marks language is directly linked to the question of finitude, or that which might be called, following Eliot, "lifedeath." If "that which is only living/Can only die," then the fragility of lifedeath, which the poet emphasizes by repeating the word "only," is something that resists division into any simple binary. To live in time is in some sense necessarily also to die, for both life and death are caught up in, and punctuate, time's general movement of difference. This difference of time then reappears in Borges's repetition of Cervantes, for what is thematized in those lines is the temporality of truth in its relation to the past, present, and future. Here it is significant how Pierre Menard, grasping one of the essential (if apparently paradoxical) implications of this movement of time, repeats Cervantes's text in such a way as to call into question the traditional opposition between identity and difference. Repetition, Borges seems to suggest, takes place strictly by way of difference. Given the negativity inherent to time, the identical reproduction of an original text cannot be said to simply mark the transition from the single to the multiple, for the original itself only appears or presents itself in its identity as irrevocably other to itself. At the essential core of an entity, in other words, there is only self-division, and the alterity and multiplicity that are produced by this division are the sole means available for the retroactive constitution of identity. Each entity exists in a state of lifedeath, for the self-division at the origin allows for the possibility of survival strictly on the condition that the specter of death appears each time an entity presents itself in its singular difference. As Pierre Menard understood, the differential tracing out of Cervantes's text risks death (i.e., the *Quixote* may henceforth no longer be recognized as Cervantes's own) in order to survive at all.

Washburn unfortunately fails to draw forth the most radical insights of Eliot and Borges, despite the fact that these works occupy pride of place in his two books on Japanese literature. His reading of "Pierre Menard, Author of the *Quixote*" minimizes the essential threat posed by the notion of differential repetition by transforming the text into a lesson for scholars of literature who confront the problem of cultural difference: "Borges's story also exposes the motivations and methods of literary critics and historians who, by merely invoking the presence of a particular cultural consciousness, can read vastly different meanings into the same words."[85] At first glance, Washburn's interpretation of Eliot appears more promising. "We can express the modern only through time," as he writes, "and so modernists are driven toward an end that makes them ever more aware of the futility of the effort to freeze the sense of presentness into a permanent state."[86] Nevertheless, the stakes involved in the critique of presence, or "presentness," are considerably vaster and more unsettling than Washburn is prepared to admit. In Washburn's view, the problem of time is to be understood primarily as an issue that plagues modernists and their anguished sense of modernity: "To be modern is to possess a heightened sense of the significance of one's present moment. . . . The central problem in a modernist narrative, then, is time."[87] In this way, time in its generality and elemental link to ontology comes to be reduced to a *particular* historical issue confronting a *particular* group of people whose own temporal identity remains accepted as self-evident. Washburn fails to consider that an interrogation of the notion of time and presence (presentness) contains direct implications for any thinking of identity. If, given the elusive moment of time, the sense of presentness can never be frozen into a permanent state, then one must now confront the fact that this insight bears dramatic consequences for a methodology that otherwise insists on positing such self-contained entities or objects as self, society, West, and non-West, etc., as well as such restricted notions as autonomy, independence, native, indigenous, and foreign. As soon as temporal difference comes into play (which is to say, in all rigor: *from always*), then these entities and notions can no longer be accepted as self-evident or self-present but must instead be fundamentally rethought.

In light of the foregoing analysis, I would like now to turn to Washburn's treatment of a major text in Japanese literature that he finds to be emblematic of Japanese modernity. Even beyond the interpretations offered of other canonical works, Washburn's reading of Natsume Sōseki's 1908 novel, *Sanshirō*, deserves comment with regard to his sustained interest in what he calls, in the subtitle of *Translating Mount Fuji*, the "ethics of identity." Washburn is to be praised for recognizing the literary value of Sōseki's work, particularly given the sharp criticism that this book has received at the hands of some critics. Edwin McClellan, for instance, judges the novel to be more or less insignificant in his early study, *Two Japanese Novelists: Sōseki and Tōson*. "It is, however, an extremely dull work," McClellan concludes. "It has almost no plot and is exasperatingly uneventful. . . . [T]he reactions of the characters to situations are a little too passive. . . . Sanshirō, the main character of the novel, is too young to move us. . . . Viewed therefore as the story of a youth whose future would be like that of the more mature heroes of the later novels, *Sanshirō* has some purpose. But by itself, it seems to be without much significance."[88] Washburn's assessment of Sōseki's text differs markedly from McClellan's uniformly negative view. He undertakes a reading of Sōseki primarily on the basis of the notion of translation, as can be seen in the title of the chapter (which is then repeated synecdochically as the title of the book itself), "Translating Mount Fuji." This apparently commonsensical if in fact difficult and elusive notion merits its place within the general architecture of *Translating Mount Fuji* because of its explanatory value in describing precisely how Japan went about incorporating the various foreign elements that derived from the West.

I would like to argue that *both* commonsensical (or dogmatic) *and* more difficult or elusive elements coexist—in both a hybrid and non- or rather prehybrid form, as it were—in Washburn's conception of translation, and that this disparity bears significant implications for his reading of *Sanshirō*. On the one hand, translation is reductively seen in historicist terms as a feature that is either present or absent in determined national entities. Because of its extensive borrowings from the West, borrowings that it sought to adapt to its own native values and traditions, Meiji Japan must be classified as what Washburn refers to as a "translation culture": "The metaphor of translation situates Sōseki's novel in a historical moment when the discourse on identity was framed by the perception that Japan had become a translation culture."[89] For Washburn, this new translational relation with the West brought about a "paradox" in urgently raising the question of the primacy of either the Western original or the Japanese translation: "[I]t makes explicit reference to the nature of Meiji-era culture, which was defined by its preoccupation with the paradox of how to translate the material culture of Western modernity into Japan without losing the essence of cultural identity."[90] On the other hand, however, Washburn boldly attempts to grasp the dynamics of translation with regard to the notions of presence and mediation: "Translation heightens the historical awareness of the parochial nature of particular languages, which in turn makes manifest issues of originality and influence, of how true the translation is to the original. This happens because the very presence of the translation mediates the original text it makes intelligible."[91] These reflections on presence and mediation, however brief and undeveloped, lead Washburn to a notion of translation centered on what he terms the "trace of difference": "The presence of the mediating barrier of the language of a translation signifies the absence or displacement of an original cultural form, thus raising the concern that the reader is blocked from a full and authentic understanding of the original. It does not matter whether we are dealing with a translation of a form from outside Japan or from the indigenous culture, for in both cases a translation acts as a trace of difference."[92]

From our perspective, everything at stake here depends on the relation between these two very different conceptions of translation. In Washburn's discussion of "translation culture," translation is viewed as a derivative or secondary movement that commences strictly *after* the constitution of the geopolitical entities Japan and the West. Since the range of this movement is restricted to the interstitial space existing between these two entities, the result, in logical terms, can only be the Westernization of Japan or the Japanization of the West. In light of Washburn's specific historical focus on the Meiji period, however, it is solely the former question regarding Japanese Westernization that is examined with a view to the various social changes experienced by Japan as a result of its translational reception of artifacts that arrived from an otherwise distant Western source. Given that the site of translation is Japan, are the original forces of the modern West to be granted primacy over the derivative Japanese translation? If so, then translational accuracy is gained at the price of cultural sensitivity, for Western elements might fit poorly into a Japanese environment that is seen as historically grounded in indigenous values and traditions. If not, however, then one runs the risk of mistranslating the original West by paying excessive attention to the demands imposed by the native environment. If in the former case Japan becomes too Westernized at the cost of sacrificing its original cultural identity (a mode of translation privileging the source text), then in the latter case Japan preserves its identity by refusing to make the necessary structural changes required for modernization (a mode of translation that privileges the target text).

However, this "paradox" is valid only insofar as one accepts the fixed or given terms of translation, and this in turn requires that one regard translation itself as a restricted movement that occurs *between*—and thus not in excess of—the preconstituted entities of, in this case, Japan and the West. Nonetheless, it is precisely this more limited, conventional notion of translation that appears to be called into question by Washburn's own account. By raising the issue of translation as an act that involves the notions of presence and mediation in such a way as to call forth a thinking of the "trace of difference," Washburn *also* points to another, far more radical understanding of translation as a form of relationality that both precedes and exceeds its given terms.[93] While it is certainly true that this latter conception of translation is not to be found in the forefront of Washburn's text, it is nevertheless also the case that he identifies the very crux of its unsettling effects. I quote once again the relevant passage: "It does not matter whether we are dealing with a translation of a form from outside Japan or from the indigenous culture, for in both cases a translation acts as a trace of difference."[94] The differential trace that is translation, in other words, inscribes itself in some way prior to the difference between the foreign and domestic. What this thought suggests is the existence of two forms or dimensions of difference: an earlier or more general form, which Washburn describes by the word *trace*, and a more limited, derivative form that functions to divide an exteriority from an interiority in the context of a particular nation-state. Despite Washburn's unswerving commitment to the notion of identity, it is possible to distinguish these two forms of difference on the basis of their fundamentally distinct engagements with this notion. To demarcate the "outside Japan" from its own "indigenous culture" is to appeal to the concept of translation as a means of confirming the traditional notion of national-cultural difference, that is, a difference grounded on the underlying unity and identity of each national culture unto itself.[95] Here the *trans-* of translation names a crossing or going beyond that is conditioned by a prior difference between two entities, a difference that is in turn conditioned by their respective forms of self-identity. As Washburn seems to suggest, however, this translational difference itself presupposes an earlier "trace of difference" that, in the absence of any fixed or given terms whereby an outside is distinguished from an inside, may be characterized as a kind of *primordial crossing or transgression of that which nevertheless only comes to appear in its identity as a derivative effect of that movement*. In contrast to a difference firmly grounded upon a prior instance of identity, translation here would be conceived as an active tracing out of forces that in their self-differentiation both create and destabilize spatial relations of exteriority and interiority.

We are now better prepared to read Sōseki. The translation that is the centerpiece of "Translating Mount Fuji" appears on the very first page of Washburn's text. The passage in question involves a dialogue between the protagonist Sanshirō and his rather iconoclastic mentor, Professor Hirota:

"How do you like Tokyo?"
"Well . . ."
"Just a big, dirty place, isn't it?"

> "Hmmm . . ."
>
> "I'm sure you haven't found a thing here that compares with Mount Fuji."
>
> Sanshirō had completely forgotten about Mount Fuji. When he recalled the Mount Fuji he had first seen from the train window, having had his attention called to it by Professor Hirota, it had indeed looked noble. There was no way to compare it with the chaotic jumble of the world inside his head now, and he was ashamed of himself for having let that first impression slip away. Just then Hirota flung a rather strange question at him.
>
> "Have you ever tried to translate Mount Fuji?"
>
> "To translate . . . ?"
>
> "It's fascinating how, whenever you translate nature, it's always transformed into something human. Noble, great, or heroic."[96]

In his analysis of these lines, Washburn dismisses the unsettling effects of the notion of translation by framing Sōseki's text within the simple opposition between individual autonomy and collective authenticity:

> Read within the historical contexts that produced the Meiji discourse on identity, Soseki's ability to conjure up Hirota's strange question—"Have you ever tried to translate Mount Fuji?"—is more readily comprehensible. The question, by its own logic, indicates the autonomy that the individual can potentially exercise in defining nation, values, and identity, and in this way carries considerable significance for the novel's story of self-discovery and socialization. At the same time, the question suggests that Mount Fuji, by virtue of its sheer natural presence, is authentic and does not symbolize false, transient, or parochial values.[97]

As we have seen, the difference between autonomy (with its privileged faculties of reason and moral intuition) and authenticity is marked by the border that distinguishes the interiority and exteriority of an individual human being. This oppositional relation, moreover, is consistently aligned by Washburn with the dichotomy between the West and Japan (non-West) in the era of modernity. In this way, the radical conception of translation as a general "trace of difference" comes to be effaced in favor of the more derivative and restricted conception based upon a thinking of difference as conditioned by a prior instance of identity. The question immediately arises, however, as to whether this latter conception of translation is able to sufficiently take into account, and hence do justice to, the act of translation that Sōseki explicitly links in *Sanshirō* with the figure of Mount Fuji. By way of response, it is necessary to first examine why Sōseki wishes to understand translation in such an idiosyncratic fashion. Moving from the Rubin translation utilized by Washburn to the "original" Sōseki text he also references,[98] we discover a surprising difference or incongruity. Whereas Sōseki employs the more commonly used characters 富士山 to signify the Mount Fuji referred to by both Professor Hirota and the omniscient narrator in the opening of this passage (respectively, "I'm sure you haven't found a thing here that compares with Mount Fuji (富士山)" and "Sanshirō had completely forgotten about Mount Fuji (富士山)"), a sudden orthographic change occurs upon the appearance of the notion of translation. In posing this unusual question of translation to a startled Sanshirō, Professor Hirota's words are rendered by Sōseki as follows: "Have you ever tried to translate Mount Fuji (不二山)?" The issue, then, is how to explain this unexpected shift in describing the same signified Mount Fuji from 富士山 to 不二山?

不二山 is a traditional appellation for Mount Fuji, one that can be found in a variety of ancient texts. In this usage, the singular nature of the mountain is emphasized by the characters 不二, literally "not two," thereby reinforcing the idea that Mount Fuji is, given its enormous size and grandeur, unqualifiedly unique, peerless, or unparalleled. There can only ever be one such mountain, as the name indicates. Indeed, Professor Hirota can be said to anticipate this particular usage by explicitly raising the question of comparison: "I'm sure you haven't found a thing here that compares with Mount Fuji," as he tells Sanshirō. Comparison involves a framework in which one subjectively estimates the relative degree of sameness or difference between distinct entities. Despite the fact that things in their particular identity naturally give themselves as different from other things, they may nevertheless be evaluated in more general terms so as to determine possible similarities existing between the properties or characteristics that they possess. It is this logic of comparison, with its appeal to the governing relation between identity and difference, that seems to motivate Professor Hirota's subsequent introduction of the notion of translation. For translation also establishes a relation of sameness between entities that are otherwise essentially distinct from one another. Following Hirota's suggestion, for example, one might decide to translate Mount Fuji with the words "noble," "great," or "heroic," as he finds occuring in the inevitably "human" translation of nature. These words are not objectively identical to Mount Fuji, of course, but their appearance is merited on the basis of their similarity of meaning when compared with the particular way in which the mountain is seen to present itself.

What is striking, however, is Hirota's insistence that Mount Fuji *cannot* be compared. And this idea of the impossibility of comparison appears to be what motivates the orthographic shift in characters from 富士山 to 不二山. The mountain is incomparable; hence, it can only be expressed as uniquely "not two." It resists the relational acts of both comparison and translation because nothing other can ever be equal to or commensurate with it. In these lines, I believe, Sōseki implicitly raises the question of translation as an *aporia*, as in other words a kind of impasse in which possibility and impossibility are complexly interwoven. On the one hand, the crossing or going beyond of "trans-lation" is impossible since, as demonstrated by the presence of Mount Fuji, an entity's appearance in the world is irreducibly singular. Here, I would like to propose that a careful reading of this passage reveals the full force of what Sōseki intends by this notion of singularity. If Mount Fuji is indeed incomparable and untranslatable, this is *not* because of its distinct natural beauty, because it is in some sense more noble, great, and heroic than any other geographic or topographic feature. To regard the mountain in such fixed terms of spatiality is to forget that it must actively present itself before others who might witness its grandeur, and *this self-presentation necessarily takes place in time.*

In these lines, Sōseki alludes to the importance of time in his description of Sanshirō's reaction upon hearing Hirota's initial remark about the incomparability of Mount Fuji. For Hirota's words return the youth to the past, to the time when he first met the professor aboard a train in the course of traveling north to Tokyo.[99] Provoked by Hirota's statement, Sanshirō is now forced to compare his first experience of seeing Mount Fuji with his present self. Although he suddenly remembers that he found the mountain noble at that time, a considerable spatiotemporal difference has since intervened, with the result that this earlier impression no longer remains within him. Rubin, as quoted by Washburn, translates the passage as follows: "He was ashamed of himself for having let that first impression slip away," but we can render these words even more literally (if awkwardly) as: "He was ashamed of himself for having, somehow during that interval of time (*itsu no ma ni ka*), lost the impression [formed] at that time (*ano toki*)." In the 1956 Iwanami edition consulted by Washburn, the character for time (*toki*) appears twice in this sentence: in the phrase "that time," of course, but also in the word *itsu*, which is written here as 何時. The phrase *itsu no ma ni ka* typically means "unwittingly" or "before one knows it," but the specific characters that form this expression signify that a temporal interval has somehow passed of which one is only dimly aware.

This introduction of time produces the effect of radicalizing Sōseki's understanding of translation. Translation, as we have seen, is ultimately impossible because the singularity of something makes it resistant to any engagement or relationality with something else. To say, as in the case of Mount Fuji, that something is "not two" is to privilege the fact of its difference to such an extent that no external likeness or sameness could ever claim to capture it. However, singularity is never to be confused with identity. If Mount Fuji is to be truly peerless or unparalleled, then it must exist as essentially divided from itself. Even before one compares it with *other* natural features or landscapes in order to arrive at the conclusion that the mountain is in fact incomparable, it must first be recognized as irrevocably *other to itself*. With his repeated references to time, Sōseki reminds us that Mount Fuji presents or gives itself in its singularity strictly within a general milieu of difference. In this particular scene of translation, significantly, Mount Fuji does not appear in the first instance as a fixed empirical object. On the contrary, the mountain exists in the narrative present merely as an "impression" (*inshō*), or rather, indeed, as a barely legible impression of an impression, since its initial marking of Sanshirō sometime in the past has since been lost or dropped (*toriotoshiteita*), with the result that the youth can now only recall the fact that he once regarded the mountain as noble but now no longer thinks of it. The notion of time allows us to understand that the sheer massiveness of Mount Fuji ultimately means little, for its recontextualization within time renders it exceedingly fragile, a mere "trace of difference," as Washburn puts it. In order to be recognized in its self-identity, the mountain is forced to depend upon the traced impressions, or impressed traces, that it leaves on others and over which it has no control. This accounts for why Sōseki, in this discussion of translation, effectuates a decisive shift away from the empirical object itself to the realm of Sanshirō's subjective interiority. "There was no way to compare it with the chaotic jumble of the world inside his head now (*tadaima jibun no atama no naka*)," as Sōseki writes.[100] The point is *not* that the subject, in its ability to abstractly reproduce things in the form of consciousness, reveals its superiority over worldly materiality, alterity, and exteriority. Directly to the contrary, Sanshirō's "translation" of Mount Fuji in the form of a residual impression shows how the crossing or going beyond of translation effectively destabilizes any fixed oppositionality between inside and outside. This impression of Mount Fuji that remains in Sanshirō belongs to neither interiority nor exteriority. Rather, it awaits, in all precariousness or fragility, *other* times and *other* spaces in which to reappear as (necessarily other to) itself.

On the other hand, however, the aporetic nature of translation as impossible *also* opens up its possibility—once again, for something to reappear or represent itself as (necessarily other to) itself. Translation is impossible, rigorously speaking, because of its singularity, its "not two" (不二), as Sōseki writes, but the essential division that underlies all identity demands that things retreat from themselves in the very movement by which they re-treat, that is, retrace themselves doubly in their coming forth into the world.[101] Such retreating of something from itself allows us to understand why translation is impossible, but the doubling or dividing movement inherent to all self-presentation also opens the possibility for things to cross over (*trans-*) and achieve phenomenalization. One of the great ironies in the foregoing passage about "translating Mount Fuji" lies in the fact that Hirota's question to Sanshirō as to whether he has ever tried to translate the mountain has indeed already been answered by the text itself. That is to say, if at one time Mount Fuji somehow doubled or crossed over from itself so as to deposit within Sanshirō a residual "impression" of itself, then translation must have already occurred. No doubt such impression is incommensurate with the mountain itself, hence explaining the latter's untranslatability, but the impossibility of reproducing the mountain in its identity strangely releases its "own" differential repetition. Paradoxically, the strict concealing or withdrawal of identity makes possible a play of sameness and difference that acts as the very element of translation.

In *Sanshirō*, Sōseki introduces this impossible possibility of translation through the unusual notion of straying, a notion that is itself a translation of the word "lost." Let us quote the famous passage involving Sanshirō and Mineko, the woman he desires:

> Still looking at him, the girl said, "*Maigo* (lost child)."
>   He did not respond.
>   "Do you know how to translate that into English?"
>   The question was too unexpected. Sanshirō could answer neither that he knew nor that he did not know.
>   "Shall I tell you?"
>   "Please."
>   "*Stray sheep*. Do you understand? . . ."
>   He thought he understood the meaning of *stray sheep*, but then, perhaps he did not . . .

> She stood up quickly, murmuring—almost intoning to herself—as she did so, *Stray sheep*. Sanshirō, of course, said nothing in reply ...
>
> "*Stray sheep*," she murmured. Sanshirō could feel her breath against him.¹⁰²

In his reading of this passage, Washburn helpfully explains the orthographic idiosyncrasy of this expression "stray sheep": "Mineko's translation uses an unusual combination of characters that are glossed in a script that announces the foreignness of the word every bit as much as romanized script."¹⁰³ He proceeds to interpret Mineko's actions as follows:

> [H]er translation of *maigo*, "lost child," as "stray sheep" is not a mistranslation, but, with its use of a Christian image, a perfect description of the guilt and perplexity she feels over who she is: a woman caught in the moral and spiritual limbo created by the hybrid culture of late Meiji Japan.¹⁰⁴

Given his methodological commitments, it is understandable why Washburn would wish to stress the link between Mineko and Christianity, for this reinforces the tension between Japan and the West that he finds to be so characteristic of Japanese modernity. In this reading, the English phrase "stray sheep" may be seen to have its roots both in Japan—given that it first appears as a translation for the Japanese term *maigo*—and in the West, since the image is traditionally Christian. And such interpretation would lend support to a conception of translation as both linguistic and cultural, as Washburn indeed argues throughout *Translating Mount Fuji*. However, the refusal to consider this notion beyond the fixed, particularistic framework of West versus non-West (Japan)—in this case, the Western cultural translation of "stray sheep" would be offset by the native Japanese linguistic translation—leaves unexplained Sōseki's notion of singular untranslatability as well as the equally important notion of straying. From Washburn's perspective, virtually everything yields to translation except the entities Japan and the West themselves. At no time does he entertain the possibility that these entities also appear in the world as a result of translation. The straying as formulated by Sōseki in this passage, then, must be of a very restricted kind, for it is forbidden in advance to exceed the fixed geopolitical points through which Washburn attempts to think Japanese modernity. Neglecting to pursue Sōseki's hints that translation be conceived of as somehow singular ("not two") and straying, Washburn proceeds in his textual analysis strictly at the level of character psychology ("the guilt and perplexity she feels") and an impressionistic, philosophically suspect historicism ("the moral and spiritual limbo created by the hybrid culture of late Meiji Japan"). Both these aspects, finally, rest on a conception of being or ontology (i.e., the question of *is*) that unfortunately remains unexamined, and thus all the more easily captured by what appears to be empirically self-evident ("a perfect description of the guilt and perplexity she feels over *who she is*: a woman caught in the moral and spiritual limbo created by the hybrid culture of late Meiji Japan").

Beyond the scope of Washburn's reading, then, we return to the question of straying as it relates to the notion of translation in its possibility. Grasped in the double sense of retreat, translation points to a receding or drawing back from presence in the very movement by which something is drawn forth in the emergence of its self-presentation. This emergence is necessarily multiple. In this regard, Washburn's comment about the translation "stray sheep" can be seen to shed an important if inadvertent light on this process: "Mineko's translation uses an unusual combination of characters that are glossed in a script that announces the foreignness of the word every bit as much as romanized script." It is advisable that we make use of this notion of "foreignness," I believe, in order to more precisely identify the place of the foreign, or exteriority, in the context of translational straying. By generalizing this term beyond the limits of a particular national language, we find that already, within the borders of the word to be translated, foreignness is present. For *maigo* to be represented by the expression "stray sheep," it must already be foreign or improper to itself. It is strictly because the word *maigo* is essentially improper or outside of itself that it can give itself in its actual appearance in the world at a particular time and place. This fundamental impropriety or foreignness that renders translation possible is, I would like to propose, what Sōseki calls "straying." The translation "stray sheep" does not exist merely outside *maigo*, supervening upon it in the form of an empirical accident. On the contrary, the word *maigo*'s essential exteriority, its general strayability from itself, is what releases translation from the enclosure of self-identity so that something may appear in the world as necessarily other to itself. Each instance of translation inscribes something singular in the world at the same time that it exceeds that singularity by appearing otherwise over the course of its different spatiotemporal inscriptions. In *Sanshirō*, Sōseki carefully marks these differences of time and space in the straying or dissemination of the phrase "stray sheep." These words, which Mineko obsessively repeats in the foregoing passage, are then repeated by

Sōseki throughout the novel in such a way as to call attention to the unruly, propagative effects of (un)translatability.[105]

Let us briefly trace the path carved out by this repetition. As a translation, the initial appearance of these words "stray sheep" reveal that the original word *maigo*, "lost child," has already begun to stray from itself. The straying of this translation from its origin involves a complex temporality, for each time it presents itself in the world it instantly wanders away from that present by referring back to the history of its past markings as well as forward to its possible future iterations. In the foregoing scene, the expression "stray sheep" seems to most immediately mark that singular moment of strangeness and intimacy shared by Sanshirō and Mineko. Slightly later in the novel, however, these words are repeated in a very different, considerably less pleasurable context when Sanshirō's classmate Yojirō discovers that Sanshirō has obsessively scribbled the phrase in his notebook during a university lecture. "You really are a 'stray sheep,'" Yojirō says in reproach.[106] The straying of these words, which began as a translation of *maigo* and have now been used by multiple characters in both vocal and written form, continues next in their transformation into a picture of two sheep that Mineko has drawn on a postcard for Sanshirō. Thereafter the words return (now in the form of a double repetition) at the end of the novel in three distinct guises: that of a cloud ("Stray sheep. Stray sheep. The cloud had taken the form of a sheep"), the scent of perfume ("The bottle of Heliotrope. The evening in Yonchōme. Stray sheep. Stray sheep"), and, in the final lines of the novel, the suggested title of a painting (" 'The title is no good.' 'What should it be, then?' Sanshirō did not answer him, but to himself he muttered over and over, 'Stray sheep. Stray sheep' ").[107] Precisely as we saw Mount Fuji stray from itself in its translated appearance as an "impression" that is initially formed on a train and then reformed, much later, in Tokyo, so too does the translated phrase "stray sheep" wander far from its original time and place, assuming different forms in different contexts, in order to instantiate itself otherwise.

By way of conclusion, let me remark that Sōseki's thinking of translation according to a logic of essential straying or self-othering (which, in turn, is complexly interwoven with the notion of singularity, the "not two") contains powerful implications for any straightforward understanding of identity. Given the internal divisibility that haunts all forms of being, how is it possible for an entity to present itself in its immediacy, as it "truly is"? This question, as our reading of Washburn has insisted, belongs as much to politics as it does to the disciplines of literature, history, and philosophy. If one is to critically interrogate the "ethics of identity," then the question of national or geopolitical identity cannot simply be accepted as self-evident but must instead be minutely scrutinized so as to determine its various ideological components. For a forceful illustration of this insight, we need look no farther than Sōseki himself. In the opening of *Sanshirō*, the protagonist, engaged in conversation by Hirota, is placed in the very uncomfortable position of listening to the professor's denunciation of Japan. As Sōseki writes, "Sanshirō had never expected to meet anyone like this after Japan's victory in the Russo-Japanese War. The man was almost not Japanese, he felt (*dōmo nihonjin ja nai yō na ki ga suru*)."[108] As with all instances of identity, Japanese identity comes to be both created and displaced on the basis of the differential inscriptions of time and space. Sanshirō's suspicion that Hirota might be somehow less than fully Japanese implicitly raises the question of the formation of Japanese identity. If this identity cannot, in all rigor, be seen as immediate or natural or objective, then one must try to make sense of the prodigious desire that it be so.

Conclusion

Analysis of the works of Suzuki, Tansman, and Washburn reveals a wide variety of differences at the level of content, and yet it is remarkable how intimately connected this scholarship remains in the broader sense of methodology. These connections, I believe, are not accidental. Failure to enter into a deeper, more sustained engagement with theoretical ideas creates the possibility of a trap in which one risks repeating the errors one initially sets out to critique. So it is that Suzuki, wishing to attack the I-novel studies of Edward Fowler and Iremela Hijiya-Kirschnereit for their common appeal to a notion of literary and cultural interiority, draws back from the powerfully disturbing effects of the concept of retroactivity in order to better consolidate the claims of Japanese national-cultural identity. In Tansman's examination of Japanese fascism, the object of criticism is not other works of Japanese literary scholarship but rather the writers and thinkers of fascism itself. Japanese fascism sought to protect the unity and identity of traditional cultural forms from what was regarded as the corruptive effects of a decadent modernity. By formulating an attack on fascist thought from a position that privileges the safeguarding of interiority, *The Aesthetics of Japanese Fascism* ends up repeating the desire for border protection that was so central to the figures Tansman critically discusses.

Just as Suzuki's *Narrating the Self: Fictions of Japanese Modernity* has no choice but to restrict the force of retroactivity that it otherwise wishes to release, so too does Tansman's work fail to recognize the general nature of the concept of binding, which it nevertheless must presuppose in order to speak of identity at all. In a similar manner, Washburn's denunciation of the identitarian ideology of Japanese nationalism can be seen to conceal an acknowledgment of all that it shares with this same ideology. If the object being contested is "the construction of idealized forms—the Japanese nation, the Japanese people, even the Japanese language," as he declares, then what is required is a methodological approach that interrogates the very division between the "indigenous" and the "foreign" to which Washburn is otherwise so firmly committed. *Translating Mount Fuji: Modern Japanese Fiction and the Ethics of Identity* seeks to condemn Japanese nationalist ideology in the same breath that it acts to structurally reinforce it. In order to resist this trap, one must attempt to think identity as essentially self-divided. In such conception, as I demonstrate above in the context of translation, what is excluded beyond the limits of identity as foreign reveals itself to be strangely present within the interiority of identity itself.

In order to avoid any misunderstanding, I want to emphasize that the studies by Suzuki, Tansman, and Washburn represent the very highest levels of North American Japanese literary scholarship in the presentation of its objects of inquiry. If this work falls prey to criticism, it does so not because of inadequate research on the I-novel, Japanese fascism, and Japanese literary modernity, respectively. Rather, the problem lies at the more general, underlying level of methodology. This problem, I insist, cannot be corrected by merely adding more references from the corpus of literary theory, for what is at stake is far more deeply rooted. My claim is that this presence of methodological shortcomings is to be found across an extremely broad range of scholarship in the field of Japanese literary studies in North America. One fails to account for these shortcomings if they are understood in a merely limited sense as pertaining to this or that individual work or this or that individual scholar. In such manner, the problematic features endemic to the discipline would be conveniently overlooked, and one would be left with the sense that the study of the national literature of Japan is in and of itself acceptable barring the work of a small number of scholars who exist outside the mainstream. My reading of the monographs of Suzuki, Tansman, and Washburn is motivated by my sense that the conclusions reached in this analysis will speak directly to the existence of larger structural problems that pervade the field as a whole.

From this standpoint, it is instructive to examine Naoki Sakai's criticism of David Pollack's 1986 book, *The Fracture of Meaning*, in his important essay (previously referred to by Washburn), "Modernity and its Critique: The Problem of Universalism and Particularism." This essay, written nearly three decades ago, remains poorly understood, and this is somewhat ironic given the fact that it has been so frequently cited and quoted. Much like Suzuki, Tansman, and Washburn, Pollack also makes liberal use of certain names and concepts drawn from literary theory, thereby calling attention to the decisive difference of his work from that of previous Japanese literary scholarship, in which no such names or concepts appeared. However, the adoption of what appears to be a more abstract, rigorous discourse, as Sakai argues, merely serves to reinforce the claims of cultural essentialism. Pollack wishes to speak about the projected nature of the Japanese image of China, but Sakai demonstrates that such framework must logically presuppose the existence of an underlying Japanese identity. The explicit thematization of Japanese discourse on China thus works to conceal the absence of any interrogation of the discursive object Japan, the assumed existence of which in turn points to Pollack's determination of his own subjective positionality as American and Western. "[H]is cultural essentialism is totally blind to the problem of subjectivity," Sakai rightly concludes.[109]

Sakai's critical engagement with Pollack helps us better grasp that it is above all the question of subjectivity that remains the most crucial for any understanding of the methodological difficulties that haunt the field of Japanese literary studies in North America. Before any overt thematization or objectivization of the subject, an implicit positing of self and other in terms of certain given or fixed identities already predetermines the methodological framework that structures and gives shape to one's research. As can be seen throughout the pages of the work of Suzuki, Tansman, and Washburn—and again, this is symptomatic of a larger institutional problem and is in no way limited to these scholars alone—this question of subjective positionality remains essentially tied to the geopolitical binary of the West and non-West. Despite the large number of literary theoretical references on display, the commitment to the West/non-West relation remains for Suzuki, Tansman, and Washburn every bit as steadfast and unquestioned as it was a generation ago for Keene, Seidensticker, and McClellan. Regardless of whether one claims for oneself the subject position of Westerner or non-Westerner (i.e., Japanese, Asian, etc.), the fact is that this prior interpellation of identity powerfully governs the particular manner in which the Japanese object of inquiry comes to be constituted.

To their credit, Suzuki, Tansman, and Washburn all attempt to engage the vital issue of Japanese modernity. It seems curious, then, why none question the validity of this simplistic duality between the West and non-West. An interrogation of the enormously complex phenomenon of modernity must at some point reckon with the fact that the division of the world into these two separate spheres is itself a legacy of modernity, one that is to be critically questioned as opposed to passively accepted. For the terms of this binary are by no means symmetrical. Historically, to be Western is to be modern, it is to be heir to civilization, it is to be endowed with reason, and it is to be white. Conversely, to be non-Western is to be premodern, it is to remain essentially barbarous, it is to possess the faculty of reason only partially or inadequately, and it is to be nonwhite. Indeed, already in the very naming of this geopolitical division the West implicitly claims for itself the position of norm, and thus what is outside the West must be understood as in some sense deviant or aberrational. In recent years, the field of Japanese literary studies in North America has seen the emergence of such important subfields as anime studies, ecology studies, and media studies, etc. These new branches of scholarship hold great promise. But insofar as they remain hostage to this same geopolitical ideology of identity, it would be difficult to regard them as anything but more of the same.

Coda

Some Brief Remarks on Responsibility

During the course of a job interview not long after completing my dissertation, I was questioned by a professor of Asian studies. "Don't you feel that these various theoretical ideas merely get in the way of our reading of primary texts?" he asked. The query was not entirely unexpected at the time. No doubt readers now will smile at the innocence or naiveté of the remark, and perhaps some might even feel a sense of pride at the considerable progress made by the field since then. While it is not my intent to deny this progress, I do believe that it is important to make a distinction between theoretical references that carry out a more or less accoutremental function and instances of conceptual engagement where premises that are typically held to be solid and secure are now placed in question, and thus returned to their original state of fragility. From the perspective of my questioner, it was an article of faith that the relation with the various textual sources of the field was one of immediacy. That is to say, the task of the scholar consisted strictly of allowing these texts to speak for themselves. What to his eyes appeared to be the recent emergence of theoretical discourse had brought about an unfortunate displacement from the object of inquiry to the scholar himself. Rather than allowing the object to come forth in all its clarity, revealing those elements that were originally present in the text itself, theoretical ideas merely beclouded the object. Let me confess that I very much share this professor's concern that inquiry must at all times endeavor to do justice to its objects. Nevertheless, I am far less confident that this goal, noble as it may be, can ever be achieved. What if, in a general sense, objects of inquiry only ever give themselves in a state of mediacy? This would be to suggest, regardless of whether one endorses or discounts theoretical scholarship, that the object comes into the light of the present as already removed from or in some sense other to itself.

One of the principal claims of the present book is that what is most immediate to the object is precisely this strange severance from itself. The result of this severance is that the object never fully appears within the parameters fixed by the subject's act of objectification. And, to follow the consequences of this chain, the object's inability to be constituted identically as itself comes to produce a disturbance at the very heart of the epistemological subject. What is under threat in this disabling of the traditional subject-object relation is the dominant mode of inquiry in Japan studies. From our standpoint, this inquiry takes as its primary goal the attainment of certitude. Whatever object may be posed before the subject, yielding this or that particular form of knowledge, all research that proceeds in this manner serves to assure the individual scholar of his subjective mastery. In calling for a rethinking of this framework that governs the production of knowledge in the field, my aim is to indicate the derivativeness of this conception of subject and object. This relation is derivative because it fails to account for the radical movement of time, which never leaves intact the logic of oppositionality upon which the subject-object relation is based. In my reading, this exposure to temporal difference or alterity must bring about a fundamental shift from the value of subjective certitude to something like a recognition of contingency, which in turn demands a reexamination of a host of received ideas and practices.

In the specific context of Japan studies, undoubtedly the most central, unshakable premise concerns the very entity Japan together with its various associated concepts (e.g., the Japanese people, Japanese culture, Japanese history, etc.). In order for scholarship in this field to commence, there must first be posited the empirical entity "Japan." Yet this entity is not merely one among equals; on the contrary, it functions as the totality within which all actual and potential objects of research are already contained. To conduct research in Japan studies, then, is to in effect consent to the validity of this premise, and this consent is given whether one wishes to or not or indeed whether one is aware of it or not. Acceptance of part of the whole, in other words, is also structurally an acceptance of the whole that determines the part qua part. An abiding aim in my writing of this work has been to draw attention to the strangeness involved in being called upon to confirm the existence of a place and people that appear to have remained more or less selfsame throughout their history. One of the most remarkable features of Japan studies can be seen in the degree with which this strangeness has been neutralized. Unasked are such preliminary questions as: What does it mean for a people to remain historically selfsame? Why must I endorse the totality "Japan" if I wish merely to consider a particular literary text or historical event? Is this act of endorsement value free or is there instead something of either positive or negative ethical import in this gesture, something that demands to be thought?

If this entity "Japan" can never be exempt from valuation, this is because its mode of appearance is continually marked by the history of its discursive instantiations. Despite the considerable empiricist prejudice in the field, the fact is that "Japan" does not give itself in its concrete, immediate presence but rather strictly through its determinations in language. Here we discover that the otherwise formalistic epistemological relation, in which the Japanese object is posed against the subjective positionality of the Japan scholar, is in fact historical through and through. Yet this relation is not historical on account of a derivative or preconstituted "Japanese history" that gives itself to objectification on the part of historians of Japan. Even prior to this—and this is an essential move in effectuating a *step back* from object to method—access to "Japan" is initially gained by participating in the history of those instances in which Japan is so named. The nature of this participation is as passive as it is active. Inasmuch as the history of these inscriptions precedes one, forming the tradition of "Japan" in its original discursivity, one receives this force passively. However, the scholar of Japan is also assigned the task of actively reshaping this history, and this is achieved through the repetition or reinforcement of certain determinations while concurrently withdrawing emphasis from others. The point I wish to make here concerns the immense responsibility placed on those who choose to participate in this discourse, for participation immediately puts one in the position of responding to this history.[1]

The discursive history of "Japan" is not an innocent one. This lack of innocence takes many forms, of course, but certainly the notion of the "Japanese people" must be recognized as one of its most potent. Is it possible for anyone in the field of Japan studies to overlook the fact that this discursive history intersects, at so many different points in time and space, with the histories of nationalism and racism? Is it possible, in other words, to posit the existence of an entity called the "Japanese people" in such a way as to entirely avoid entanglement with the interrelated problems of nation and race? I pose these questions because it appears to me impossible to separate from these political issues any object of inquiry in Japan studies, no matter how apparently neutral or dissimilar in nature. In conceptual terms, this discursive history of "Japan" that concerns me forms a line that continues from past to present, and the discrete points through which this line is diachronically traced out are thus bound together essentially. Each new instance of language in which "Japan" is designated must consequently be understood as a response to previous instances, for the identity of the former is fundamentally dependent upon that of the latter. More concretely, each object produced in this field bears within it this history of nationalism and racism. No doubt it is tempting to claim immunity from such history by pointing, for example, to one's own politically progressive engagement with the object or perhaps to the object's own rootedness in an era prior to the emergence of national and racial discourses. However, my point touches upon the more general dimension of language: regardless of the individual scholar's political stance or the individual object's moment of appearance, the very act of writing on Japan immediately places one in the position of respondent to its past discursive instantiations.

What this signifies, in my account, is a hyperbolization of responsibility—again, in the precise sense of responding to a history that has already claimed one. Responsibility must be hyperbolized from the particular level of object to the vastly more general level of method in order to render explicit and so confront those unseen premises in Japan studies that govern research. The haste with which one dismisses methodological questions as needlessly abstract and irrelevant serves merely to strengthen their hold over thinking. Similarly, exclusive attention to the specific object of inquiry, regardless of how vigilantly one polices its borders, does not prevent broader issues of method from infiltrating and announcing their presence from the inside. In the case of nationalism, for example, it is surely possible to claim that the massive efforts devoted to condemning this phenomenon while also celebrating the heroic instances of resistance to it have succeeded in striking a decisive blow against this political evil. If we were to assess this type of scholarship in more structural terms, however, an alternative interpretation appears that views it, at best, as contributing to an increase in objective knowledge that allows the Japanese nation-state to more fully consolidate itself in the expansion of its historical self-consciousness and, at worst, as confirmation of the Orient's inability to raise itself to the level of reason as exemplified by the West. My point here is not to dismiss this research, much of which is indeed valuable. Yet there is always a risk of not seeing the forest for the trees, and the only chance to avoid this trap consists in asking how such widespread critiques of nationalism might possibly come to be appropriated by the nation at a deeper level. Here let us keep in mind that the attack on Japanese nationalism has been accommodated quite comfortably by the discipline of Japan studies.

A similar point can be made with regard to racism. Despite appearances, the emergence of racism in the field cannot be restricted to its explicit thematization in the form of individual essays or monographs. More broadly, the very framework in which an entity called the "Japanese people" comes to serve as the object of knowledge for a subject that determines itself as "Western" must be recognized as already racist. The problem, in other words, is a structural or institutional one, and involves the way in which the production of knowledge has come to be organized in the modern era. This insight, however, need not lead to hand wringing and vows of repentance. On the contrary, by *assuming* this history—that is to say, by acknowledging it as a structural feature of the discipline, one that itself responds to the larger geopolitical dynamics of modernity—one begins to understand that the complex mechanism of racism in no way exists outside Japan studies but rather informs it essentially. Such assumption of a history that has already taken place, and that moreover has already claimed one in the course of its development, opens the possibility of combating issues of race more effectively.

In light of these remarks on nationalism and racism as these phenomena have historically shaped the field, I would like now to briefly touch upon the issue of tone. Readers will observe certain fluctuations or modulations of tone throughout this book, and for this I can perhaps do nothing but endeavor in future work to "fail better," as Beckett says. In partial defense, however, let me note that the several scholars whose work I read and attempt to explicate all have very different things to say about such crucial topics as subjectivity, time, and ethics. The sheer difficulty of these concepts demands that they be treated with care and rigor, and I believe it is important to indicate those moments when such care is lacking, and rather than genuine conceptual inquiry one finds merely a conventional scholarship in which the glitter of theoretical references serves poorly to conceal the proximity to the Orientalism and philosophical disregard of the past. One doesn't wish to sound shrill and scolding, and the fact is that conceptual labor puts one at constant risk of failing to measure up to the complexity and gravity of these ideas. I do believe that this difficulty must be treated as generously as possible. Nevertheless, it is vital to recognize that the engagement with concepts is not only additive but also, significantly, subtractive. By this I mean that the departure point for abstract thinking is not to be located simply at the site of the object whose constitution has already taken place in accordance with the existing conventions of the field. As I have indicated in certain chapters of this book, evidence of such an approach can unfortunately be found in abundance throughout Japan studies, and this is a problem that needs to be addressed rather than politely or diplomatically ignored. In contrast to this additive outlook, a properly subtractive conceptual practice includes within its scope both the individual object of inquiry and the larger methodological presuppositions that so formatively shape research. Above all, this subtractive dimension of conceptual work is centered upon the act or movement of reflection. The scholar does not encounter the object as a blank slate but rather from the position of subjective prejudice, a prejudice that also springs from a variety of institutional rules and protocols. Inquiry that proceeds on the basis of conceptual or theoretical reflection provides the chance—not the guarantee, but merely the opportunity—of more critically evaluating these prejudices, thereby allowing one to better disturb the cycle of institutional replication.

Here it should be clear that I am not advocating a greater degree of theoretical rigor merely for its own sake. Ultimately, there can be no opposition between a theoretical approach and one based on the empiricism or positivism that remains so dominant throughout the field. And this for the simple reason that the latter is forced to conceal from itself the depth of its own theoretical commitments. To assume as one's departure point an empirical entity called "Japan" is to reveal both a theoretical and practical investment in the notion of identity, one that manifests itself in the terms of nationality, race, and ethnicity. It is precisely this attachment to identity that a more substantial theoretical or conceptual engagement is able to problematize, thereby showing that the otherwise innocuous epistemological relation with the individual Japanese object is indicative of a much broader level of subjective participation in the discourses of nation and race that so powerfully shape modernity. If the present volume can be said to be guided by an ethicopolitical vision, then such vision is most consistently directed to the question of identity as it grounds Japan studies.

It is in order to intervene in this tradition of Japan studies that I have sought in the foregoing pages to displace attention from the level of object to that of method. The *question* of method, more precisely, for the problem is that methodological procedures in the field have become so entrenched and naturalized that it is important now to disinter these and subject them to conceptual examination. To this end I have been consistently guided (or, to speak more truthfully, haunted) by one principal notion and one principal image, and the various textual analyses in the book represent my attempt to pursue what I believe are the enormous implications of these. The notion I refer to is that of originary diffusion or dispersion, while the image is that of the line as formed by a series of points. In the former instance, my thinking was provoked by the need to respond to the repeated appeal to the notion of presence that I found in all of the works I consider. While evidence of this engagement can be found most visibly in chapter 2, the fact is that the detailed treatment of the notion of subjectivity that appears in the first and third chapters situates this problematic of the subject at the more general level of presence. The substratum that encounters difference while remaining itself identical in its capacity to underlie or ground those forces that otherwise threaten to overwhelm it is nothing other than subjective presence. This subjective presence is centered on reason and consciousness, and so my reading unfolds by showing how such presence is scattered from itself in primordial fashion. This approach slightly differs in chapter 2, where I underscore the effects of dispersion through focus on the interrelated questions of time and ontology.

In the latter instance, by contrast—that of the image of the line—I wanted to respond to the sizeable pressure brought to bear on myself and all scholars of Japan studies by the tradition that forms this field. In chapter 3, in particular, it was striking to me how similar the underlying methodologies appear in the work of the scholars I discuss. These diverse points (i.e., textual instances) themselves form a line, but my familiarity with the research of the generations both prior and subsequent to these scholars convinces me that the extension of this line shows no clear signs of abating. Since I myself am implicated in this history given my own disciplinary affiliation, it seemed important to rethink the basic, if deceptively complex, relation between point and line. A pure stance of resistance vis-à-vis the field is impossible because one's positionality (or punctuality, as it were) is from the beginning corrupted by the tradition or inheritance that has partially claimed one's identity. To the degree that one participates in the field, in other words, one is already compromised. And yet such present entanglement can also be seen as providing the necessary purchase, or foothold, from which to begin to formulate a response to the past, thereby inventing a different kind of future. In this way, it seems to me, one creates the possibility not of destroying but rather of distorting or disfiguring the line.

How might one envision a more critical Japan studies, one that allows itself to be guided by the awareness that any engagement with the object already presupposes certain commitments at the logically prior level of method? It seems important, in the interest of cultivating an anticipatory response to the future, to keep this question as open and undetermined as possible. Nonetheless, let me at least suggest that research begin to rethink its conviction that it is anchored at some ultimate point to Japan (the Japanese people, Japanese history, Japanese culture, etc.) as an empirical entity. Such conviction, I believe, severely underestimates the power of language to shape our understanding of external reality. To say that "Japan" never gives itself immediately is to begin to recognize that this entity exists most originally as a product of a modernity that has organized the world on the basis of discrete nation-states, each endowed with its own individual history and culture. This history, which involves an irreducible moment of language and mediation, disallows any access to the Japanese object as such and instead calls for a more metacritical engagement with those forces that produced, and continue to produce, this entity. With its meticulous archival work and untiring discoveries of new themes and subject matter, scholarship in Japan studies has played a leading role in consolidating this production. A reflective step back from this activity will reveal that the space of this national interiority is in fact created by forces that exist both alongside and below it. A modernity that has formed the nation-state as the privileged agent of history owes its success to underlying assumptions about identity that a properly conceptual approach is equipped to expose and dismantle.

Notes

Introduction

1. Takeuchi Yoshimi, *Takeuchi Yoshimi zenshū* [Collected works of Takeuchi Yoshimi], vol. 5 (Tokyo: Chikuma shobō, 1980), 90–115; Richard F. Calichman, trans., *What is Modernity? Writings of Takeuchi Yoshimi* (New York: Columbia University Press, 2005), 149–165.

2. Richard F. Calichman, *Beyond Nation: Time, Writing, and Community in the Work of Abe Kōbō* (Stanford, CA: Stanford University Press, 2016). I am referring specifically to chapter 4 of this work, where I attempt to show how problems of national-culturalism found in Donald Keene's reading of Abe come subsequently to be repeated in the work of John Treat.

3. Here my project follows directly from the pioneering work of Naoki Sakai, whose critique of Japan studies—and of area studies more generally—merits continued attention insofar as it addresses many of the theoretical problems still found throughout the field. See especially *Translation and Subjectivity: On "Japan" and Cultural Nationalism* (Minneapolis: University of Minnesota Press, 1997).

4. As Harry Harootunian convincingly argues in slightly different terms, "History is not memory, the conservation of the archive. . . . It is, I believe, only history if the interventions force moments of critique and make possible the realization of promises transmitted and recovered by tradition." See Harry Harootunian, "Japan's Long Postwar: The Trick of Memory and the Ruse of History," in "Millennial Japan: Rethinking the Nation in the Age of Recession," ed. Tomiko Yoda and Harry Harootunian, special issue of *South Atlantic Quarterly* 99, no. 4 (Fall 2000): 734.

5. My decision to focus on these particular scholars is based on their considerable prominence in the field, as determined by such factors as scholarly achievement, institutional affiliation, and training of graduate students. No doubt this choice can be questioned, but one of my central arguments is that the conceptual shortcomings that mark their work must ultimately be understood in broadly structural rather than individual terms. I am uncertain that, barring several notable exceptions, a different selection would yield fundamentally dissimilar results.

Chapter 1

1. Murakami Haruki, *Umibe no Kafuka* (Tokyo: Shinchōsha, 2004), 2:97; trans. Philip Gabriel, *Kafka on the Shore* (New York: Vintage International, 2006), 284–285. Translation slightly modified.
2. Komori Yōichi, *Murakami Haruki ron: 'Umibe no Kafuka' wo seidoku suru* (Tokyo: Heibonsha shinsho, 2006), 7.
3. Komori, *Murakami Haruki ron*, 9.
4. Komori, *Murakami Haruki ron*, 12–13. Murakami, *Umibe no Kafuka*, 2:429; trans. Gabriel, *Kafka on the Shore*, 467. Kawai's speech appears in the December 2002 issue of the literary journal *Shinchō*. Here it is germane to note that this journal is published by Shinchōsha, which is of course the same publisher of Murakami's *Umibe no Kafuka*.
5. Komori, *Murakami Haruki ron*, 13.
6. Komori, *Murakami Haruki ron*, 14.
7. Komori Yōichi, *Kōzō to shite no katari* (Tokyo: Shinyōsha, 1992), 466–469. Emphasis in the original.
8. Komori, *Kōzō*, 469.
9. Komori Yōichi, *Buntai to shite no monogatari* (Tokyo: Chikuma shobō, 1994), 276.
10. Komori, *Murakami Haruki ron*, 131.
11. Komori, *Kōzō*, 8–9. In this context, it is important to note a certain inconsistency in Komori's conception of the relation between writer and reader. The difference or gap that separates the acts of writing and reading is at times presented as a logical or structural feature. At other times, however, this difference is problematically regarded in mere historicist terms. For instance, immediately prior to the above passage the following lines appear: "Even if the writer hands over to the reader a signed copy of his book, there exists behind this apparently immediate and intimate act of communication the marking of a spatiotemporal gap, which can in no way be filled, created between the writer and reader under the system of modern capitalism" (see Komori, 7–8).

It goes without saying that this difference between the acts of writing and reading remains irreducible to any determined or positive empirical factor, as appears here in the reference to modern capitalism. While Komori's attention to the socioeconomic aspects of writing is certainly of interest, the implication is that such difference somehow comes to supervene upon an earlier period of immediate intimacy between writer and reader. Here we find evidence of a kind of communalism that, I believe, haunts Komori's project throughout the course of his writing. It is true that Komori will go on to condemn Murakami's *Umibe no Kafuka* for fostering this same type of communality (*kyōdōsei*) (see *Murakami Haruki ron*, 11), but my point is that Komori can be seen to unwittingly repeat this tradition.

12. Komori, *Murakami Haruki ron*, 11.

13. See Georg Wilhelm Friedrich Hegel, *Phenomenology of Spirit*, trans. A. V. Miller (Oxford: Oxford University Press, 1977), 118–119. As Hegel writes, "For, in fashioning the thing, the bondsman's own negativity, his being-for-self, becomes an object for him only through his setting at nought the existing *shape* confronting him. But this objective *negative* moment is none other than the alien being before which it has trembled. Now, however, he destroys this alien negative moment, posits *himself* as a negative in the permanent order of things, and thereby becomes *for himself*, someone existing on his own account. . . . Through this rediscovery of himself by himself, the bondman realizes that it is precisely in his work wherein he seemed to have only an alienated existence that he acquires a mind of his own." Italics in the original.

14. For Murakami's own views on Sōseki's novel and its particular influence on his work, see Murakami, introduction to *The Miner*, trans. Jay Rubin (London: Aardvark Bureau, 2015), ix–xxiii.

15. Komori Yōichi, *Dekigoto to shite no yomu koto* (Tokyo: Tokyo daigaku shuppankai, 1996), 2–6. Emphasis in the original.

16. See here Derrida's account in "*Ousia* and *Grammē*: Note on a Note from *Being and Time*," in *Margins of Philosophy*, trans. Alan Bass (Chicago: University of Chicago Press, 1982), 29–67. For a persuasive analysis of the complex issues raised in this essay, see Martin Hägglund, *Radical Atheism: Derrida and the Time of Life* (Stanford, CA: Stanford University Press, 2008) and from a different perspective, John Protevi, *Time and Exteriority: Aristotle, Heidegger, Derrida* (Lewisburg, PA: Bucknell University Press, 1994).

17. Murakami, *Umibe no Kafuka*, 1:63; trans. Gabriel, *Kafka on the Shore*, 38.

18. Matthew Carl Strecher describes the issue of Nakata's memory loss in terms of time. Nakata, as he writes, "has lost the ability to remember anything from his past or to form new memories. Put in a slightly different way, he is no longer a being in 'time,' divided into past, present, and future, but of Time, that unified eternity in which past and future are bound up in an endless present." See *The Forbidden Worlds of Haruki Murakami* (Minneapolis: University of Minnesota Press, 2014), 51. The aim to call attention to the theme of time in *Umibe no Kafuka* is laudable, but Strecher's division between the concepts of "time" and Time, as he sees it, remains highly problematic.

19. Murakami, *Umibe no Kafuka*, 1:103; trans. Gabriel, *Kafka on the Shore*, 61.

20. Murakami, *Umibe no Kafuka*, 1:107–108; trans. Gabriel, *Kafka on the Shore*, 64. Translation slightly modified.

21. Murakami, *Umibe no Kafuka*, 1:20; trans. Gabriel, *Kafka on the Shore*, 13. This appearance of the secret is already anticipated several pages earlier in the Kafka narrative, where we read: "The omen was always there, like dark, secretive (*himitsu no*) water." Murakami, *Umibe no Kafuka*, 1:16; trans. Gabriel, *Kafka on the Shore*, 10. Translation slightly modified.

22. Murakami, *Umibe no Kafuka*, 1:21, 1:12; trans. Gabriel, *Kafka on the Shore*, 14, 8. Translation slightly modified. The passage in question very distinctly lists the device's audio function immediately after reference to a notebook and pen, thus signaling to the reader the importance of the issue of inscription or recording for a deeper understanding of the novel as a whole. In an otherwise fine translation, this detail is unfortunately omitted in the English.

23. Murakami, *Umibe no Kafuka*, 1:20, 1:103; trans. Gabriel, *Kafka on the Shore*, 13, 61. Translation slightly modified.

24. Murakami, *Umibe no Kafuka*, 1:20; trans. Gabriel, *Kafka on the Shore*, 13.

25. Murakami, *Umibe no Kafuka*, 1:119–120; trans. Gabriel, *Kafka on the Shore*, 70–71. Translation slightly modified.

26. Murakami, *Umibe no Kafuka*, 1:124; trans. Gabriel, *Kafka on the Shore*, 73. Translation slightly modified.

27. Murakami, *Umibe no Kafuka*, 1:148, 154; trans. Gabriel, *Kafka on the Shore*, 87, 90. Translation slightly modified.

28. Murakami, *Umibe no Kafuka*, 1:337–338; trans. Gabriel, *Kafka on the Shore*, 132. In this scene, Murakami explicitly calls attention to the multiple or diffusive nature of the trace, for in the Eichmann book Kafka finds a penciled note left by Ōshima at an earlier time. As Kafka reflects, "I knew that the handwriting (*hisseki*: literally, writing or brush traces [*seki/ato*]) was Ōshima's."

29. Murakami, *Umibe no Kafuka*, 2:246; trans. Gabriel, *Kafka on the Shore*, 367. Translation slightly modified.

30. Murakami, *Umibe no Kafuka*, 2:333; trans. Gabriel, *Kafka on the Shore*, 414–415. Emphasis in the original; translation slightly modified. Also see Komori, *Murakami Haruki ron*, 172–173.

31. Komori, *Murakami Haruki ron*, 173.

32. Let me provide several examples of this hyperbole, which regrettably borders on the irrational: "Insofar as we readers do not consciously recall memory so as to resist the erasure and execution of memory as performed by the text of the novel *Kafka on the Shore*, we become complicit without realizing how memory and history have been distorted" (Komori, *Murakami Haruki ron*, 206); and "As someone involved in the linguistic practice called literature, I would like as a matter of responsibility to emphasize that there exists what might be called a criminal social role in the best-selling novel *Kafka on the Shore*, which provided national 'solace' when published in the year 2002" (Komori, *Murakami Haruki ron*, 256). Many similar passages can be found throughout the text.

33. Komori, *Murakami Haruki ron*, 63.

34. Komori, *Murakami Haruki ron*, 28. For Komori, this identity in infancy between the toddler and mother is in truth just an extension of the initial identity experienced in the womb, a period that he describes as "perhaps the most blissful in a person's life" (Komori, *Murakami Haruki ron*, 31).

35. Komori, *Murakami Haruki ron*, 38.

36. Komori, *Murakami Haruki ron*, 38–39.

37. One example among others: "To lead readers toward pardoning or accepting the youth Kafka's desire for violence is, I believe, a fundamental desecration of human beings as creatures with a command of language. It is also a betrayal of the linguistic art of the novel, which is grounded on myths, folk tales, and narratives." See Komori, *Murakami Haruki ron*, 55. This language of pathologization—"desecration" (*bōtoku*), "betrayal" (as with the earlier quoted reference to the novel as "criminal")—is, I believe, far more revealing of Komori's conceptual and methodological biases than it is of Murakami's work.

38. Murakami, *Umibe no Kafuka*, 1:65; trans. Gabriel, *Kafka on the Shore*, 39. Translation slightly modified.

39. Murakami, *Umibe no Kafuka*, 1:88; trans. Gabriel, *Kafka on the Shore*, 52.

40. Murakami, *Umibe no Kafuka*, 2:174–175; trans. Gabriel, *Kafka on the Shore*, 328. Emphasis in the original.

41. Murakami, *Umibe no Kafuka*, 2:290–291; trans. Gabriel, *Kafka on the Shore*, 391–392. In his reading of these lines, Komori finds evidence of a deep current of misogyny that he believes runs throughout the novel as a whole. Comparing this collapse of paradise to the biblical story of Adam and Eve, Komori concludes that the implicit message in *Umibe no Kafuka* is that "being a woman is itself a 'sin.'" He continues his analysis with reference to Japanese history of the 1960s (see Komori, *Murakami Haruki ron*, 212–213):

> The Garden of Eden as "paradise," however, was not destroyed by Saeki's "sin." As she says, "We grew up, and times changed. Parts of the circle fell apart, the outside world came rushing into our private paradise, and things inside tried to get out." In addition to the surface meaning that the young boy and girl grew up and assumed a social existence, which made it impossible for just the two of them to stay in this self-contained world, there exists another meaning. The fact that the "circle" "fell apart" was also brought about by the circumstances of the "times." The "baby boomer generation" became adults in the late 1960s. In terms of collective memory, the phrase "the outside world" "came rushing into our private paradise" while "things inside tried to get out" signifies that the consumer culture centered in Tokyo quickly rushed into the rural areas through the spread of television (particularly following the Tokyo Olympics of 1964). In the midst of rapid economic growth, large companies in Japan fiercely stirred up middle-school graduates as the "golden egg," enacting a large-scale mobilization of labor to the cities. As a result, rural labor power underwent a radical decrease, Japanese agriculture declined, and the gulf widened between the city and countryside.... Saeki's individual "sin" is in no way inherent in these circumstances.

42. This point bears emphasis given the complex political stakes involved. Komori's scholarship is profoundly marked by his "leftist" activism, and this, I believe,

is an admirable feature of his work. The fact remains, however, that the prelapsarian logic that at least partially informs his notion of ethics is also used extensively by the "right." For a wartime illustration of this logic, see the 1942 symposium *kindai no chōkoku*, in *Overcoming Modernity: Cultural Identity in Wartime Japan*, ed. and trans. Richard F. Calichman (New York: Columbia University Press, 2008).

43. In her informative chapter on Komori, Atsuko Sakaki locates in Komori's work an intriguing shift from structuralism to deconstruction. See Atsuko Sakaki, *Recontextualizing Texts: Narrative Performance in Modern Japanese Fiction* (Cambridge, MA: Harvard University Asia Center, 1999), 48. While her argument concerning Komori's structuralism is indeed persuasive, her claim that the self-referentiality found in his later essays should be seen as proof of a "deconstructionist Komori" remains somewhat unconvincing.

44. Komori, *Murakami Haruki ron*, 58.

45. Despite the consistent appeal in Komori's work to the notion of alterity (*tashasei*), which he regards as the very touchstone of ethics, the belief in the autonomy of the subject is never fundamentally questioned. As he argues in his discussion of Sōseki with reference to Adorno's analysis of fascism, "The 'anger' and 'opposition' that one displays upon receiving from the other a command that goes against one's will is nothing other than an expression of man's autonomy and individuality as a creature with a command of language who can say 'No!' It is precisely this that is proof of the independence of the self." See Komori, *Murakami Haruki ron*, 168–169. A more radical conception of alterity would immediately reveal the impossibility of such subjective autonomy or independence. For this to occur, however, the *other* needs to be thought beyond the level of merely other (autonomous) human beings.

46. Komori, *Murakami Haruki ron*, 220, 255, 201, and 140, respectively.

47. Komori, *Murakami Haruki ron*, 144–146.

48. Komori, *Murakami Haruki ron*, 137. As Mizumura writes, "Throughout modern Japanese literature, it is only in Sōseki's work that women breathe as spiritual human beings." See Mizumura Minae, "'Otoko to otoko' to 'otoko to onna': Fujio no shi" ['Man and man' and 'man and woman': Fujio's death] *Hihyō kūkan* [Critical space], July 1992. Following the Latin root of this term, Mizumura here aligns the notion of spirit with that of breath. Toward the end of *Murakami Haruki ron*, Komori will return to this issue in denouncing the misogyny he finds at the core of *Umibe no Kafuka*. There he expands upon Mizumura's determination of women on the basis of spirit (breath) by rehabilitating the notion of voice. It is through the voiced narration and singing of women, Komori argues, that they are able to recall authentic memory and thus resist the inauthentic historical accounts written by men. In this way, the conceptual chain of woman-victim-voice-memory is directly opposed to that of man-power-writing-forgetting (see Komori, *Murakami Haruki ron*, 258–262). While what appears to be the ethicopolitical intent of Komori's attack on misogyny is certainly noble, one must wonder if power relations ever follow such a straightforward division and if such formulation does not indeed obfuscate rather

than reveal certain mechanisms of power. Further, the explicit linking of women with spirit (breath, voice) itself runs the risk of enlarging the scope of misogyny.

49. Komori, *Murakami Haruki ron*, 148. The passage from Murakami appears in *Umibe no Kafuka*, 2:92; trans. Gabriel, *Kafka on the Shore,* 281. Translation slightly modified.

50. Murakami, *Umibe no Kafuka*, 1:147, 172, 218, 256, 265; trans. Gabriel, *Kafka on the Shore*, 87, 100, 126, 148, 153. Translation slightly modified.

51. The specific term that Komori uses here is *mubaikaiteki*, literally "unmediated." As he writes: "I have repeatedly criticized this 'unmediated bonding.' Why? Because there is here a dynamics that cause a cessation of thought regarding the logical and rational relation between cause and effect. That is, the novel *Kafka on the Shore* represents an attempt to execute causal thinking itself, it possesses a function that causes all readers who advance through the text to stop thinking. Also, I criticize this point precisely because the ability on the part of human beings to think causal relations involves the foundation of human beings as creatures with a command of language." See Komori, *Murakami Haruki ron*, 160–161.

Chapter 2

1. Harry Harootunian, *History's Disquiet: Modernity, Cultural Practice, and the Question of Everyday Life* (New York: Columbia University Press, 2000), 103.

2. Harry Harootunian, *Toward Restoration: The Growth of Political Consciousness in Tokugawa Japan* (Berkeley and Los Angeles: University of California Press, 1970); Harry Harootunian, *Things Seen and Unseen: Discourse and Ideology in Tokugawa Nativism* (Chicago: University of Chicago Press, 1988); and Harry Harootunian, *Marx After Marx: History and Time in the Expansion of Capitalism* (New York: Columbia University Press, 2015).

3. David Williams, "Modernity, Harootunian and the Demands of Scholarship," in *Japan Forum* 15, no. 1 (2003): 154–155. Italics in original.

4. Harry Harootunian, *Overcome by Modernity: History, Culture, and Community in Interwar Japan* (Princeton, NJ: Princeton University Press, 2000), 90.

5. Harootunian makes exactly this point in his review of Williams's *Defending Japan's Pacific War: The Kyoto School Philosophers and Post-white Power* (London: RoutledgeCurzon, 2004). Employing the racialized language first articulated in Williams's argument, Harootunian remarks, "Moreover, the same philosophers who supplied, according to Williams, the template for a future figure of non-White power and multi-cultural and multi-ethnic utopia had no trouble in insisting on Japan's leadership in the coming reconstruction of Asia, which invariably meant developing a national community on the Japanese model. As for the empire of Yellow power that had already taken shape by 1942 it was fully committed to force and violence and to a studied indifference toward those subject peoples without subjectivity who

were now being asked to participate in the great 'cooperative' enterprise." See Harry Harootunian, "Returning to Japan: Part Two," in *Japan Forum* 18, no. 2 (2006): 281.

6. Andrew Gordon, "Rethinking Area Studies, Once More," *Journal of Japanese Studies* 30, no. 2 (2004): 418.

7. Gordon, "Rethinking Area Studies," 423.

8. Masao Miyoshi and H. D. Harootunian, eds., *Learning Places: The Afterlives of Area Studies* (Durham, NC: Duke University Press, 2002), 151.

9. Harootunian repeats this important claim in much the same language in *History's Disquiet*: "It has been one of the enduring ironies of the study of Asia that Asia itself, as an object, simply doesn't exist. While geographers and mapmakers once confidently named a sector on maps, noting even its coordinates as if in fact it existed, this enmapped place has never been more than a simulacrum of a substanceless something." See Harry Harootunian, *History's Disquiet*, 25.

10. Ethan Kleinberg, *Haunting History: For a Deconstructive Approach to the Past* (Stanford, CA: Stanford University Press, 2017), 1.

11. Kleinberg, *Haunting History*, 9.

12. Harootunian, *Marx After Marx*, 21–23.

13. Two important examples of such interpretation can be found in Jacques Derrida, *Specters of Marx: The State of the Debt, the Work of Mourning, and the New International*, trans. Peggy Kamuf (New York and London: Routledge, 1994); and the less well known but equally provocative William Haver, "For a Communist Ontology," in *The Politics of Culture: Around the Work of Naoki Sakai*, eds. Richard F. Calichman and John Namjun Kim (London and New York: Routledge, 2010), 105–120.

14. Harry Harootunian, "Visible Discourses/Invisible Ideologies," in *Postmodernism and Japan*, eds. Masao Miyoshi and H. D. Harootunian (Durham, NC: Duke University Press, 1989), 87. This phrase appears in the context of Harootunian's discussion of the social critic and China scholar Takeuchi Yoshimi.

15. Harootunian, *Things Seen and Unseen*, 243. The following italics are mine.

16. Harootunian, *Things Seen and Unseen*, 234.

17. Harootunian, *Things Seen and Unseen*, 332.

18. Harootunian, *Things Seen and Unseen*, 434.

19. In Tomiko Yoda and Harry Harootunian, eds., "Millennial Japan: Rethinking the Nation in the Age of Recession." Special Issue of *South Atlantic Quarterly* 99, no. 4 (Fall 2000): 717.

20. Harootunian, *Overcome by Modernity*, 30 and 216.

21. Harootunian, *Marx After Marx*, 36 and 67.

22. See Harry Harootunian, *Confronting Capital and Empire: Rethinking Kyoto School Philosophy*, eds. Viren Murthy, Fabian Schäfer, and Max Ward (Leiden: Brill, 2017), 52.

23. This understanding of time, I believe, can ultimately be traced to Hegel's repetition of Aristotle in thinking through the basic relation between point and line, as Jacques Derrida convincingly shows in "Ousia and Grammē: Note on a Note from *Being and Time*," *Margins of Philosophy*, trans. Alan Bass (Chicago: University

of Chicago Press, 1982), 29–67. For an excellent analysis of these issues, see Martin Hägglund, *Radical Atheism: Derrida and the Time of Life* (Stanford, CA: Stanford University Press, 2008).

24. Harootunian, *Overcome by Modernity*, 297–298.

25. Harootunian, *Things Seen and Unseen*, 451, n. 23. Italics mine.

26. Harootunian, *Overcome by Modernity*, 270. Italics mine.

27. Harootunian, *Marx After Marx*, 31. Italics mine.

28. Jean-François Lyotard, *The Postmodern Condition: A Report on Knowledge*, trans. Geoff Bennington and Brian Massumi (Minneapolis: University of Minnesota Press, 1984).

29. Harootunian, *Overcome by Modernity*, 180.

30. Harootunian, *Overcome by Modernity*, xxiv.

31. Yoda and Harootunian, "Millennial Japan," 734–735.

32. Yoda and Harootunian, "Millennial Japan," 736–737. A nearly verbatim account appears in the final pages of Harootunian, *History's Disquiet*, 157–158.

33. Yoda and Harootunian, "Millennial Japan," 735.

34. Jacques Derrida, "Force of Law: The 'Mystical Foundation of Authority,'" in *Deconstruction and the Possibility of Justice*, ed. Drucilla Cornell et al. (London: Routledge, 1992), 3–67.

35. Two examples among many others found throughout his work: "When Japanese ethnology became committed to Japan as signified as a condition for effacing both the practice of the body (the signifier) and its endless trek toward the place of the Other, when it moved to completely remove the Other—the different—it could never hope to become anything more than an incurable nostalgia, which yearned to freeze what had been process into a timeless presence." See Harootunian, *Things Seen and Unseen*, 418; and "With this move Yanagita supplied native ethnology, if not the modern Japanese consciousness, with a structure of desire for an origin that could never be reached and opened the way for a nostalgia driven by irretrievable loss." See Harootunian, *Overcome by Modernity*, 324.

36. "The practice of reading that I have tried to apply in this book contests the institutional limits that have defined the disciplinary boundaries of history . . . by raising questions concerning the aporetic nature of historical understanding itself. Ideally, such an approach should lead to what might nervously be called a 're-exoticization' of the historical past, which emphasizes its difference from, not its identity with, the present and reminds us of how narrative seduces us into believing that the past leads to the present. It would also, however, oblige us to concede our recognition of the genuine otherness of texts we stand in a position to 'receive' from *times and cultures distant from our own*." See Harootunian, *Things Seen and Unseen*, 20. Italics mine.

A question immediately arises upon reading these lines: if time, following Harootunian's reading of Marx, is essentially multiple and heterogeneous, then how can it ever be possible for us to determine that which is "our own?" What is called here "genuine otherness" cannot truly be an alterity insofar as it allows me to continue to confirm my own identity in opposition to that which exists outside of, or "distant from," me. Only when my knowledge of what is mine and what is other is disrupted does both time and otherness appear together in the general movement of temporal difference.

37. See, for example, "In no time at all, Japan, a former foe, was transmuted into friend but not full-fledged partner, *an autonomous nation into a dependent client* of a newly emerging, postwar imperium." Harry Harootunian, *The Empire's New Clothes: Paradigm Lost, and Regained* (Chicago: Prickly Paradigm, 2004), 79. Italics mine.

38. Harootunian, *History's Disquiet*, 141. Similar expressions can be found throughout Harootunian's *Overcome by Modernity*.

39. Harootunian, *History's Disquiet*, 103.

40. Harootunian, *History's Disquiet*, 113.

41. Harootunian, *History's Disquiet*, 99. Harootunian returns to this point of Heidegger's lack of "sociological specificity" in *Overcome by Modernity* in the context of his discussion of Watsuji Tetsurō: "Watsuji was quick to point out that Heidegger's account of human existence lacked sociological and historical specificity." See Harootunian, *Overcome by Modernity*, 268.

42. Martin Heidegger, *Being and Time*, trans. John Macquarrie and Edward Robinson (San Francisco: Harper and Row, 1962), 22.

43. As we witnessed earlier, Harootunian shrewdly targets the constitutive blind spot of Asian studies by arguing that "Asia" is, in fact, "substanceless." I fully concur with this argument but disagree with the restriction of the notion of substancelessness to the level of empirical history, such that certain things may be determined as substantial in contrast to other things that are determined as substanceless. The notion of substancelessness, I believe, must be raised to the general level of ontology. As goes without saying, this does *not* mean that nothing exists. Directly to the contrary, it means that the question of ontology must be openly or explicitly reconceived, failing which one risks falling back upon traditional (i.e., conservative) interpretations.

44. Harootunian, *Marx After Marx*, 233. Here the challenge to Heidegger proceeds through negative comparison with Marx: "Marx was concerned with a temporality that derived from the present, from the activity of labor itself, whereas Heidegger conceived of a temporality that came from the future; Marx secularized everyday time, while Heidegger 'resacralized' time as Being's destiny toward death." This notion of "Being's destiny toward death" seems to indicate a confusion between Being and Dasein. Graham Parkes points to this difficulty in Harootunian's treatment of Heidegger in the essay "Heidegger and Japanese Fascism: An Unsubstantiated Connection": "Harootunian's frequent discussions of Heidegger nonsensically conflate his fundamental distinctions between Being and beings (*Sein und Seiendes*: what Heidegger calls 'the ontological difference'), and between Being and Dasein" See Graham Parkes, "Heidegger and Japanese Fascism: An Unsubstantiated Connection" 257, n. 9, accessed July 5, 2018, https://nirc.nanzan-u.ac.jp/nfile/2131.

45. Heidegger, *Being and Time*, 47.

46. Harootunian, *History's Disquiet*, 100–101.

47. Theodor W. Adorno, *The Jargon of Authenticity* (Evanston, IL: Northwestern University Press, 1973). In *Overcome by Modernity*, Harootunian indeed quotes Adorno against Heidegger: "Authentic historicality must be discovered in Dasein's 'primordial temporality,' a mode of existence that would, according to Adorno, 'immobilize history in the unhistorical realm' and sanction a freezing of culture as primordial existence for Japanese theorists in the 1930s." See Harootunian, *Overcome by Modernity*, 223.

48. Harootunian, *Overcome by Modernity*, 96. Harootunian returns to this point later in the same text: "The Heideggerian narrative, plotting the ascent from inauthenticity to authenticity and Being's resolute decision for death that would produce a desired, ecstatic unity of time—past, present, and future—provided a powerful model for new forms of representation and memorative communication that managed to avoid development, as such" (see Harootunian, *Overcome by Modernity*, 229). (Once again, the phrase "resolute decision for death" should refer to Dasein rather than to Being.)

49. Beyond question, the nature of this retort to Heidegger brings Harootunian very close to the thinking of Tosaka Jun. In *Overcome by Modernity*, for instance, we read the following lines: "Tosaka's conception of custom, whose behavior he assimilated to the commodity form, converged with his elevation of the category of everydayness (*nichijōsei*). Like custom, everydayness had simply been taken for granted as unworthy of further reflection. . . . The commonsense understanding of everyday life saw it as simply 'customary' and 'vulgar,' dull routine, prompting philosophers to juxtapose it to the 'transcustomary' (*chōtsūzokumono*), which they privileged as a proper object for philosophical speculation . . . [P]hilosophy, in Tosaka's view, discounted the everyday because of its triviality, insignificance, for a world that exceeded the common and customary. He appeared concerned with the way philosophy had turned away from the reality of contemporary custom, the world of everyday life that was being figured in mass media and lived on the streets, removing its 'experience' from serious consideration" (see Harootunian, 122–123).

For a further example of Harootunian's perceptive reading of Tosaka, see Harry Harootunian, "The Darkness of the Lived Moment," introduction to *Tosaka Jun: A Critical Reader*, eds. Ken C. Kawashima, Fabian Schäfer, and Robert Stolz (Ithaca, NY: Cornell East Asia Series, 2013), pp. xv–xxxv.

50. In his "Visible Discourses/Invisible Ideologies" essay, for example: "Yet this discounting of historical change, denying history as the site of genuine difference, prefigured the assertion that, once the modern has been surpassed, the age of culture and the new middle class will finally realize their exemption from the uncertainties of change and the caprice of history." See Harootunian, "Visible Discourses," 84.

51. Heidegger, *Being and Time*, 377.

52. "The time that Heidegger named as vulgar and inauthentic, Benjamin, as we shall see, qualified as progressive. Both, however, envisaged in time a succession and accumulation of presents and thus saw modernity as the temporality called the 'new' and the end of the present." See Harootunian, *History's Disquiet*, 100.

53. Given the colossal importance of this line, it is helpful to provide other translations where the emphasis can be seen to have slightly shifted. In, for example, David Farrell Krell's *Ecstasy, Catastrophe: Heidegger from* Being and Time *to the* Black Notebooks (Albany: State University of New York Press, 2015), 22, we find: "Temporality is not prior to that a being that only later emerges out of *itself*; rather, its essence is temporalization in the unity of the *ecstases*"; whereas in Michael Inwood, *A Heidegger Dictionary* (Oxford: Blackwell, 1999), 221, Inwood renders it thusly: "It is not first an entity, which only later steps outside itself; its essence is to extemporize in the unity of the ecstases."

54. Harootunian, *Things Seen and Unseen*, 20.

Chapter 3

1. Takeuchi Yoshimi, "Kindai toha nanika (Nihon to Chūgoku no baai)" [What is modernity? (The case of Japan and China)], *Takeuchi Yoshimi zenshū* [The complete works of Takeuchi Yoshimi] (Tokyo: Chikuma shobō, 1980), 4:146–147; trans. Richard F. Calichman, *What is Modernity? Writings of Takeuchi Yoshimi* (New York: Columbia University Press, 2005), 65.

2. As Yoshikuni Igarashi argues in *Bodies of Memory: Narratives of War in Postwar Japanese Culture, 1945–1970* (Princeton, NJ: Princeton University Press, 2000), 29: "The relationship between the United States and Japan in the postwar melodrama is highly sexualized. The drama casts the United States as a male and Hirohito and Japan as a docile female, who unconditionally accepts the United States' desire for self-assurance. As a good enemy that is also constructed as a docile woman, Japan provides the United States with a reflection of its own power."

3. Doubtless the most representative example of this early presence of literary theory in Japan would be Natsume Sōseki's 1907 *Bungakuron*, translated as *Theory of Literature and Other Critical Writings*, eds. Michael K. Bourdaghs, Atsuko Ueda, and Joseph A. Murphy (New York: Columbia University Press, 2010).

4. Donald Keene, *Dawn to the West: Japanese Literature in the Modern Era: Fiction* (New York: Henry Holt, 1984), 506.

5. Tomi Suzuki, *Narrating the Self: Fictions of Japanese Modernity* (Stanford, CA: Stanford University Press, 1996), 9.

6. Suzuki, *Narrating the Self*, 4.

7. Suzuki, *Narrating the Self*, 51.

8. Suzuki, *Narrating the Self*, 6. Italics mine.

9. Michael Naas, *Taking on the Tradition: Jacques Derrida and the Legacies of Deconstruction* (Stanford, CA: Stanford University Press, 2003), xviii. As Naas writes, "With each reception [of tradition] comes the possibility of rethinking what is our own by receiving it before either we or it have been wholly constituted."

10. Suzuki, *Narrating the Self*, 3.

11. Keene, *Dawn to the West*, 4.
12. Edward Fowler, *The Rhetoric of Confession: Shishōsetsu in Early Twentieth-Century Japanese Fiction* (Berkeley: University of California Press, 1988), xviii.
13. Suzuki, *Narrating the Self*, 6.
14. Suzuki, *Narrating the Self*, 10.
15. Suzuki, 160; *Tanizaki Jun'ichirō zenshū* [The complete works of Tanizaki Jun'ichirō] (Tokyo: Chūōkōronsha, 1966–1970), 10:4.
16. Suzuki, *Narrating the Self*, 161.
17. This retroactive formation of identity appears forcefully in the work of Abe Kōbō as well. In his 1957 novel, *Kemonotachi ha kokyō wo mezasu* [Beasts head for home], a work that focuses on the irreducible complexity of all racial, ethnic, and national forms of identity, the protagonist Kuki Kyūzō at one point attempts to determine the identity of the character Kō. As Abe writes: "'So you're Japanese. I thought you might be,' [Kō] whispered in a low, dry voice while shooting a glance outside. He spoke Japanese easily. When Kyūzō looked at him again, the features of a Japanese person rose to the surface on the man's face (*aratamete minaosu to, otoko no kao ni nihonjin no rinkaku ga ukabideru*)." Precisely as with Tanizaki, Abe detects a certain linguistic contamination to be already at work in all sensory perception. See *Abe Kōbō zenshū* [The complete works of Abe Kōbō] (Tokyo: Shinchōsha, 1997–2000), 6:329–30; trans. Richard F. Calichman, *Beasts Head for Home: A Novel* (New York: Columbia University Press, 2017), 37.
18. Suzuki, *Narrating the Self*, 53; italics mine. This prospect of a negation of Japanese identity is perceived by Suzuki as threatening, which may account for the strange repetition of these lines nearly verbatim later on in the text: "The Shirakaba group in fact tended to accept Western discourse as universal. For them, there were no Japanese: there was only Humanity (*ningen*), or Mankind (*jinrui*), which stood side by side with such 'universal' notions as Love, Art, Nature, Justice, Beauty, and Life. All these notions were defined in relation to Humanity." See Suzuki, *Narrating the Self*, 94.
19. Suzuki, *Narrating the Self*, 10.
20. Suzuki, *Narrating the Self*, 102.
21. Suzuki, *Narrating the Self*, 107–108.
22. Suzuki, *Narrating the Self*, 108–109.
23. Sigmund Freud, "Inhibitions, Symptoms, and Anxiety," in *The Standard Edition of the Complete Psychological Works of Sigmund Freud*, ed. James Strachey (London: Hogarth and the Institute of Psycho-Analysis, 1974), 20:17.
24. Suzuki, *Narrating the Self*, 168; *Tanizaki Jun'ichirō zenshū*, 10:155.
25. Suzuki, *Narrating the Self*, 170; *Tanizaki Jun'ichirō zenshū*, 10:84.
26. Suzuki, *Narrating the Self*, 170.
27. Etienne Balibar, "Racism and Nationalism," in *Race, Nation, Class: Ambiguous Identities*, ed. Etienne Balibar and Immanuel Wallerstein, trans. Chris Turner (London: Verso, 1991), 49.

28. Suzuki, *Narrating the Self*, 171.
29. Keene, *Dawn to the West*, 746.
30. This geopolitical pairing is precisely what the cultural theorist Stuart Hall has called "the West and the Rest." See, among his various other works, "The West and the Rest: Discourse and Power," in *Modernity: An Introduction to Modern Societies*, ed. Stuart Hall, et al. (Cambridge, MA: Blackwell, 1996), 184–227.
31. Suzuki, *Narrating the Self*, 171.
32. Suzuki, *Narrating the Self*, 172.
33. Georg Wilhelm Friedrich Hegel, *The Philosophy of History*, trans. J. Sibree (New York: Wiley, 1900), 103.
34. Alan Tansman, *The Aesthetics of Japanese Fascism* (Berkeley: University of California Press, 2009), 18–19.
35. Tansman, *Aesthetics*, 166.
36. Alan Tansman, *The Writings of Kōda Aya, a Japanese Literary Daughter* (New Haven, CT: Yale University Press, 1993), 11–12.
37. Tansman, *Aesthetics*, 10.
38. Tansman, *Aesthetics*, 9.
39. Tansman, *Aesthetics*, 15.
40. Tansman, *Aesthetics*, 289, n. 46.
41. Tansman, *Aesthetics*, 15.
42. Sigmund Freud, "Beyond the Pleasure Principle," in *The Standard Edition of the Complete Psychological Works of Sigmund Freud*, ed. James Strachey (London: Hogarth and the Institute of Psycho-Analysis, 1974), 18:62. For an incisive reading of the Freudian notion of binding, see Martin Hägglund, *Dying for Time: Proust, Woolf, Nabokov* (Cambridge: Harvard University Press, 2012), 110–145.
43. Martin Heidegger, *Being and Time*, trans. John Macquarrie and Edward Robinson (New York: Harper & Row, 1962), 308.
44. Tansman, *Aesthetics*, 58. The footnote on Steiner appears on page 305, n. 31.
45. Nishida Kitarō, *An Inquiry Into the Good*, trans. Masao Abe and Christopher Ives (New Haven, CT: Yale University Press, 1990), xxx; *Nishida Kitarō zenshū* [The complete works of Nishida Kitarō] (Tokyo: Iwanami shoten, 1987–1989), 1:4.
46. Tansman, *Aesthetics*, 291. The translation of *Research on Zen* appears on page 329, n. 29. In this context, we should note that Tansman privileges the will as an important means of resistance against fascism. It remains unclear, however, how this idea is to be reconciled with the fact that fascism also drew extensively upon the resources of the will, as can be seen most notoriously in Leni Riefenstahl's 1935 propaganda film *Triumph of the Will*.
47. Tansman, *Aesthetics*, 6.
48. Tansman, *Aesthetics*, 8; italics mine. In *Narrating the Self*, Suzuki reveals herself to be more sensitive to the trap of subjective interiority as informs such appeal to the value of directness. As she argues, "Both detractors and eulogizers of

the I-novel, who unwittingly collaborated in characterizing the I-novel as direct, immediate, and factual as opposed to fictional, projected these same notions of directness and factuality on the so-called indigenous tradition" (see Suzuki, *Narrating the Self*, 3).

49. Tansman, *Aesthetics*, 338, n. 8.

50. Tansman, *Aesthetics*, 10.

51. Tansman, *Aesthetics*, 3.

52. Tansman, *Aesthetics*, 128–129.

53. Tansman, *Aesthetics*, 240.

54. Tansman, *Aesthetics*, 101.

55. At the same time, we must be attentive to the various ways in which this state project was itself internally contradictory. Tansman's desire to partly determine Japanese fascism on the basis of the claims of ethnic purity ignores the entire question of empire and the related problematic of *kōminka*, or "imperial subjectivization as Japanese." For a reading of Yasuda that focuses on these questions while also taking strong issue with Tansman's interpretation, see Takeshi Kimoto, "The Standpoint of World History and Imperial Japan" (PhD diss., Cornell University, 2010).

56. Tansman, *Aesthetics*, 235.

57. Tansman, 130.

58. Tansman, 195.

59. "The desire to dispense with the communicative function of language, a desire that would become so central to writers in this study." Tansman, 41.

60. Jacques Derrida, "My Chances/*Mes Chances*: A Rendezvous with Some Epicurean Stereophonies," in *Taking Chances: Derrida, Psychoanalysis, and Literature*, eds. Joseph H. Smith and William Kerrigan, trans. Irene Harvey and Avital Ronnell (Baltimore: Johns Hopkins University Press, 1988), 1–32.

61. Tansman, *Aesthetics*, 55.

62. Tansman, *Aesthetics*, 46; italics mine.

63. Tansman, *Aesthetics*, 262.

64. Dennis C. Washburn, *The Dilemma of the Modern in Japanese Fiction* (New Haven, CT: Yale University Press, 1995), 266–267. As a footnote in the introduction makes clear, these words are in fact a veiled criticism of Naoki Sakai's article "Modernity and Its Critique: The Problem of Universalism and Particularism," in *Postmodernism and Japan*, eds. Masao Miyoshi and H. D. Harootunian (Durham, NC: Duke University Press, 1989), which Washburn faults for being "excessively reductive" (Washburn, *Dilemma*, 271, n. 12).

65. Washburn, *Translating Mount Fuji: Modern Japanese Fiction and the Ethics of Identity* (New York: Columbia University Press, 2007), xii.

66. Washburn, *Translating*, 207.

67. Washburn, *Translating*, 208.

68. Washburn, *Translating*, 24.

69. Washburn, *Translating*, 23.

70. Washburn, *Translating*, 3. Similar formulations can be found throughout *Translating Mount Fuji*.

71. Washburn, *Translating*, 83. Washburn is attempting in this passage to provoke a dialogue between Okakura Kakuzō and Barbara Johnson concerning the nature of translation.

72. Washburn, *Translating*, 5, 20, 27, respectively.

73. Maruyama Masao, *Nihon no shisō* (Tokyo: Iwanami shoten, 1961).

74. Maruyama, *Nihon*, 25.

75. Washburn, *Translating*, 32. Washburn here draws upon Maruyama's *Studies in the Intellectual History of Tokugawa Japan*, trans. Mikiso Hane (Princeton, NJ: Princeton University Press, 1974).

76. Inconsistencies regarding this position of scholarly neutrality or impartiality naturally appear, however. Two examples: (1) "Looking back over the history of Japan during the first half of the twentieth century, it seems that there was no way to easily resolve these contradictions. The aesthetically powerful appeal to a common identity was one way to relieve the individual from the burden of a modern ethical consciousness which demanded skepticism over belief and the struggle for independence of spirit over the comforts of conformity" (Washburn, *Translating*, 16); and (2) "Making authenticity the starting point for discussions of identity is one way to overcome the self-consciousness required for reflection" (Washburn, *Translating*, 22).

It seems clear in these passages that Washburn is himself advocating a stance of "modern ethical consciousness," which values "skepticism over belief and the struggle for independence of spirit over the comforts of conformity," thereby creating a space for "the self-consciousness required for reflection." Given the binaristic framework to which Washburn appeals that aligns individual autonomy with the West and collective authenticity with Japan or the non-West, however, it is worth asking how he manages to avoid the trap of modernization theory in its claim for the superiority of so-called Western values. In this regard, I believe, a certain anxiety may be detected throughout the pages of both *The Dilemma of the Modern* and *Translating Mount Fuji* that the reader might possibly equate Washburn's position with that of modernization theory and that of Eurocentrism more generally.

77. Washburn, *Translating*, 137–138, italics mine. It should be noted that Washburn repeats this sentence (and the paragraph in which it is situated) nearly verbatim in his translator's postscript to *Shanghai: A Novel by Yokomitsu Riichi* (Ann Arbor: Center for Japanese Studies, University of Michigan, 2001), 219.

Washburn appears to borrow this phrase "original sin" in its specific reference to a fallen Japanese modernity from the literary critic Maeda Ai, whom he quotes in the following passage: "Maeda situates [Higuchi] Ichiyo's story in the process by which the latter festival, in which the movement of people in a modern capitalist society divorces them from agricultural time and space, overtakes the former. He sees the modern arising in the change from the agricultural space of play to an ethos of hard work and determination to succeed, and he calls this 'our original sin' (*wareware no genzai*)" (Washburn, *Translating*, 262, n. 3).

An English translation of Maeda's essay by Edward Fowler appears in *Text and the City: Essays on Japanese Modernity*, ed. James A. Fujii (Durham, NC: Duke University Press, 2004), 109–143.

78. In a quite different context, and without recourse to the concept of original sin, the literary critic and China scholar Takeuchi Yoshimi memorably referred to this historical phenomenon as the "double structure of the Meiji state," which he describes as follows: "Japan's basic state policy throughout the Meiji period was the realization of complete independence. The complete repeal of the unequal treaties forced upon the country at the time of its opening up (tariff autonomy) had been put off until 1911. Meanwhile, however, Japan forced unequal treaties upon Korea as early as 1876. This imposition of unequal treaties upon Korea and China corresponded with Japan's own attempt to free itself from those unequal treaties imposed upon it." See Takeuchi Yoshimi, "Kinda no chōkoku" [Overcoming modernity], in *Takeuchi Yoshimi zenshū* (Tokyo: Chikuma shobō, 1980), 8:51; *What is Modernity?*, 136.

79. In his perceptive review of *Translating Mount Fuji*, Michael Bourdaghs also calls attention to the flaw of Washburn's notion of hybridity: "The result is what Washburn calls the hybridity of modern Japanese culture. But is there any culture (including our own) that is not the product of translation or that is not hybrid? If not, then in what sense are these terms especially meaningful for a discussion of Japanese modern literature?" *Journal of Japanese Studies* 34, no. 1 (Winter 2008): 219.

80. Washburn, *Translating*, 3. In *Dilemma of the Modern*, Washburn quotes the philosopher Charles Taylor to more or less the same effect. For Taylor, the difference between the premodern and the modern appears most crucially as the distinction between the outside and inside of the individual subject: "For the modern I am a natural being, I am characterized by a set of inner drives. . . . The horizon of identity is an inner horizon. For the pre-modern, I want to argue, I am an element in a larger order. . . . The order in which I am placed is an external horizon" (Washburn, *Dilemma*, 9).

Washburn can be said to map this temporal-historical distinction between the premodern and modern onto the explicitly spatial-geographical opposition between the non-West and West. Let me quickly add, however, that this is an extremely common (if erroneous and, I believe, ultimately racist) formulation, and Washburn is by no means alone in grasping the dynamics of global modernity in these terms. On the contrary, his work testifies to the need to understand such geopolitical issues at an *institutional* rather than merely *individual* level. In this regard, Washburn's scholarship, much like that of Suzuki and Tansman, must be regarded in the broader psychoanalytic sense as a symptom.

81. Ferdinand de Saussure, *Course in General Linguistics*, trans. Wade Baskin (New York: McGraw-Hill, 1966), 117.

82. This important insight returns us directly to Takeuchi Yoshimi. As Takeuchi writes in the 1948 essay "Kindai toha nanika" in the context of a discussion of European imperialist expansion in Asia: "Simply being Europe does not make Europe Europe. The various facts of history teach that Europe barely maintains itself through the tension of its incessant self-renewals." *Takeuchi Yoshimi zenshū*, 4:130; *What is Modernity?*, 54.

83. Washburn, *Dilemma*, 1.

84. Washburn, *Translating*, ix.

85. Washburn, *Translating*, x.

86. Washburn, *Dilemma*, 2. Washburn gives the name transcendence to this illegitimate freezing of time into a state of presence. Compare here Tansman, whose methodology, conceptual understanding, and indeed overall project share a great many commonalities with those of Washburn. As, for example, Tansman writes in *The Aesthetics of Japanese Fascism*: "For many writers of the fascist aesthetic, transforming language into incantation was a way of tapping into materiality, and this was a way to evoke a realm untouched by will and undisturbed by time. Theirs was a language with no practical ends, free from mediation, grounded in the material in order to connect directly with the transcendent. Its feeling of material permanence—concrete yet transcendent—was an imaginative shield against the tyrannical fracturing of the senses and of the movement of time" (Tansman, *Aesthetics*, 38–39).

87. Washburn, *Dilemma*, 1.

88. Edwin McClellan, *Two Japanese Novelists: Sōseki and Tōson* (Chicago: University of Chicago Press, 1969), 31–32. McClellan's inability to grasp the importance of *Sanshirō* appears somewhat surprising when judged against the background of his very elegant translation of the 1912 novel *Kokoro*. For a recent evaluation of some of the limitations of this translation, however, see J. Keith Vincent, "Sexuality and Narrative in Sōseki's *Kokoro*," in *Perversion and Modern Japan: Psychoanalysis, Literature, Culture*, eds. Nina Cornyetz and J. Keith Vincent (London: Routledge, 2010), 222–240.

89. Washburn, *Translating*, 73.

90. Washburn, *Translating*, 73.

91. Washburn, *Translating*, 83.

92. Washburn, *Translating*, 28.

93. As is well known, this problematic is as old as the history of philosophy itself. William Haver forcefully determines its Marxist inflection as follows: "The relation, Marx repeatedly insists, determines the relata. Indeed, it would make no sense to appeal to the dialectic, any dialectic, if it were not to claim the priority of relation over relata. The Marxist dialectic is precisely an insistence upon the absolute priority of relation as differential articulation." See William Haver, "For a Communist Ontology," in *The Politics of Culture: Around the Work of Naoki Sakai*, eds. Richard F. Calichman and John Namjun Kim (London: Routledge, 2010), 107.

94. These words must be seen as structurally analogous to the lines previously quoted and analyzed from Suzuki: "The I-novel is best defined as a mode of reading

that assumes that the I-novel is a single-voiced, 'direct' expression of the author's 'self' and that its written language is 'transparent'—characteristics hitherto regarded as 'intrinsic' features of the I-novel. The I-novel, instead of being a particular literary form or genre, was a literary and ideological paradigm by which a vast majority of literary works were judged and described. *Any text can become an I-novel if read in this mode.*" Suzuki, *Narrating the Self*, 6; italics mine.

In both cases, Washburn's and Suzuki's, an idea is formulated within the framework of the larger argument that strangely reveals itself to be more general than, and hence directly threatening to, the argument itself. This idea thus resides uncomfortably within the scope of the argument presented, since the latter is unable to contain it strictly within itself.

95. In the field of Japan studies and beyond, the most rigorous examination of this problem is to be found in Naoki Sakai, *Translation and Subjectivity: On "Japan" and Cultural Nationalism* (Minneapolis: University of Minnesota Press, 1997).

96. Washburn, *Translating*, 71. Washburn here uses Jay Rubin's translation in *Sanshirō: A Novel* (Seattle: University of Washington Press, 1977).

97. Washburn, *Translating*, 75.

98. Washburn notes that he has also consulted *Natsume Sōseki zenshū* [The complete works of Natsume Sōseki], vol. 7 (Tokyo: Iwanami shoten, 1956). In this edition, the discussion of Mount Fuji appears on pp. 61–62. Washburn, *Translating*, 257, n. 1.

99. The reference to Mount Fuji then is described in the voice of Professor Hirota as follows: "Oh yes, this is your first trip to Tokyo, isn't it? You've never seen Mount Fuji. We go by it a little farther on. Have a look. It's the finest thing Japan has to offer, the only thing we have to boast about. The trouble is, of course, it's just a natural object. It's been sitting there for all time. We didn't make it." See Natsume Sōseki, *Sanshirō*, trans. Jay Rubin (London: Penguin Classics, 2009), 15–16.

100. The dislocating presence of time *within* the subject is carefully noted by Sōseki: "The chaotic jumble of the world inside his head *now*." Significantly, this insight into the subject's participation in the constitution of the world already appears in the first reference to the singular Mount Fuji (still written as 富士山). Immediately after advising Sanshirō to view the mountain from the train window, Professor Hirota turns to the complex question of the subject-object relation: "But then the man said, 'Tokyo is bigger than Kumamoto. And Japan is bigger than Tokyo. And even bigger than Japan . . .' He paused and looked at Sanshirō, who was listening intently now. 'Even bigger than Japan is the inside of your head.'" *Natsume Sōseki zenshū*, 7:19; *Sanshirō*, 16.

It is perhaps no accident in this context that Sōseki, having now established the fact of the subject's participation in the constitution of the world, then broaches the question of the subject's national affiliation: "Don't ever surrender yourself—not to Japan, not to anything. You may think that what you're doing is for the sake of the nation, but let something take possession of you like that, and all you do is bring it down." Clearly these words cannot be reduced to any simple victory of subjective autonomy over the repression and conformity of collective authenticity. On the contrary, I believe that they must be seen as directly relevant to any thinking that insists on understanding national affiliation in purely objective terms.

101. As Philippe Lacoue-Labarthe and Jean-Luc Nancy write, tracing out a logic already developed in Heidegger and Derrida, "First, the other only ever '*is*' its own withdrawal, its own proper-improper withdrawal. . . . The Other is not at first the identical other, but the withdrawal of this identity—the originary *alteration*." Philippe Lacoue-Labarthe and Jean-Luc Nancy, "La panique politique," in *Retreating the Political*, ed. Simon Sparks (London: Routledge, 1997), 27.

102. Washburn quotes this passage in a slightly more truncated form in *Translating Mount Fuji*, 101–102. See also *Natsume Sōseki zenshū*, 7:106–109; *Sanshirō: A Novel*, 93–94.

103. Washburn, *Translating*, 102.

104. Washburn, *Translating*, 104.

105. Limited space prevents me from further pursuing this line of reading, but it seems clear that Sōseki wishes to think this excessive movement of translation as a kind of propagation. Hence the fascinating reference in the text to *reiyoshi*, or what Rubin skillfully translates as "A. Propagule," in the sense of those parts of a plant that can be removed in order to create new plants, thereby indicating the presence of a self-generating difference in the interior of identity. *Natsume Sōseki zenshū*, 7:110; *Sanshirō*, 103.

106. Sōseki, 102; *Sanshirō*, 109.

107. Sōseki, 238–242; *Sanshirō*, 223–228.

108. Sōseki, 18; *Sanshirō*, 16.

109. See Miyoshi and Harootunian, *Postmodernism and Japan*, 104.

Coda

1. In order to avoid the trap of moralism, I should state that this notion of responsibility is to be translated into Japanese less by the common term *sekinin* than by the more recent *ōtō kanōsei*, that is, the "possibility of response."

Bibliography

Abe Kōbō. *Kemonotachi ha kokyō wo mezasu* [Beasts head for home]. In *Abe Kōbō zenshū* [The complete works of Abe Kōbō]. Vol. 6. Tokyo: Shinchōsha, 1997–2000.

Adorno, Theodor W. *The Jargon of Authenticity*. Evanston, IL: Northwestern University Press, 1973.

Balibar, Etienne. "Racism and Nationalism." In *Race, Nation, Class: Ambiguous Identities*, edited by Etienne Balibar and Immanuel Wallerstein. Translated by Chris Turner. London: Verso, 1991.

Bourdaghs, Michael. "Review of Translating Mount Fuji." *The Journal of Japanese Studies* 34, no. 1 (Winter 2008).

Calichman, Richard F., trans. *Beasts Head for Home: A Novel*. New York: Columbia University Press, 2017.

———. *Beyond Nation: Time, Writing, and Community in the Work of Abe Kōbō*. Stanford, CA: Stanford University Press, 2016.

——— ed. and trans. *Overcoming Modernity: Cultural Identity in Wartime Japan*. New York: Columbia University Press, 2008.

——— ed. and trans. *What is Modernity? Writings of Takeuchi Yoshimi*. New York: Columbia University Press, 2005.

Derrida, Jacques. "Force of Law: The 'Mystical Foundation of Authority.'" In *Deconstruction and the Possibility of Justice*, edited by Drucilla Cornell, et al. New York and London: Routledge, 1992.

———. *Margins of Philosophy*. Translated by Alan Bass. Chicago: University of Chicago Press, 1982.

———. "My Chances/Mes Chances: A Rendezvous with Some Epicurean Stereophonies." In *Taking Chances: Derrida, Psychoanalysis, and Literature*, edited by Joseph H. Smith and William Kerrigan. Translated by Irene Harvey and Avital Ronnell. Baltimore: Johns Hopkins University Press, 1988.

———. *Specters of Marx: The State of the Debt, the Work of Mourning, and the New International*. Translated by Peggy Kamuf. New York and London: Routledge, 1994.

Fowler, Edward. *The Rhetoric of Confession: Shishōsetsu in Early Twentieth-Century Japanese Fiction*. Berkeley: University of California Press, 1988.

Freud, Sigmund. "Beyond the Pleasure Principle." In *The Standard Edition of the Complete Psychological Works of Sigmund Freud*, edited by James Strachey. Vol. 18. London: Hogarth Press and the Institute of Psycho-Analysis, 1974.

———. "Inhibitions, Symptoms, and Anxiety." In *The Standard Edition of the Complete Psychological Works of Sigmund Freud*. Vol. 20. London: Hogarth Press and the Institute of Psycho-Analysis, 1974.

Fujii, James A, ed. *Text and the City: Essays on Japanese Modernity*. Durham, NC: Duke University Press, 2004.

Gordon, Andrew. "Rethinking Area Studies, Once More." *Journal of Japanese Studies* 30, no. 2 (2004).

Hägglund, Martin. *Dying for Time: Proust, Woolf, Nabokov*. Cambridge, MA: Harvard University Press, 2012.

———. *Radical Atheism: Derrida and the Time of Life*. Stanford, CA: Stanford University Press, 2008.

Hall, Stuart. "The West and the Rest: Discourse and Power." In *Modernity: An Introduction to Modern Societies*, edited by Stuart Hall, et al. Cambridge, MA: Blackwell, 1996.

Harootunian, Harry. *History's Disquiet: Modernity, Cultural Practice, and the Question of Everyday Life*. New York: Columbia University Press, 2000.

———. "Japan's Long Postwar: The Trick of Memory and the Ruse of History." In *Millennial Japan: Rethinking the Nation in the Age of Recession*, edited by Tomiko Yoda and Harry Harootunian. Special issue of *South Atlantic Quarterly* 99, no. 4 (Fall 2000).

———. *Marx After Marx: History and Time in the Expansion of Capitalism*. New York: Columbia University Press, 2015.

———. *Overcome by Modernity: History, Culture, and Community in Interwar Japan*. Princeton, NJ: Princeton University Press, 2000.

———. "Philosophy and Answerability: The Kyoto School and the Epiphanic Moment of World History." In *Confronting Capital and Empire: Rethinking Kyoto School Philosophy*, edited by Viren Murthy, Fabian Schäfer, and Max Ward. Leiden: Brill, 2017.

———. "Postcoloniality's Unconscious/Area Studies' Desire." In *Learning Places: The Afterlives of Area Studies*, edited by Masao Miyoshi and H. D. Harootunian. Durham, NC: Duke University Press, 2002.

———. "Returning to Japan: Part Two." In *Japan Forum* 18, no. 2: 2006.

———. "The Darkness of the Lived Moment." In *Tosaka Jun: A Critical Reader*, edited by Ken C. Kawashima, Fabian Schäfer, and Robert Stolz. Ithaca, NY: East Asia Program, Cornell University, 2013.

———. *The Empire's New Clothes: Paradigm Lost, and Regained*. Chicago: Prickly Paradigm, 2004.

---. *Things Seen and Unseen: Discourse and Ideology in Tokugawa Nativism.* Chicago: University of Chicago Press, 1988.

---. *Toward Restoration: The Growth of Political Consciousness in Tokugawa Japan.* Berkeley and Los Angeles: University of California Press, 1970.

---. "Visible Discourses/Invisible Ideologies." In *Postmodernism and Japan*, edited by Masao Miyoshi and H. D. Harootunian. Durham, NC: Duke University Press, 1989.

Haver, William. "For a Communist Ontology." In *The Politics of Culture: Around the Work of Naoki Sakai*, edited by Richard F. Calichman and John Namjun Kim. London and New York: Routledge, 2010.

Hegel, Georg Wilhelm Friedrich. *Phenomenology of Spirit.* Translated by A.V. Miller. Oxford: Oxford University Press, 1977.

---. *The Philosophy of History.* Translated by J. Sibree. New York: John Wiley, 1900.

Heidegger, Martin. *Being and Time.* Translated by John Macquarrie and Edward Robinson. San Francisco: Harper and Row, 1962.

Igarashi Yoshikuni. *Bodies of Memory: Narratives of War in Postwar Japanese Culture, 1945–1970.* Princeton, NJ: Princeton University Press, 2000.

Inwood, Michael. *A Heidegger Dictionary.* Oxford: Blackwell, 1999.

Keene, Donald. *Dawn to the West: Japanese Literature in the Modern Era: Fiction.* New York: Henry Holt, 1984.

Kimoto, Takeshi. "The Standpoint of World History and Imperial Japan." PhD diss., Cornell University, 2010.

Kleinberg, Ethan. *Haunting History: For a Deconstructive Approach to the Past.* Stanford, CA: Stanford University Press, 2017.

Krell, David Farrell. *Ecstasy, Catastrophe: Heidegger from Being and Time to the Black Notebooks.* Albany: State University of New York Press, 2015.

Komori Yōichi. *Buntai to shite no monogatari* [Narrative as literary style]. Tokyo: Chikuma shobō, 1994.

---. *Dekigoto to shite no yomu koto* [Reading as event]. Tokyo: Tokyo daigaku shuppankai, 1996.

---. *Kōzō to shite no katari* [Narration as structure]. Tokyo: Shinyōsha, 1992.

---. *Murakami Haruki ron: 'Umibe no Kafuka' wo seidoku suru* [On Murakami Haruki: A close reading of 'Kafka on the Shore']. Tokyo: Heibonsha shinsho, 2006.

Lacoue-Labarthe, Philippe, and Jean-Luc Nancy. "La panique politique." In *Retreating the Political*, edited by Simon Sparks. London: Routledge, 1997.

Lyotard, Jean-François. *The Postmodern Condition: A Report on Knowledge.* Translated by Geoff Bennington and Brian Massumi. Minneapolis: University of Minnesota Press, 1984.

Maruyama Masao. *Nihon no shisō* [Japanese thought]. Tokyo: Iwanami shoten, 1961.

---. *Studies in the Intellectual History of Tokugawa Japan.* Translated by Mikiso Hane. Princeton, NJ: Princeton University Press, 1974.

McClellan, Edwin. *Two Japanese Novelists: Sōseki and Tōson*. Chicago: University of Chicago Press, 1969.

Mizumura Minae. " 'Otoko to otoko' to 'otoko to onna': Fujio no shi" ['Man and man' and 'man and woman': Fujio's death]. *Hihyō kūkan* [Critical space], July 1992.

Murakami Haruki. "Introduction." In *The Miner*. Translated by Jay Rubin. London: Aardvark Bureau, 2015.

———. *Umibe no Kafuka* [Kafka on the shore]. Tokyo: Shinchōsha, 2004. Translated by Philip Gabriel. New York: Vintage International, 2006.

Naas, Michael. *Taking on the Tradition: Jacques Derrida and the Legacies of Deconstruction*. Stanford, CA: Stanford University Press, 2003.

Natsume Sōseki. *Sanshirō*. In *Natsume Sōseki zenshū* [The complete works of Natsume Sōseki]. Vol. 7. Tokyo: Iwanami shoten, 1956.

———. *Sanshirō: A Novel*. Translated by Jay Rubin. Seattle: University of Washington Press, 1977.

———. *Sanshirō*. Translated by Jay Rubin. London: Penguin Classics, 2009.

———. *Theory of Literature and Other Critical Writings*. Edited by Michael K. Bourdaghs, Atsuko Ueda, and Joseph A. Murphy. New York: Columbia University Press, 2010.

Nishida Kitarō. *Nishida Kitarō zenshū* [The complete works of Nishida Kitarō]. Vol. 1. Tokyo: Iwanami shoten, 1987–1989.

———. *An Inquiry Into the Good*. Translated by Masao Abe and Christopher Ives. New Haven, CT: Yale University Press, 1990.

Parkes, Graham. "Heidegger and Japanese Fascism: An Unsubstantiated Connection." https://nirc.nanzan-u.ac.jp/nfile/2131.

Protevi, John. *Time and Exteriority: Aristotle, Heidegger, Derrida*. Lewisburg, PA: Bucknell University Press, 1994.

Sakai, Naoki. "Modernity and its Critique: The Problem of Universalism and Particularism." In *Postmodernism and Japan*, edited by Masao Miyoshi and H. D. Harootunian. Durham, NC: Duke University Press, 1989.

———. *Translation and Subjectivity: On "Japan" and Cultural Nationalism*. Minneapolis: University of Minnesota Press, 1997.

Sakaki, Atsuko. *Recontextualizing Texts: Narrative Performance in Modern Japanese Fiction*. Cambridge, MA: Harvard University Asia Center, 1999.

Saussure, Ferdinand de. *Course in General Linguistics*. Translated by Wade Baskin. New York: McGraw-Hill, 1966.

Strecher, Matthew Carl. *The Forbidden Worlds of Haruki Murakami*. Minneapolis: University of Minnesota Press, 2014.

Suzuki, Tomi. *Narrating the Self: Fictions of Japanese Modernity*. Stanford, CA: Stanford University Press, 1996.

Takeuchi Yoshimi. "Hōhō to shite no Ajia" [Asia as method]. In *Takeuchi Yoshimi zenshū* [Collected works of Takeuchi Yoshimi]. Vol. 5. Tokyo: Chikuma shobō, 1980.

———. "Kinda no chōkoku" [Overcoming modernity]. In *Takeuchi Yoshimi zenshū* [Collected works of Takeuchi Yoshimi]. Vol. 8. Tokyo: Chikuma shobō, 1980.

———."Kindai toha nanika (Nihon to Chūgoku no baai)" [What is modernity? (The case of Japan and China)]. In *Takeuchi Yoshimi zenshū* [Collected works of Takeuchi Yoshimi]. Vol. 4. Tokyo: Chikuma shobō, 1980.

Tanizaki Jun'ichirō. *Chijin no ai* [A fool's love], in *Tanizaki Jun'ichirō zenshū* [The complete works of Tanizaki Jun'ichirō]. Vol. 10. Tokyo: Chūōkōronsha, 1966–1970.

Tansman, Alan. *The Aesthetics of Japanese Fascism*. Berkeley: University of California Press, 2009.

———. *The Writings of Kōda Aya, a Japanese Literary Daughter*. New Haven, CT: Yale University Press, 1993.

Vincent, J. Keith. "Sexuality and Narrative in Sōseki's Kokoro." In *Perversion and Modern Japan: Psychoanalysis, Literature, Culture*, edited by Nina Cornyetz and J. Keith Vincent. London: Routledge, 2010.

Washburn, Dennis C., trans. *Shanghai*. Ann Arbor: Center for Japanese Studies, University of Michigan, 2001.

———. *The Dilemma of the Modern in Japanese Fiction*. New Haven, CT: Yale University Press, 1995.

———. *Translating Mount Fuji: Modern Japanese Fiction and the Ethics of Identity*. New York: Columbia University Press, 2007.

Williams, David. "Modernity, Harootunian and the Demands of Scholarship." *Japan Forum* 15, no. 1 (2003).

Index

Abe Kōbō, 3, 189, 201
Alterity, 7, 20, 27, 50, 52–54, 74–75, 84, 89, 100–101, 105, 142, 144–146, 149–150, 157–158, 163–164, 172, 182, 194, 197
Althusser, Louis, 144

Benjamin, Walter, 96–97, 154, 199
Bergson, Henri, 13, 27, 69, 72
Binarity, 6–7, 15–17, 36, 43, 62, 68, 76, 83–85, 89, 100, 116, 118, 121, 123–124, 139, 144, 146–147, 158, 162–164, 179–180, 204
Binding, 7, 35, 133–142, 149–150, 178, 202
Borges, Jorge, 163–164

Consciousness, 10–17, 19–25, 27–29, 35–36, 39, 41–43, 48–49, 51, 55, 57, 82, 132, 143, 146, 159, 161, 165, 172, 184, 187, 197, 204
Contingency, 5, 16, 31, 42, 66, 78, 114–115, 134, 141, 182

Death, 14, 17–19, 23–24, 32, 47–48, 73, 98, 142, 164, 194, 198–199
Derrida, Jacques, 12, 27, 67–68, 149, 191, 196–197, 200, 203, 207

Eliot, T. S., 163–165

Ethics, 2, 5–6, 17, 38–44, 46–49, 51–54, 59, 81, 83–85, 89, 93, 104–106, 158, 162, 165, 177, 185, 193–194
Event, 21, 23, 26–39, 45, 47, 67–68, 71, 77, 85, 87, 126, 158, 183

Fascism, 7, 60, 110–111, 133–147, 149, 177–178, 194, 198, 202–203
Finitude, 98, 124, 143, 164
Fowler, Edward, 112–113, 115–116, 118, 121–122, 127, 177, 200, 204
Freud, Sigmund, 15, 27, 128, 142, 201–202
Future, 4, 9, 21, 24–25, 33, 35, 37–38, 57, 64, 74, 78, 85–86, 90, 94, 99, 102–106, 113–114, 117, 120, 124, 126, 163–164, 166, 176, 185, 187–188, 191, 195, 198–199

Ghost, 3, 68
Gordon, Andrew, 6, 59, 62–66, 195

Haunting, 3, 37, 66–68, 73, 148, 160, 176, 179, 186, 190
Harootunian, Harry, 5–6, 57–106, 189, 195–200, 203, 208
Hegel, Georg Wilhelm Friedrich, 18, 27, 94, 132, 191, 196, 202

Heidegger, Martin, 6–7, 59, 69, 72, 95–106, 142–143, 191, 198–199, 202, 207
Hijiya-Kirschnereit, Iremela, 112–113, 115, 118, 121–122, 127, 177
Historiography, 27, 59, 66–68, 70–72, 74
Human, 22, 30–31, 35, 39, 41, 44–45, 48, 50–54, 81–82, 122, 131–133, 141, 144, 147, 158, 169–170, 192, 194–195, 198, 201

Identity, 1, 7, 14, 19, 24–25, 27, 32–33, 35, 38–41, 44, 46, 52–55, 61–62, 68, 70–71, 74–76, 79–81, 84–86, 88, 90, 94, 102–105, 108–110, 112–114, 116–133, 135, 138–147, 149, 151, 153, 155–170, 172–173, 175–180, 184, 186–188, 192, 197, 201, 204–205, 207–208
Imamura Shōhei, 6, 86–91, 93–95, 97, 101
Inheritance, 4–5, 8, 42, 45, 67, 75, 187
Isoda Kōichi, 144

Kakuta Mitsuyo, 10–11, 13, 15
Katō Norihiro, 87–89
Kawai Hayao, 11–12, 15, 190
Keene, Donald, 110–111, 115–116, 118, 121–122, 127, 130, 179, 189, 200–201
Kleinberg, Ethan, 67–68, 70, 73, 196
Kobayashi Hideo, 134, 146–150
Kōda Aya, 7, 110, 137, 143, 150, 202
Komori Yōichi, 5–6, 9–55, 190–195

Lejeune, Philippe, 117–118
Line, 4, 38, 184, 187, 196
Loss, 28–29, 39–40, 45–47, 105, 124, 141, 145, 157, 159–160, 191, 197

Maruyama Masao, 158–159, 203
Marx, Karl, 57, 68, 70–71, 73, 75, 77–78, 82–83, 90, 195–198, 206
Materiality, 12–14, 17–22, 24–25, 35–36, 41, 51–52, 55, 65, 80, 95, 97, 100, 124, 145–146, 149, 172, 206
McClellan, Edwin, 110, 165–166, 179, 206
Memory, 10–12, 15–16, 20–22, 24–25, 27–28, 31, 35, 37–39, 41, 43, 49, 77, 99, 126, 189, 191–194
Method, 1–3, 6–8, 12, 15, 20, 26, 28, 48, 57–59, 63–66, 69, 80, 95, 102, 106, 109–112, 115, 118, 120, 127, 130–131, 134, 140–141, 151–152, 154–157, 160–163, 165, 174, 177–179, 183–184, 186–187, 192, 205
Miyoshi, Masao, 62, 195–196, 203, 208
Mizumura Minae, 50, 194
Mori Ōgai, 151, 153–154
Murakami Haruki, 5, 9–55, 190–195

Naas, Michael, 116, 200
Nationalism, 1–2, 7–8, 85, 122–123, 155–156, 178, 183–185, 189, 201, 207
Natsume Sōseki, 10, 20–21, 50, 151, 165–166, 168–177, 191, 194, 200, 206–208
Negativity, 18, 23–25, 28, 42, 47–48, 54, 75, 77–79, 91, 99–100, 103, 124, 163–164
Nishida Kitarō, 7, 143, 202

Ontology, 22, 27, 38–40, 53, 67–68, 70, 75, 96–98, 102, 123, 137–138, 141–142, 157–159, 162, 165, 175, 187, 196, 198, 206

Past, 3–4, 6, 9–10, 12, 21–22, 24–28, 30–31, 35, 38, 47, 57, 63–64, 67–68, 70–72, 74–75, 78, 80, 86, 90, 99, 103–106, 108, 113–114, 117, 120, 123–126, 147–148, 150, 160, 163–164, 171–172, 176, 184–185, 187, 191, 196–197, 199
Pollack, David, 179
Prelapsarianism, 6, 46–47, 53, 81, 83, 105, 161, 193
Presence, 2–3, 6–7, 15, 31, 33, 38–39, 44–45, 47–49, 53, 64–66, 68, 75, 79, 86, 88, 90, 92, 94–95, 97–99, 102–106, 113, 120–121, 123–124, 128, 131, 136, 141, 154, 156–157, 160–162, 165–167, 169, 171, 175, 178, 183–184, 187, 197, 200, 205, 207–208

Race/Racism, 107–108, 126–128, 130–133, 183–186, 201
Reading, 12–14, 17–18, 20–25, 36, 38, 40, 43, 51, 94, 102, 111–118, 120–121, 128, 131, 190, 197, 206
Repetition, 14, 31–33, 36, 76, 86, 90, 96, 99, 115, 122, 125, 134, 143, 164, 173, 176, 183, 196, 201
Retroactivity, 7, 28, 71, 85, 94, 111–121, 123, 126, 128–131, 134, 148, 164, 177–178, 201
Rubin, Jay, 170–171, 191, 207–208

Sakai, Naoki, 179, 189, 196, 203, 206–207
Saussure, Ferdinand de, 162–163, 205
Secret, 26, 30–32, 37–38, 191
Shiga Naoya, 124–126
Singularity, 5, 25, 85, 93, 109, 155, 171–173, 175–176
Space, 6–7, 13–18, 19–24, 26–27, 30–33, 35–37, 40, 66, 75–85, 90–93, 103–104, 106, 108, 112–113, 115, 120, 124–125, 127, 157–159, 167–168, 171, 173, 175, 177, 183, 188, 204–205
Spirit, 19–20, 35, 49–52, 54, 144, 162, 174–175, 194, 204
Subjectivism, 5, 19, 28, 54, 71, 138, 142, 144
Subjectivity, 6, 7, 13, 16–18, 20, 22–23, 27–28, 36, 39, 48–49, 54, 92, 101, 107, 110–111, 124–128, 132–139, 141, 143–144, 148–150, 179, 185, 187, 189, 195, 207
Succession, 13–14, 23–25, 27, 42, 54, 75, 77–78, 91, 99, 103, 199
Suzuki, Tomi, 7, 111–133, 162, 177–180, 200–202, 205–206

Takeuchi Yoshimi, 2, 107, 189, 196, 200, 204–205
Tanizaki Jun'ichirō, 108, 119–121, 128–132, 200–201
Tansman, Alan, 7, 110, 133–150, 162, 177–180, 202–203, 205–206
Time, 5–7, 13–33, 35–40, 42–43, 47–48, 52–54, 57, 66–86, 88–95, 97–99, 101–106, 112–117, 119–121, 124–126, 128–130, 132, 134, 143, 147–148, 157, 161, 163–165, 171–173, 175–177, 182–183, 185, 187, 190–191, 196–199, 205–207
Trace, 10, 12, 14, 24–25, 29–30, 34–38, 61, 77, 105, 120, 123–124, 126, 166–169, 172–173, 192
Tradition, 8, 28, 45, 61, 75, 84, 87, 93, 97–98, 100, 102, 104, 108, 112–116, 121–123, 126–127, 130–131, 150–151, 153, 155, 161, 166–167, 183, 186–187, 189–190, 200, 202
Translation, 166–176, 178, 205, 208

Trauma, 28, 30, 35, 37, 43, 45

Violence, 10–11, 13, 15, 28, 31, 33–34, 38–40, 43, 45, 48–49, 51–52, 62, 73, 84, 111, 133, 135, 142, 145–147, 149, 155, 157, 159–160, 192, 195

Washburn, Dennis, 7, 110, 150–180, 203–208
Watsuji Tetsurō, 82–83, 198

Williams, David, 6, 59–62, 195
Writing, 12–15, 17–28, 30, 35–36, 38, 51, 85, 88, 93–94, 96, 105, 112, 114–118, 124–125, 184, 190, 192, 194

Yasuda Yojūrō, 134, 146, 148–150, 203
Yokomitsu Riichi, 12–15, 17–19, 21–22, 28, 36, 151, 204

www.ingramcontent.com/pod-product-compliance
Lightning Source LLC
Chambersburg PA
CBHW020653230426
43665CB00008B/421